Massive Open Online Courses - Learning Frontiers and Novel Innovations

Edited by Sam Goundar

Published in London, United Kingdom

Massive Open Online Courses - Learning Frontiers and Novel Innovations
http://dx.doi.org/10.5772/intechopen.1003428
Edited by Sam Goundar

Contributors
Abdelaziz Ouajdouni, Anke Schüll, Eli Alejandra Garcimarrero Espino, George Katete, Heidy Yelní Díaz Oviedo, José Enrique Díaz Camacho, José Luis Rosales Barrero, María Elena Palma Moreno, Patricia Núñez Mercado, Sabila Naseer, Sam Goundar, Silvia Rodriguez-Donaire, Soyoung Park, Veronika Yarnykh, Zanub Ansari

First published in London, United Kingdom, 2025 by IntechOpen
IntechOpen is the global imprint of INTECHOPEN LIMITED, registered in England and Wales, registration number: 11086078, 167-169 Great Portland Street, London, W1W 5PF, United Kingdom

For EU product safety concerns: IN TECH d.o.o., Prolaz Marije Krucifikse Kozulić 3, 51000 Rijeka, Croatia, info@intechopen.com or visit our website at intechopen.com.

British Library Cataloguing-in-Publication Data
A catalogue record for this book is available from the British Library

Massive Open Online Courses - Learning Frontiers and Novel Innovations
Edited by Sam Goundar
p. cm.
Print ISBN 978-0-85014-796-4
Online ISBN 978-0-85014-795-7
eBook (PDF) ISBN 978-0-85014-797-1

If disposing of this product, please recycle the paper responsibly.

Meet the editor

Professor Dr. Sam Goundar is an international academic and researcher with over 35 years of teaching experience across 13 universities in 11 different countries. He specializes in emerging technologies such as Artificial Intelligence, Blockchain, Educational Technologies, Data Science and Cyber Security. As Editor-in-Chief of multiple international journals, including the *International Journal of Blockchains and Cryptocurrencies* and the I*nternational Journal of Fog Computing*, he has made significant contributions to academic publishing. Dr. Goundar has authored and edited 20 books and published over 140 research articles in reputable journals and book chapters. His research excellence is reflected in his global collaborations and innovative contributions to advancing technology-driven education. He is renowned for his work in equitable and transformative education.

Contents

Preface

The evolution of Massive Open Online Courses (MOOCs) represents one of the most transformative movements in the history of education. Emerging in the early 21st century, MOOCs began as experimental platforms to provide free access to high-quality educational content. Over time, they evolved into robust systems capable of delivering structured, scalable, and personalized learning experiences to millions of learners worldwide. Fueled by technological advancements and the increasing demand for accessible education, MOOCs have become a cornerstone of the digital learning revolution.

The significance of MOOCs lies in their ability to democratize education. By breaking down barriers of cost, geography, and institutional access, they have made learning opportunities available to individuals who might otherwise be excluded from traditional educational systems. Whether a student in a rural community is gaining knowledge in data science or a professional in a developing country is upskilling to compete in the global workforce, MOOCs exemplify the power of technology to bridge divides and create equitable opportunities for learning.

The inspiration for this book, *Massive Open Online Courses – Learning Frontiers and Novel Innovations*, comes from my own journey as an educator and researcher. Over the years, I have witnessed firsthand how MOOCs have empowered learners from diverse backgrounds, providing them with tools to not only acquire knowledge but also transform their lives. The rapid proliferation of MOOCs and their adoption by institutions, corporations, and governments underscore their immense potential. However, with this growth comes the need to explore their evolving dimensions, including innovative pedagogies, technological integration, and their impact on societal progress.

Through this book, I aim to provide a platform for thought leaders, educators, and technologists to share their insights on the latest advancements in MOOCs. It is a culmination of my desire to address pressing questions about the future of online education and to explore the untapped possibilities that MOOCs offer. I hope this book not only serves as a resource for understanding MOOCs but also inspires a new wave of innovation and collaboration in the field of education.

The primary objective of *Massive Open Online Courses – Learning Frontiers and Novel Innovations* is to explore the cutting-edge frontiers of MOOCs, investigating their transformative potential in reshaping education for the 21st century and beyond. MOOCs have evolved from their initial role as platforms for broad access to learning into dynamic ecosystems that enable scalable, personalized, and innovative educational experiences. This book seeks to unravel the depth of this transformation, providing insights into the strategies, technologies, and pedagogical innovations propelling MOOCs to the forefront of global education.

In an era where education must adapt to an increasingly digital, interconnected world, MOOCs stand out as a critical solution to address the challenges of equity, accessibility, and lifelong learning. This book uncovers how these tools redefine the learner's journey by examining the intersection of emerging technologies such as Artificial Intelligence, Blockchain, and Learning Analytics with MOOC platforms. It also highlights the innovative methodologies that foster collaboration, critical thinking, and learner engagement, providing pathways for deeper, more meaningful learning experiences.

This book is designed to serve as a comprehensive resource for a wide audience:

- Educators: This book equips educators with practical strategies and innovative approaches to design and deliver engaging MOOCs. By incorporating cutting-edge methodologies, it offers tools to enhance teaching effectiveness and learner outcomes in both online and blended learning environments.

- Students: As the primary beneficiaries of MOOCs, students can use this book to better understand the structure and opportunities these platforms offer. The chapters address the evolving landscape of MOOCs, highlighting ways learners can optimize their educational experiences and achieve their goals.

- Technologists: For those at the forefront of educational technology development, this book provides insights into integrating emerging technologies such as AI, learning analytics, and digital storytelling into MOOC platforms. It bridges the gap between theoretical innovation and practical application, offering inspiration for new technological solutions.

- Researchers: The book is a rich resource for scholars investigating the impact of MOOCs on education. Its chapters explore diverse themes, from collaborative learning and motivation to the application of analytics and emerging pedagogical approaches, fostering new research directions.

- Policymakers: Focusing on global educational challenges, the book offers valuable guidance for shaping policies that prioritize equity, access, and innovation. Policymakers will find actionable insights to support the creation of inclusive and effective online learning ecosystems.

This book fills a critical gap in the literature by addressing not only the "how" of MOOCs but also the "why" behind their continued evolution. It provides actionable knowledge and thought leadership on the future of MOOCs, equipping stakeholders with the tools and frameworks needed to harness their full potential.

By bringing together contributions from leading researchers, educators, and technologists, *Massive Open Online Courses – Learning Frontiers and Novel Innovations* aspires to spark new conversations, inspire forward-thinking approaches, and stimulate interdisciplinary collaborations. It is not just a collection of chapters but a collective vision for a future where learning is inclusive, transformative, and attuned to the diverse needs of a rapidly changing world. This book is a call to action for all stakeholders in education to embrace MOOCs as a cornerstone of the digital learning revolution.

The book *Massive Open Online Courses – Learning Frontiers and Novel Innovations* is organized into a cohesive sequence of chapters, each addressing a critical dimension of MOOCs and their transformative impact on education. This structure is designed to guide the reader through the evolution, current innovations, and future potential of MOOCs, while highlighting the diverse perspectives and interdisciplinary approaches that define their relevance in today's educational landscape.

The book opens with an Introductory Chapter which introduces us to the evolution, transformational role, Challenges and opportunities of Massive Open Online Courses.

Chapter 2 investigates the implementation and evaluation of an online course at a Mexican university, where technology and best teaching practices were used to develop critical, reflective, and self-regulated undergraduate students. Surveys and data analysis were conducted, and it is concluded that student outcomes can be positively influenced by effective teaching techniques.

Chapter 3 "Design Elements for Gamified E-Learning: On Fueling Intrinsic Motivation by Digital Storytelling and Challenges", investigates how instructional design elements, such as storytelling and constructive feedback, can fuel intrinsic motivation and improve learning outcomes in self-paced MOOCs.

Chapter 4, "Digital Teaching and Learning: Trust and Intuition in Universities in Kenya", provides a unique perspective by examining how trust and intuition influence the adoption and success of digital education initiatives, particularly in the context of Kenyan universities. This chapter underscores the cultural and contextual factors that shape the effectiveness of MOOCs in diverse regions.

Chapter 5, "Transition in the Concept of Scaffolding", focuses on the role of data and analytics in improving MOOC effectiveness. By leveraging learning analytics, educators and technologists can better understand learner behaviour and optimize courses for greater impact.

Chapter 6 examines the increasing importance of e-learning in Moroccan educational contexts and worldwide. Morocco's e-learning environment is analyzed, with terminology and primary methods for assessing the efficacy of information systems being emphasized. The mechanisms for enhancing the effectiveness of e-learning are discussed through the use of models such as the Technology Acceptance Model (TAM), user satisfaction, e-learning quality, and DeLone and McLean's Information Systems Success Model. Factors influencing the success of e-learning systems are explored, and valuable insights are provided to help educators and policymakers improve e-learning strategies in Morocco.

Chapter 7 "Influence of Prompts Structure on the Perception and Enhancement of Learning through LLMs in Online Educational Contexts", delves into the role of Large Language Models (LLMs) in shaping online learning experiences. It examines how prompt design influences learning and explores the integration of LLMs into MOOCs for enhanced engagement and understanding.

Chapter 8 "Intention of Hybrid Learning for Students Deprived of Liberty (Inmates of the San Roque de Sucre Penitentiary)", highlights a unique application of MOOCs, examining how hybrid learning models can be adapted for incarcerated learners. This chapter demonstrates the far-reaching potential of MOOCs to provide education in unconventional and restricted settings.

Chapter 9, "Perspective Chapter: New Approaches for Learning Design – Course Architecture and Media Educational Technologies", highlights innovative methodologies in course design. It explains how MOOCs employ cutting-edge media technologies and course architectures to create immersive and effective learning experiences.

Chapter 10, "Perspective Chapter: Collaborative Learning Benefits and Its Role in Critical Thinking", explores the transformative potential of collaborative learning in MOOCs. It discusses strategies to foster critical thinking skills, emphasizing how interaction and teamwork can enhance learner outcomes.

Each chapter is a vital piece of the puzzle, collectively building a comprehensive narrative around the innovations, challenges, and opportunities that define the MOOC ecosystem. Together, these contributions provide readers with a multifaceted understanding of how MOOCs shape the future of education, offering practical insights and a roadmap for continued evolution.

As you explore the insights shared in *Massive Open Online Courses – Learning Frontiers and Novel Innovations*, I encourage you to envision how these advancements can shape the future of education in your own context. This book highlights the transformative potential of MOOCs and the opportunities they present to overcome challenges in accessibility, engagement, and scalability.

The lessons and innovations captured here are meant to inspire educators, technologists, researchers, and policymakers to take bold steps in applying these strategies to real-world contexts. At the same time, the evolving nature of MOOCs underscores the need for continued exploration and research. By building on the knowledge shared in these chapters, we can push the boundaries of what MOOCs can achieve and ensure they remain at the forefront of global education.

Sam Goundar
RMIT University,
Hanoi, Vietnam

Chapter 1

Introductory Chapter: Massive Open Online Courses – Learning Frontiers and Novel Innovations

Sam Goundar

1. Introduction

Over the past decade, education has undergone an extraordinary transformation, driven by rapid technological advancements and a growing demand for accessible and flexible learning opportunities. At the heart of this shift are Massive Open Online Courses (MOOCs), which have disrupted traditional education systems and redefined how knowledge is disseminated. MOOCs have empowered millions of learners by offering access to world-class courses from leading institutions, breaking barriers of cost, geography, and infrastructure that have historically limited educational opportunities [1].

The rise of MOOCs reflects a broader global trend toward digital transformation and remote learning. During the COVID-19 pandemic, when schools and universities worldwide faced closures and disruptions, MOOCs became a lifeline for learners and educators alike. Platforms like Coursera and edX reported record enrollments, as individuals turned to these tools to continue their education and acquire new skills amidst the crisis. This unprecedented reliance on MOOCs underscored their scalability and adaptability in meeting diverse learning needs during challenging times [2].

MOOCs are more than just a response to immediate crises—they represent a paradigm shift in education. By leveraging technology, MOOCs have made it possible to reach learners in the most remote corners of the globe. They have become an integral part of a world that values continuous learning, offering opportunities not just for academic achievement but also for personal growth and career advancement. The transformative potential of MOOCs lies in their ability to adapt to the evolving needs of society, making education more inclusive, accessible, and future-ready.

2. Exploring the evolution of MOOCs

The origins of Massive Open Online Courses (MOOCs) can be traced back to the early 2010s when platforms like Coursera, edX, and Udacity began offering free, high-quality online courses from top universities. The initial vision behind MOOCs was simple yet ambitious: to democratize education by making it accessible to anyone, anywhere. Over time, these platforms evolved beyond offering basic video lectures to include interactive learning elements such as quizzes, peer reviews, and discussion forums. This shift reflected the growing demand for engagement and interactivity in online learning environments [3].

A critical milestone in the evolution of MOOCs was the incorporation of professional certifications and degree pathways. This development transformed MOOCs from supplemental educational tools into integral components of career and academic growth. Platforms began partnering with universities and corporations to offer micro-credentials and industry-recognized certifications, enabling learners to enhance their professional skills or pursue new career opportunities. By integrating these features, MOOCs became a bridge between academia and industry, addressing the skills gap in an increasingly competitive job market [4].

The evolution of MOOCs mirrors the broader transformation of education itself. From their inception as experimental platforms for sharing knowledge, MOOCs have grown into dynamic ecosystems that cater to diverse learner needs. They now leverage advanced technologies, such as artificial intelligence and machine learning, to provide personalized learning experiences. These innovations, combined with the scalability of MOOCs, position them as a cornerstone of global education, capable of adapting to the rapidly changing demands of modern society.

3. The transformational role of MOOCs

Massive Open Online Courses (MOOCs) have emerged as powerful tools for democratizing education on a global scale. By breaking down traditional barriers such as cost, geographic location, and access to infrastructure, MOOCs have opened the doors of learning to millions of individuals. For instance, rural learners with limited access to universities or professionals seeking flexible upskilling options can now access courses from some of the world's top institutions. This transformation has redefined education as a public good, shifting its accessibility from being exclusive to inclusive [5].

One of the most transformative aspects of MOOCs is their ability to foster collaboration between educational institutions and industries. By aligning course content with real-world skills and market demands, MOOCs have bridged the gap between academia and employment. This collaboration has resulted in tailored micro-credentials and modular degrees that address workforce shortages in technology, health care, and other critical sectors. For example, recent collaborations between Google and Coursera have created IT certification programs that have successfully placed thousands of learners into technology roles, further showcasing the role of MOOCs in workforce development [6].

MOOCs have also played a significant role in promoting global educational equity. Through multilingual courses and culturally adaptive content, these platforms ensure that learners from diverse backgrounds feel included and supported. Additionally, MOOCs are increasingly incorporating features like offline downloads and mobile-friendly interfaces to accommodate learners in areas with poor Internet connectivity. These efforts highlight how MOOCs are not only transforming the education landscape but also contributing to the broader goals of equity and inclusivity in a rapidly globalizing world.

4. Challenges and opportunities

While the impact of Massive Open Online Courses (MOOCs) has been revolutionary, their journey has not been without challenges. One of the most prominent issues is the low course completion rate. Research indicates that fewer than 10% of learners who enroll in MOOCs complete their courses, primarily due to a lack of motivation, inadequate interaction with instructors, and insufficient peer engagement. This challenge is particularly significant when compared to traditional education, where structured environments and accountability mechanisms support learner persistence [7]. Addressing these issues requires innovative approaches to engagement and support systems within the MOOC framework.

Another critical challenge lies in the digital divide. Although MOOCs have democratized education, their reach is still limited in areas with poor Internet connectivity or inadequate digital infrastructure. Learners in low-income or rural regions often face barriers to accessing online content, further widening existing inequities. Additionally, the lack of localized and culturally relevant content can make it difficult for some learners to relate to the material. This underscores the importance of designing MOOCs with inclusivity and accessibility in mind, ensuring they cater to the diverse needs of a global audience [8].

Despite these challenges, the opportunities for innovation in MOOCs are immense. Advances in artificial intelligence (AI) and machine learning are enabling personalized learning experiences tailored to individual needs and progress. AI-powered chatbots, for example, provide real-time feedback and support, while adaptive learning systems adjust content delivery based on the learner's pace and proficiency. Furthermore, the integration of immersive technologies like augmented reality (AR) and virtual reality (VR) is transforming the way MOOCs deliver experiential learning, particularly in technical and scientific disciplines. These advancements not only enhance engagement but also help overcome some of the limitations inherent in traditional online education.

5. Lifelong learning and non-traditional learners

In an era of rapid technological change and shifting workplace demands, lifelong learning has become a necessity rather than a choice. MOOCs have emerged as a key enabler of this paradigm, providing flexible, cost-effective, and high-quality education to learners of all ages. Unlike traditional educational systems that cater primarily to younger students, MOOCs empower individuals to learn at their own pace, on their own schedule, and in alignment with their personal or professional goals. This accessibility makes MOOCs particularly valuable for professionals seeking to reskill or upskill, as well as for those exploring entirely new career paths.

Non-traditional learners, such as working parents, caregivers, veterans, and individuals with disabilities, often face unique barriers to education. These learners benefit significantly from the self-paced nature of MOOCs, which allow them to balance their educational pursuits with personal and professional responsibilities. Furthermore, MOOCs are increasingly incorporating features like closed captioning, multilingual content, and mobile accessibility to ensure inclusivity. Such advancements cater to diverse learner needs and promote equitable access to education, even in underserved communities [9].

MOOCs have also revolutionized how education is perceived, shifting the focus from formal degree programs to skills-based learning. This is particularly relevant for older learners or those re-entering the workforce, who may not require a degree but need targeted knowledge or certifications. By offering courses in emerging areas such as artificial intelligence, digital marketing, and blockchain, MOOCs not only meet individual learning needs but also align with broader workforce demands. These programs demonstrate how MOOCs can contribute to a culture of lifelong learning, equipping learners to thrive in a rapidly changing world.

6. A vision for the future

The future of Massive Open Online Courses (MOOCs) is closely tied to the integration of emerging technologies that promise to enhance the learning experience. One of the most exciting frontiers is the metaverse, which could transform online education by creating immersive and interactive learning environments. Imagine virtual classrooms where learners from across the globe can collaborate in real time or simulated labs where they can conduct experiments safely and efficiently. Additionally, the adoption of gamification in MOOCs offers a unique way to engage learners by incorporating rewards, challenges, and interactive elements. These innovations have the potential to make learning more dynamic, personalized, and enjoyable, ultimately addressing some of the current limitations of MOOCs [10].

Moreover, the role of artificial intelligence (AI) in MOOCs will continue to expand, providing learners with adaptive pathways and real-time feedback. By analyzing learner behavior and progress, AI-driven systems can recommend tailored content and identify areas requiring additional support. This level of personalization ensures that MOOCs cater to individual learning needs, making education more accessible and effective for diverse audiences. As these technologies mature, MOOCs will not only improve learner outcomes but also redefine the boundaries of traditional education, creating a system that is flexible, inclusive, and future-ready.

Beyond technological advancements, the future of MOOCs lies in fostering meaningful collaborations among educators, policymakers, and technology developers. These partnerships will be essential for scaling innovations, addressing global challenges, and ensuring that MOOCs remain inclusive and equitable. For instance, public–private partnerships can fund infrastructure improvements in underserved regions, while educational institutions can work with industry leaders to create job-relevant content. By focusing on inclusivity and collaboration, MOOCs can evolve into a truly transformative force in global education, shaping a future where lifelong learning is accessible to all.

Author details

Sam Goundar
RMIT University, Melbourne, Australia

*Address all correspondence to: sam.goundar@gmail.com

References

[1] Goglio V. The Diffusion and Social Implications of MOOCs: A Comparative Study of the USA and Europe. Routledge; 2022

[2] Shahriar SHB, Akter S, Sultana N, Arafat S, Khan MMR. MOOC-based learning for human resource development in organizations during the post-pandemic and war crisis: A study from a developing country perspective. Journal of Research in Innovative Teaching & Learning. 2023;**16**(1):37-52

[3] Barbetta PM. Technologies as tools to increase active learning during online higher-education instruction. Journal of Educational Technology Systems. 2023;**51**(3):317-339

[4] Alenezi M, Akour M, Alfawzan L. Evolving microcredential strategies for enhancing employability: Employer and student perspectives. Education Sciences. 2024;**14**(12):1307

[5] Chowdhury SA, Dey M, Cross B. Rethinking education in the era of fourth industrial revolution (4IR): Perspective of less developed countries. In: Future-Oriented Learning and Skills Development for Employability: Insights from Singapore and Some Asia-Pacific Contexts. Singapore: Springer Nature Singapore; 2024. pp. 35-52

[6] Sharma R, Jones K, Anderson W, Inthiran A, Tabatabaee M. The digital transformation of higher education–"uni for nothin', MOOCs for free"? Journal of Information Technology Case and Application Research. 2022;**24**(1):34-60

[7] Goopio J, Cheung C. The MOOC dropout phenomenon and retention strategies. Journal of Teaching in Travel & Tourism. 2021;**21**(2):177-197

[8] Mrayhi S, Khribi MK, Belhadj H, Jemni M. Designing future education for all: Principles and frameworks. In: Envisioning the Future of Education Through Design. Singapore: Springer Nature Singapore; 2024. pp. 147-177

[9] Chong SW, Khan MA, Reinders H. A critical review of design features of LMOOCs. Computer Assisted Language Learning. 2024;**37**(3):389-409

[10] Rohan R, Pal D, Funilkul S, Chutimaskul W, Eamsinvattana W. How gamification leads to continued usage of MOOCs? A theoretical perspective. IEEE Access. 2021;**9**:108144-108161

Chapter 2

MOOC for Lifelong Learning: Training Critical, Reflective and Self-Regulating Students at University Level

José Enrique Díaz Camacho,
Eli Alejandra Garcimarrero Espino,
Patricia Núñez Mercado and Heidy Yelní Díaz Oviedo

Abstract

This project presents a report on the implementation of a course enriched with information and communication technologies aimed at the training of more critical, reflective and self-regulated undergraduate students in a Mexican university. With this objective in mind, this study used the best online teaching practices, as defined in a previous study, applying them in an enriched, supported and technology-based learning environment through online university courses. The instrument developed in the previous project was used to evaluate the teacher's performance as a measure of educational gain using a statistical correlational methodology. This survey was administered to students from a Mexican university to obtain an account of the best teaching practices and correlate them with student performance. Once the data was collected, the results were analysed and graphed, and the corresponding reports were prepared. It can be concluded that by using appropriate teaching techniques and methods, it is possible to prepare critical, reflective and self-regulating students.

Keywords: lifelong learning, online education, critical students, reflective students, self-regulating students, educational effectiveness

1. Introduction

A Chinese proverb says "Tell me and I will forget, show me and I may remember, involve me and I will understand" [1] referring to the fact that learning occurs in different sensory modalities and that when only the auditory modality intervenes, one is more prone to forget; however, when demonstrated, one will remember for a longer period of time; and when practiced, learning will be permanent. Indeed, when more sensory, attitude-driven and value modalities are involved, what is learned will last longer. But when more pedagogical strategies come into play, such as those classified as best practices in online education, not only will learners be able to retain learning for longer, but they will also maintain it in the form of schemes or prototypes that they can use in the future to continue learning, thus achieving lifelong learning.

In fact, since 1997, Albert Bandura [2] referred to learning as what teachers do to equip students with intellectual tools, self-belief and self-regulation capabilities as well as capacity, will and mental skills transformed into academic skills and strategies, in other words, a series of skills to self-manage your learning process that involve the handling of different cognitive tools. Similarly, Schunk and Zimmerman [3] already proposed that learning is a process through which students maintain emotional behaviour and affections oriented towards achieving goals. This implies self-regulation of behaviour, motivation, affection and cognition.

Likewise, Schunk [4] argues that learning is a lasting change in behaviour and the ability to behave in a certain way; that is, it is the result of practice and other forms of experience in which self-knowledge, the subject or task, the learning strategies, the contexts in which learning will be applied and the personal project, self-discipline and will are all involved. In short, learning consists not only in the acquisition and more or less permanent strengthening of a response, and if there is learning, it is not only the classical and instrumental conditioning of a response; in any case, it is always the conditioning of the organism as a whole [5], and it involves attitudes, values, motivations, perceptions, emotions, affections and, of course, the capacity for critical analysis and self-regulation. Therefore, learning and hence education should be seen as a process to train people with the ability to perform critical analysis and display self-regulated behaviour and not merely as an act of transmitting information from teacher to student.

This study addresses the issue of multiple learning modes by attempting to teach students not only to review and repeat the learning content but also to conduct a critical analysis of this content as well as reflecting on its implications. This way they can solve personal problems and strengthen their individual capacities to continue learning for life. In other words, the aim is to promote critical, reflective and self-regulated learning.

2. Background

Critical learning involves students questioning the concepts or information they are being taught. The questioning can be not only about the concepts or the information they are being provided but also about the source from which that information comes, that is, the person who teaches them. The most common form of questioning is when you ask how confident you are. The most common form of questioning consists in querying the reliability of the information provided and the trustworthiness of the person who provides this information.

Some authors have identified critical learning as a type of learning transfer. Learning transfer has been considered to be the ability to apply, in practice, theoretical learning acquired in situations or tasks that are not familiar [6]. However, it has also been referred to as those changes in behaviour that occur over time. Others understand it as the application of the theory in practice [7].

Additionally, Haskell [8] affirms that learning transfer requires the learning of new behaviours. He also asserts that, if something new is not learned, learning should be considered simply as an application. In the same way, Roumell [9] emphasises the differences between learning transfer and transformational learning maintaining that "learning transfer involves practicing the application of knowledge, perspectives and skills across contexts, while transformation would involve a complete integration of knowledge and perceptions into a new world of perspectives" (p. 2). Critical learning has been studied by Nkansah [10] when teaching students to develop a critical awareness of the socio-economic development policies of the Government of Ghana, for instance.

Reflective learning occurs when the learner relates what has been learned to other domains of content other than the object of that learning, especially when they relate it to previous learning that already exists in their behavioural repertoire. Thus, reflective learning is related to metacognition, that is, the fact of being aware of learning itself. As Flavell [11] points out, "meta-cognition can be regarded as knowledge about the cognitive activities and their regulation during the learning process" (p. 233).

Students engage in cognitive mental activities when they think about what they have learned, how they have learned it or how they can relate what they learned to their personal past experiences. From here on, students who develop these skills should show more appropriate strategies to know what to do to learn. Accordingly, understanding and controlling these cognitive processes is considered an essential skill, and as such teachers should encourage students at all levels of education to develop it [12].

Self-regulated learning has been used in a wide variety of situations and conditions under study, as well as in a large diversity of populations. In one study, self-regulated learning was used to promote the learning of basic ideas of Muslim religion in a population of African children [13]. It is also related to self-discipline for the exercise of different behaviours as in a study conducted by Li et al. [14] to strengthen physical skills during sports practice with undergraduate students. Furthermore, its role as an independent variable has been studied to determine its effect on understanding, motivation and self-regulation skills in elementary-level children [15].

In the same way, it has been used to teach the minimum professional skills for the litigant lawyer who is incorporated into his professional practice through the solution of scheduled online activities through the social network LinkedIn [16]. Türkben [17] used it to evaluate the effects of self-regulation-based reading on understanding, reading motivation and self-control skills in fifth-year elementary school children. Jansen et al. [18] conducted a study with undergraduate students from a German university and compared two methods to measure the effect of a Massive Open Online Course (MOOC) course on students' self-regulation skills.

Bort-Mir [19] developed a learning guide journal with different purposes, (1) defining the general and specific goals of the content to be taught, (2) developing the metacognitive skills of students through content questions and (3) promoting the development of important competencies such as self-critical and autonomous learning, self-evaluation and ability to improve. This learning guide journal also allows teachers to conduct self-assessments, thus facilitating the supervision and improvement of both the course content and the didactic methodology.

For the purposes of this study, critical learning is understood as the ability of students to question the reliability of the information they are receiving in their education, including the analysis of the credibility they can give to the person or persons in charge of their education. Reflective learning is understood as the ability of students to analyse the education in which they participate and where they play the leading role as people undergoing training. Among the aspects that they can reflect on is their own cognitive activity, that is, realising how they are learning as well as how much they are learning. This is what is called metacognition: making your own learning process explicit.

As for self-regulated learning, we understand it as the learning that takes place from the planning that students make of the conditions, strategies that they will employ, the implementation of the actions that they consider important and their own awareness of how successful it has resulted.

The problem that this study addresses deals with the effectiveness of MOOCs in training critical, reflective and self-regulating students who are able to reflect on the quality of education they receive at university, and who also feel in a position to continue learning for life. This is opposed to the fact that they are not just students able to repeat the knowledge they are taught.

The Massive Open Online Courses (MOOCs) system has been identified as one of the best online educational practices by Díaz Camacho and Núñez [20]. According to the authors, "this modality offers a flexible model that makes it possible for universities to reach the previously unattended population, thus enabling a personalized learning experience" (p. 9).

MOOCs have revolutionised access to higher and continuing education, providing an accessible and flexible alternative to traditional education, thereby helping lifelong learning. This has enabled programmes such as EdX and Coursera to integrate the efforts of institutions such as the University of Berkeley, the Massachusetts Institute of Technology (MIT) and Harvard University to broaden the educational impact [21, 22].

Coursera is a system offering online university courses that can be taken for free by anyone in the world. It also offers academic programs such as diploma courses, certifications and technical degrees designed and built by prestigious institutions. It was founded in 2012 by Andrew Ng and Daphne Koller, professors of computer science at Stanford University.

Coursera offers courses on a wide variety of topics, such as mathematics, humanities and sciences, as well as technology, presenting educational materials in different formats including images, audio and video. Provided that anyone with an Internet connection can access them, Coursera contributes to achieving equity for the citizens of the world in terms of access to education and lifelong learning [23]. It has exponentially grown in the last few years by incorporating a large number of universities and courses. To date, there are more than 200 universities involved, of which at least four Mexican universities stand out.

The MOOC model is used in the present study to improve the outcome of education, not only to convey knowledge but to train critical, reflective and self-regulating students capable of achieving lifelong learning.

3. Method

Online learning has increased exponentially in recent years [24], which was greatly promoted by the global pandemic of COVID-19 in the years following 2020. This has meant that students from those years on are now faced with a series of decisions that were not normally made by them taking classes in educational institutions. Certainly, in the loneliness of their desktop computer, students had to decide details of their academic life that they did not have to do before. Now they have to plan their academic life: what subjects to take, at what hours, with what other topics the subject they are interested in relates, how many topics they can take in the time that they dedicate to study, etc. This forced the students to assume their responsibilities as independent students, problem solvers, critical thinkers, entrepreneurs and capable to improve their communication skills. In embracing this change, students who come from a traditional system must adapt and improve their learning style in line with the conditions of the more active forms of learning.

In a previous study [25], a system of online courses to train better-prepared pupils to be more critical, reflective and self-regulating was described, which allowed for a report on the best practices of online education presented at a European research forum [20]. Such a system was supported by a computing system called SIABEV, which allows to create diverse learning experiences based on problems, cases or projects developed to guide the learning process [26].

The course system described was implemented in the early years of a bachelor's degree through online courses, as well as in the senior courses. For students in the first semesters, this system served as a corrective system to overcome some of the difficulties that students typically drag from secondary school, while for senior students, the courses aimed at preparing students for their coming encounter with a work environment, training them for their professional performance and in lifelong learning. In both cases, the objective was to analyse whether students could acquire the skills for self-regulated learning and be able to critically analyse and reflect on their personal situation at school and provide the elements to plan their professional life.

3.1 Purpose

The purpose of this study was to determine whether it was possible to offer a formative education option that would train critical, reflective and self-regulating students through an online instruction modality by using MOOCs as a learning strategy.

3.2 Design

It was an ex post facto quasi-experimental transversal study of a descriptive nature, with intact groups. The groups were formed with those students registering for the course through the online institutional registration system. The online course followed the syllabus designed for it, and a single measurement method was used at the end to gather data.

3.3 Instrument

The data collection instrument was a Likert scale questionnaire to measure 30 different behavioural categories: 10 on critical learning, 10 on reflexive learning and 10 on self-regulated learning.

3.4 Participants

The participating subjects consisted of two groups, one of newly enrolled students and the other of students who were about to complete their bachelor's degree. The first group was made up of 32 students, and the second group consisted of 14 students. The subjects were selected considering their own interest in taking the course during the institutional online registration system of the university before the beginning of each semester.

3.5 Preparing the courses

The courses consisted of a series of exercises, called learning objects such as problems, cases or projects. These exercises differ from each other by the extent of their linguistic content and consist of open questions that the student must answer considering real or hypothetical situations and pondering the advantages and disadvantages of performing one or another action. In the case of problems, the student had to understand the problem and propose one or more solutions seemingly relevant alternatives to solve the problem from the teacher's perspective.

When dealing with cases, the student should understand the case, imagine that they were the protagonist of the given case and describe one or more possible forms of behaviour based on similar events that they had experienced in the past. Finally, for developing a project, the student had to set a goal, establish the background from the literature on similar projects conducted by other people and describe how their own project would be conducted.

3.6 Procedure: implementing the courses

Courses were delivered online. After promoting them through social networks on the Internet, students enrolled through the university online registration system. Courses were delivered using the zoom video conferencing system in three and two-hour sessions, combining the tools for online courses offered by the institutional platform called *Eminus*, YouTube videos and HTML pages, which are some of the external tools compatible with the institutional platform. Midterm evaluations were uploaded as text in the corresponding sections in *Eminus.* Instructional design was delivered through templates from the institutional platform available for such purpose.

The courses lasted 16 weeks, having two sessions a week. The data collection instrument was administered during the last session using Google forms and the data was stored using the same system. Subsequently, data were statistically processed and students' response percentages were obtained for each of the three learning categories that were assessed.

4. Results

The courses were conducted normally, and participants attended regularly. The age of the students ranged between 19 and 22 years old; the average age was 20 years and 8 months old. Regarding gender, 60% of participants were women and 40% were men. The students were highly motivated and constantly participated in the discussions for the learning objects consisting of problems. The learning objects consisting of cases and projects were mandatory for everyone. One case was conducted for each topic of the course and one project throughout the course. At the end of each course, the instrument was administered to all students. The instruments were rated and the scores obtained by each student were concentrated on an Excel spreadsheet and analysed with the *Statistica* computing package.

As can be seen in **Figure 1**, the students obtained the highest score in the critical learning questions (93%), and they received the second highest score in the reflexive learning questions (87%) and got the lowest score in the self-reflective learning questions (81%). However, in every question category, the score percentages were higher than 80%, which means an acceptable and very high overall performance.

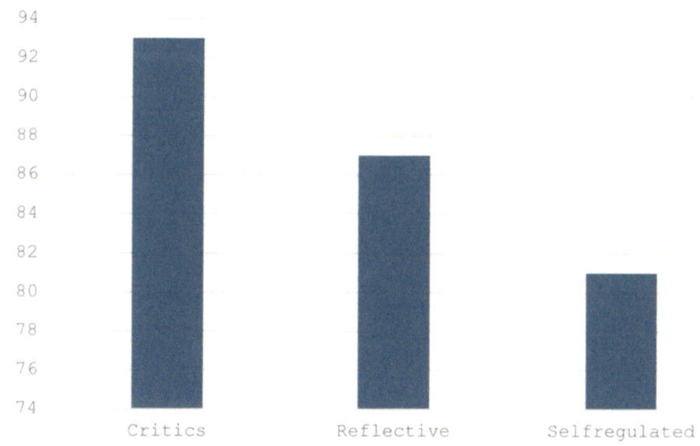

Figure 1.
Questionnaire results.

5. Discussion

As Jean Piaget [27] states, all people have a natural tendency to create a rational representation of their world and their living conditions. This means that all individuals form a rational representation of their environment and their position in it. The representation of each person is unique and different from that of the others. It is a representation that depends on the personal history of each individual, their cognitive structure and learning and education experiences. Therefore, what is learned in an instructional process is incorporated into a cognitive structure in processes called critical learning, reflective learning and self-regulated learning.

Critical learning occurs when students evaluate the information received and contrast it with the knowledge they already have. Reflective learning occurs when students relate the content of learning received to the particular conditions of their own life and apply it. Finally, self-regulated learning occurs when students take every episode of their education to continue learning, achieving lifelong learning and thus are able to plan how new learning will come about.

Throughout history, many of the educational models that have been used consist of a teacher instructing a group of students by transmitting knowledge organised according to a specific curriculum. This instruction model implies a top-down dynamic where, during a session, the teacher provides a small dose of knowledge and gradually makes the students acquire this knowledge, which constitutes the teaching goal.

However, these educational models encounter several problems. In many cases, not all students have the same level of knowledge or have the same cognitive structure at the beginning of a course, neither do all students have the same ability to learn, and consequently, nor all learn at the same pace.

Therefore, it is wrong to assume that the exact same teaching approach would be effective for all students. Ideally, every single student requires different educational strategies and methods so as to achieve meaningful learning, but such a level of personalisation would be almost impossible to accomplish in traditional learning environments. There is some hope placed in new technologies to achieve such individualised teaching appropriate to the capacities of each student, considering their cognitive structure, their initial level of knowledge and their particular learning pace, as well as their own goals, expectations and future learning scenarios.

MOOCs are an excellent tool for achieving active learning for the future. They not only proved their effectiveness for education purposes during the COVID-19 pandemic lockdown, but also in studies like the one described in the present study, which constitute a different learning scenario. Nonetheless, further research needs to be conducted to examine its educational effectiveness in greater detail. Particularly, it is important to study and analyse how recent developments in Artificial Intelligence may contribute to personalise and individualise teaching when using MOOCs; therefore, it would be necessary to replicate the present study including them.

6. Conclusions

From the results in this study, we can mainly conclude that by using the appropriate educational methods and techniques, students can achieve critical, reflective and self-regulated learning. In this particular case, using MOOCs as a teaching strategy proved to be useful in developing the expected critical analysis, reflective thought and self-regulated learning.

A second conclusion relates to the objects of active learning: problems, cases and projects. All of them were very motivating for the students, who showed great creativity in analysing the learning objects and relating them to events that occurred in their own lives. This indicates that when appropriate learning methods and techniques are selected, students will show greater critical, reflective and self-regulated analysis.

Thirdly, it can also be concluded that MOOCs are an excellent technique to broaden the scope of the impact of education to greater educational coverage among the world's population by facilitating the development of self-regulated and long-life learning. However, as Chong et al. [28] point out, due to the recent popularisation of MOOCs and their rapid development, a detailed evaluation of the courses offered by Coursera is required.

Finally, it is possible to conclude that the activities and research procedures in the present study were consistent and satisfactorily corroborate the usefulness of MOOCs as a learning strategy to promote critical, reflective and self-regulating learning.

Author details

José Enrique Díaz Camacho*, Eli Alejandra Garcimarrero Espino,
Patricia Núñez Mercado and Heidy Yelní Díaz Oviedo
Universidad Veracruzana, Xalapa, Veracruz, Mexico

*Address all correspondence to: joseenriquedc@gmail.com

References

[1] Godos R. Optimizando la Enseñanza Universitaria: Estrategias Pedagógicas, Recursos Digitales y Herramientas Tecnológicas Para Fomentar el Aprendizaje Activo [Optimizing University Education: Pedagogical Strategies, Digital Resources and Technological Tools to Promote Active Learning]. México: Editorial Amazon; 2024

[2] Bandura A. Self-Efficacy: The Exercise of Control. New York: Freeman and Company; 1997

[3] Schunk DH, Zimmerman BJ, editors. Self-Regulation of Learning and Performance: Issues and Educational Applications. Hillsdale, NJ: Lawrence Erlbaum Associates, Inc.; 1994

[4] Schunk DH. Social-self interaction and achievement behavior. Educational Psychologist. 1999;**34**(4):219-227. DOI: 10.1207/s15326985ep3404_3

[5] Schoenfeld WN. Conditioning the whole organism. Integrative Physiological and Behavioral Science. 1966;**31**(3):258-260. DOI: 10.1007/bf02691457

[6] Christie B, Beames S, Higgins P. Context, culture and critical thinking Scottish secondary school teachers' and pupils' experiences of outdoor learning. British Educational Research Journal. 2016;**42**(3):417-437. DOI: 10.1002/berj.3213

[7] Makransky G, Bonde MT, Wulff JSG, Wandall J, Hood M, Creed PA, et al. Simulation based virtual learning environment in medical genetics counseling: An example of bridging the gap between theory and practice in medical education. BMC Medical Education. 2016;**16**(1):1-9. DOI: 10.1186/s12909-016-0620-6

[8] Haskell RE. Transfer of Learning Cognition, Instruction, and Reasoning. Maine, USA: Academic Press; 2001. DOI: 10.1016/B978-012330595-4/50003-2

[9] Roumell EA. Priming adult learners for learning transfer: Beyond content and delivery. Adult Learning. 2019;**30**(1):15-22. DOI: 10.1177/1045159518791281

[10] Nkansah JN. The future of education in Ghana: Critical education for socio-economic development. Journal of Interdisciplinary Studies in Education. 2021;**10**(SI):57-78. Available from: https://www.ojed.org/index.php/jise/article/view/2889

[11] Flavell JH. Metacognitive aspects of problem solving. In: Resnick LB, editor. The Nature of Intelligence. Hillsdale, NJ: Erlbaum Associates; 1976. pp. 231-235

[12] Anderson NJ. The Role of Metacognition in Second Language Teaching and Learning. ERIC Digest. Washington, DC: ERIC Clearinghouse on Languages and Linguistics; 2002. Available from: https://eric.ed.gov/?id=ED463659

[13] Mustajab M, Baharun H, Fawa'iedah Z. Adapting to teaching and learning during Covid-19: A case of Islamic school's initiative of self-regulated learning. Nadwa. 2020;**14**(2):241-264. DOI: 10.21580/nw.2020.14.2.6515

[14] Li K, Onyon N, Choichareon T, Charoontham O. Physical education course based on self-regulated learning to improve Students' physical literacy. International Journal of Sociologies and Anthropologies Science Reviews

(IJSASR). 2023;**3**(3):143-152. DOI: 10.14456/jsasr.2023.42

[15] Türkben T. The effect of self-regulated strategy education on the writing skills of middle school students. International Journal of Education & Literacy Studies. 2021;**9**(2):52. DOI: 10.7575/aiac.ijels.v.9n.2p.52

[16] Chin C, Puteri S. Self-regulated lifelong learning in law using LinkedIn. International Journal of Curriculum and Instruction. 2020;**12**(Special Issue): 172-184. Available from: https://eric.ed.gov/?id=EJ1245136

[17] Türkben T. The effect of self-regulation based strategic reading education on comprehension, motivation, and self-regulation skills. International Journal of Progressive Education. 2019;**15**(4):27-46. DOI: 10.29329/ijpe.2019.203.3

[18] Jansen R, van Leeuwen A, Janssen J, Kester L. A mixed method approach to studying self-regulated learning in MOOCs: Combining trace data with interviews. Frontline Learning Research. 2020;**8**(2):35-64. Available from: https://eric.ed.gov/?id=EJ1252768

[19] Bort-Mir L. Using Penzu™ for academic online diaries to enhance metacognitive skills in higher education. The EuroCALL Review. 2020;**29**(2):50-63. DOI: 10.4995/eurocall.2020.12756

[20] Díaz-Camacho JE, Núñez P. Best practices of online education [conference presentation]. In: VIth Leipzig-Evora Zwickau Scientific Meeting in Psychology and Health Sciences: New Horizons, New Paradigms in Health and Human Development. Zwickau, Germany; 2023

[21] Tanış H, Arif Akçay A, Nursel Yılmaz N, Fatih Yiğit M, Tüzün H. How usable is coursera? A usability analysis through eye-tracking and authentic tasks. Participatory Educational Research. 2022;**9**(4):379-395. DOI: 10.17275/per.22.96.9.4

[22] Thao Ho NT, Lim Abdullah M, Idrus RTHB, Sivapalan S, Pham HH, Dinh VH, et al. Acceptance toward coursera MOOCs blended learning: A mixed methods view of Vietnamese higher education stakeholders. SAGE Open. 2023;**13**(4):1-18. DOI: 10.1177/21582440231197997

[23] Ayoub A, Amin R, Wani ZA. Contribution of developed countries towards MOOCs: An exploration and assessment from a representative platform Coursera. Asian Association of Open Universities Journal. 2020;**15**(2):251-262. DOI: 10.1108/aaouj-03-2020-0016

[24] Allen IE, Seaman J. Online Report Card: Tracking Online Education in the United States. Wellesley, MA: Babson Survey Research Group and Quahog Research Group, LLC; 2016. Available from: https://eric.ed.gov/?id=ED572777

[25] Díaz-Camacho JE, Reynoso AV. Implementación de un sistema de cursos mediados por las tecnologías de la información y la comunicación que permita mejorar la calidad de la educación formando alumnos más críticos, reflexivos y auto-regulados [Implementation of a system of courses mediated by information and communication technologies to improve the quality of education by training more critical, reflective and self-regulating students] [Conference presentation]. In: Congreso Internacional del Centro de Investigación de Estudios Comparados de América Latina (CIECAL); Mexico City, Mexico. 2018

[26] Díaz-Camacho JE, Andrade CCDP, Velázquez DA. Sistema de Aprendizaje

Basado en Entornos Virtuales: proyectos, casos y problemas [Virtual Environment-Based Learning System: Projects, Cases and Problems]. Mexican Patent 03-2012-032711025300-01. México: Registro Público del Derecho de Autor. S. E. P.; 2012

[27] Piaget J. The Child's Conception of the World. London: Rowman & Littlefield Publishers, Inc.; 1973

[28] Chong SW, Khan MA, Reinders H. A critical review of design features of LMOOCs. Computer Assisted Language Learning. 2022;**37**(3):1-21. DOI: 10.1080/09588221.2022.2038632

Chapter 3

Design Elements for Gamified E-Learning: On Fueling Intrinsic Motivation by Digital Storytelling and Challenges

Anke Schüll

Abstract

In recent years, gamified e-learning earned its place in higher education. Aligned to the audience, the content and the learning goals design elements are orchestrated around the backbone of any gamified intervention: the story. The art of storytelling is old and well-established, but digital storytelling is not yet fully explored. To narrow the gap, this chapter derives a solution space for design parameters for digital storytelling from key literature. Informed by this solution space, the next iteration of a gamified e-learning environment on procurement, manufacturing, and sales supported by the Enterprise Resource Planning System SAP S/4 HANA could evolve to add to the body of knowledge. This solution space can inform teachers, e-learning designers, and researchers and accelerate the creative process of digital storytelling.

Keywords: gamified e-learning, gamification, learning from mistakes, challenges storytelling, intrinsic motivation, business information systems, design elements

1. Introduction

Triggered by the social distancing regulations enforced by the pandemic, e-learning gained a foothold in higher education. A new culture of teaching and learning evolved that promotes active and autonomous learning [1, 2], with positive impacts reported on engagement and intrinsic motivation [3, 4] but also with high dropout rates [5, 6]. Gamification provides enrichment to e-learning that fosters active and engaging learning, giving a "fun spirit to academic activities" [7–9]. Even though promising, gamification is a path that needs to be threaded carefully in higher education. To avoid what critics call "chocolate-dipped broccoli" [10–12], studies for meaningful gamification are called for [13, 14].

Storytelling can be a powerful tool to endorse meaning, but even though the art of storytelling is an old and well-established teaching/learning method, meaningful digital storytelling in e-learning and/or gamified learning environments is not yet fully explored [15]. And even though recent research provides a broad spectrum of case studies from cybersecurity [16], law- and policy-making [17] to climate change [18, 19], cultural heritage [20], and heart failure [4, 21] in digital formats ranging from immersive virtual reality [16], mobile augmented reality [22], to real-life supported, for example, by escape boxes [23], a comprehensive overview of design parameters for storytelling related to e-learning is lacking.

This chapter is a continuation of previous Educational Design Research on gamified self-paced e-learning explored in real-life situations at a German university [24, 25] and explores design elements that the growing maturity of gamification suggests as promising for deeper learning: storytelling and challenges [26]. The research discussed in this chapter aims to contribute to the body of knowledge by providing a solution space of design parameters for digital storytelling evaluated within the scientific community. It is relevant to inform teachers, e-learning designers, and researchers by facilitating the innovative digital storytelling process and laying the groundwork for further research. This is guided by one question: Which design parameters for digital storytelling were evaluated by the scientific community?

The chapter adds to the body of knowledge a case study for using this solution space to design the digital storytelling of the next iteration of a gamified e-learning environment on business information systems. The story is related to the content and aims to endorse a sense of meaning and to make it more intriguing. In an experimental approach to evolving a real-life learning situation, the deployment will be followed by quantitative and qualitative evaluations grounded primarily on the flow theory. The design of the next iteration of this e-learning environment will thus be guided by two questions: Will broadening the options for "learning from mistakes" make the learning scenarios more realistic and more challenging? Can 3D storytelling improve a sense of meaning by taking students deeper into a (virtual) reality represented by the data processed within the scenarios?

With Educational Design Research, an iterative approach has been chosen to actively solve complex real-world educational problems grounded on education and technology research and directed toward expanding the body of knowledge [27]. Educational Design Research is innovative and experimental, based on a sound pedagogical and technical understanding, systematic evaluations, and continuous improvement of solutions. An optimal solution to an educational problem should be creative and innovative but also usable within the specific context of interest [28]. It is innovative if an idea, practice, or object is new to an industry, to a firm, to a customer [29, 30], or to an educational problem. Educational design research can be driven by research motives, design motives and/or motives to change educational practices that constantly and concurrently influence the research and design decisions [28].

Within this chapter, the complex real-world educational problem arose during the pandemic, when hands-on training on business processes in SAP S/4 HANA had to work from a distance. Aligned with the course's learning goals, a rich media self-paced e-learning environment with gamification elements evolved [24, 25] without compromises regarding the complexity or scope of the content. Due to the positive students' response, the solution perpetuated into a blended learning environment that allows students to learn in their own pace anywhere and anytime. Following an iterative approach to this real-world educational problem led to several iterations. The iteration discussed in this chapter is grounded on observations of student's feedback and guided by flow theory and the theory of persuasion. Adjustments are evaluated toward a deeper sense of meaning by providing a more intriguing story and as part of a realistic learning experience: broader options to fail and learn from failure.

The chapter is structured as follows: Section 2 gives a short overview of the flow theory and persuasion in e-learning; Section 3 provides background information on gamification and challenges that come with the freedom to fail. In Section 4 a solution space for design parameters for digital storytelling in e-learning is derived from key literature. Section 5 presents a case study informed by the solution space. The paper ends with a conclusion (Section 6).

2. Flow theory and persuasion in e-learning

Distance Learning is an old and well-established learning concept for education delivery. It replaces the same-time, same-place, face-to-face environment of a traditional classroom by delivering education over a distance [31]. E-learning creates, fosters, delivers, and facilitates learning, anytime and anywhere, with the use of interactive network technologies and can be understood as the next evolutionary step of distance learning [32]. A shift toward blended learning by opening e-learning to local students is widely supported [33]. E-learning enables learners to prepare or revisit a lecture and to reinforce the knowledge construction process [33]. A successful enhancement of learning experiences by digital design elements requires a complex blend of technological, pedagogical, and organizational components [34]. Within a recent literature review, two important continuums for e-learning in higher education were identified: an active learning continuum and an authentic learning continuum [35].

Learning is an individual, personal experience and, thus, should be student-centered [36]. Within student-centered learning environments, intrinsic motivation is the most important aspect. The theory most often referred to in this context is the flow theory. Flow is a mental state of deep concentration in which an individual is totally absorbed by an activity [37]. The focus on this activity is so complete that people within this state of flow get lost in it [37], so deep in concentration that they lose their sense of time and become unaware of their surroundings. The state is temporary, perceived as pleasant, and free of anxiety, boredom, or pressure [38]. It is a state of total immersion and engagement [39]. Within this state of flow, skills and challenges are perfectly balanced [38], and the tendency is high to grow with the challenge and learn new skills [40]. The achievement of this state could be fostered by authentic learning settings, allowing learning to happen as an interactive experience embedded in an ecosystem called a classroom or learning space [41]. The concept of flow in education has often been studied in combination with other theories and aspects like intrinsic motivation, or self-determination theory, social cognitive theory, self- and collective efficacy, or self-regulation [41]. Flow theory provides additional explanatory aspects on psychological determinants of commitment and persistence for adults and for lifelong learning [41].

Persuasion is an intervention directed toward a change in behavior by changing someone's mental state and attitude [42]. Persuasive technologies can induce informal learning by applying persuasive design principles [43]. Case studies on persuasive learning environments on various topics indicate that these principles also work for more formal learning objects [44, 45]. For the design of persuasive technology directed to a change in behavior or attitude, eight steps are recommended [46]:

1. Goals: Simple goals for a start instead of big, ambitious objectives.

2. Audience: Receptive, not resistant.

3. Identification of barriers to behavioral change.

4. Technology: Deciding on a technology the target group is familiar with.

5. Best Practices: Evaluate successful examples of persuasive technology.

6. Imitation of Successful Examples.

7. Small, rapid tests.

8. Expand.

3. Gamification and the freedom to fail

The term gamification refers to the application of design elements from game contexts in non-game contexts [47]. In contrast to plays, games have a goal and a purpose [48] and cannot be judged by the same criteria as games [48]. In a learning context, the achievement of learning goals is the main priority, without compromising for the sake of playfulness [11, 12]. Instead, gamified interventions should be understood as an enrichment of an intervention by game elements, accompanied by a game-like surface [49]. Gamification aims at increasing users' intrinsic and extrinsic motivation and assists in processing information to improve the achievement of goals [23] and/or to change their behavior [39]. When the intention is directed toward a behavioral change, gamified interventions belong to a subset of persuasive technologies and should apply persuasion design principles [50]. In a learning context, gamified interventions aim to engage learners, using elements directed toward scarcity, commitment, and consistency [51] and a persuasive narrative, "The design of a gamified intervention is complex" [52]:

- elements and mechanics of games cannot be transferred so easily to another context,
- directing gamified interventions toward increased (intrinsic) motivation requires some knowledge of motivational psychology and
- if the gamified intervention is directed toward a change of behavior in real life, this adds another layer of complexity.

Recent publications voiced some doubts regarding the benefits of playful or gamified learning environments with a strong focus on extrinsic motivation and instead pleaded for a playful engagement with particular contexts and objects in tune with the purposes and goals of that object and context [53]. The goal or challenge should be clear from the start and broken down into smaller goals, challenges, or missions. The achievement of a goal or the completion of a mission can be rewarded with a badge, points, virtual currency, etc. [49], to encourage the user to pursue. The most important requirements for gamified interventions are [52]:

- sound understanding of users, their motivation and needs and the characteristics of the context,
- clear goals of the gamification project,

- early tests and evaluation (iterative and user-centered approach),
- holistic approach including motivation theories and game design,
- early consideration of legal and ethical constraints,
- a consideration of cheating, and
- continuous monitoring and optimization.

Design principles for gamification and persuasive systems can be clustered into individual behavior principles, social behavior principles, hedonic experience principles, and context principles [54]. Gamification design is tailored to suit a specific context, the problem to solve, the desired effects, and the target group [51]. The problem to solve can be fictional but should be aligned with the learning goals. The challenge should be adjusted to the skills, allowing learners to take decisions. Choices are an important element of a game: the options to choose and to provide an idea of control [50]. This includes the choice to participate, to accept a challenge, and to fail.

Beyond supporting student's engagement, gamified approaches, educational games, and gamification techniques can provide opportunities to learn from failure [53]. Students, who fail in a safe environment, self-reflect, learn from the experience, and will gain self-confidence. Failure in a problem-solving learning process can be process-oriented or solution-oriented [55]. Failure as part of a learning process can support flexibility, induce reflective reasoning, and broaden the search for alternative approaches [55]. To initiate reflective reasoning, students must be aware of failures in their learning process or the solution [55]. Failure can also lead to frustration, low confidence, and disengagement, so guidance and assistance are recommended [55]. Failure or mistakes can lead to a perception of scarcity. Scarcity is an important principle of persuasion [51]: things hard to get are perceived as more valuable and more precious than those that come easily.

4. Design options for digital storytelling in e-learning

Gamification requires a game-like surface, visual stimulation, and visual clues to imbue an atmosphere, a theme, or a situation [50]. The graphics, in combination with an appropriate orchestration of persuasive techniques, initiate the perception of an intervention as a gamified intervention [49, 50]. Avatars, illustrations, and simulations are among the most frequently used graphical elements documented in game-based learning [56]. Virtual or augmented reality can be perceived as a design element for a game-like learning approach that can trigger curiosity [57].

3D-representations of teachers and/or students within a virtual scene can avoid a sense of isolation and instead lead to high degrees of perceived presence in the virtual world, the copresence of teachers and/or other students [57]. When people are the subject of learning, 3D representations of these people can raise the interest of students and their engagement when a virtual representation allows them to interact with these persons. A treasure hunt in historical scenes accompanied by virtual humans reveals the power of storytelling supported by seamless integration of 360-degree videos, 3D artifacts, and virtual human engagement to establish an emotional connection with users, providing a meaningful learning experience [58].

Gamification design should pick up the discipline and the content, "play" with it, and eventually build up a narrative around it [51]. Narrative-based learning is an active learning methodology that is driven by a narrative using any medium [59].

To evaluate successful examples or best practices of persuasive technology for digital storytelling, research of design options for storytelling in e-learning environments was conducted on Scopus using the search criterion ("design elements") AND (storytelling OR narrative) AND (education OR learning OR teaching). The inclusion criteria were as follows:

- publications in English,
- peer review,
- final publication stage,
- published 2021 onwards, and
- (higher) education.

Excluded were reviews. Only research accessible as full text could be considered. The remaining 23 papers were dominated by the subject areas of Computer Science, Social Sciences, and Engineering. Grounded on this and on literature from adjacent fields, a morphological field of design parameters (**Table 1**) was constructed by

Dimension	Design parameters			
Audience	Children [15, 60–62]	Adolescents [63, 64]	Adults [64–67]	
Narrator	Students [67]		Teacher [18, 68–70]	
Degree of Activity	Interactive [58, 70–74]		Non-interactive [16, 66]	
Situation	Face-to-face [75]	Distance [76, 77]	Blended Learning [75]	
Degree of collaboration	Collaborative [62, 78, 79]		Individual [66, 74]	
Topic [80]	Personal narratives [20, 66, 67]	Historical documentaries [81]	Stories related to a particular concept or practice [18, 20, 74, 77, 82, 83]	
Perspective	Character-based [73, 79, 83, 84]		Plot-based [73, 74]	
Approach	Social-emotional learning [60]		Problem-based learning [23, 71, 72, 82, 83]	
Realism	Autobiographical [20, 66, 67]	Documentary [18, 74, 85, 86]	Fictional [84, 86, 87]	
Medium	Text [74]	Audio/Speech	Illustration [74, 83]	Video [74, 77, 85]
3D Visualization	People/Avatars [58, 61, 62, 70]	Scenes [57, 58, 70, 79, 84, 88]	Concepts [20, 23, 70, 82, 88, 89]	
Scale of virtuality	Reality [83, 88]	Augmented Reality [19, 22]	Virtual reality [16]	

Table 1.
Selection of design elements for digital storytelling in e-learning with example references.

examining configurations in this field to identify a possible, viable, practical, or interesting subset of configurations: the solution space [90, 91].

This solution space provides a selection of design parameters suitable for the purpose and evaluated within the scientific community. Even though this morphological approach might restrain creativity, it can accelerate the creation of innovative ideas. There are relationships and constraints between the design parameters, for example, due to legal constraints: there is a minimum age for fully immersive VR, forbidding its deployment for younger children. Other relationships and constraints should be analyzed thoroughly and would require further exploration.

Digital storytelling refers to stories on a specific theme or topic by blending a mixture of rich media into a digital format accessible via a computer or any other device capable of playing videos [15]. Digital stories can be personal narratives, historical documentaries, or stories related to a particular concept or practice [80] and are a powerful tool to endorse a sense of meaning. This sense of meaning is paramount for teaching/learning environments: The whole construction of knowledge is built through the process of meaning-making [92]. That is the point of education: that students learn something from someone, and they learn it for a reason; it is about content, purpose, and relationships [93].

Within a teaching/learning context, the role of the narrator is another criterion of differentiation. Teachers create educational digital storytelling that can increase interest in new ideas or clarify abstract or conceptual content [80]. Based on a systematic literature review, eight types of outcomes for educational digital storytelling by students were identified: affective, cognitive, conceptual, academic, technological, linguistic, ontological, and social outcomes [15]. Social-emotional learning by storytelling aims at stimulating the social part of the brain by activating learners' emotions, thus increasing their receptiveness to information [94]. Students playing an active role in the learning process can have a positive impact on their perception of knowledge [59]. Interactive learning concepts are, for example, simulated, case-based, problem-based, or scenario-based learning [33].

The search for meaning is a part of human nature, a quest spoken to by storytelling [94]. A story refers to a succession of events and actions that take place in a scenario represented by a narrative [95]. "Meaningful storyfication" enriches online learning with an engaging, motivating story [96] that students perceive as relevant to their personal goals [18]. The story must be intrinsically linked to the content [16]. Meaningful learning can be supported by excitement, stimulation, and engagement in the learning process [38]. 3D-design elements could add to the learning experience by providing immersive experiences, improving a sense of reality, and raising interest and curiosity.

5. Case study

The audience of the case study presented in this chapter is undergraduate students in business administration and business law. Students are adult learners, self-directed human beings who expect to be perceived as such [97]. They cannot be fed knowledge against their will but are alive and learn in an attempt to create meaning [98]: they are a receptive, non-resistant audience. Adults possess higher physical, cognitive, and mental abilities than children [24] and should be supported in their quest for meaning-making in their learning activities. Adult learning should thus be oriented on situations and on solving problems [99]. It should be life-centered and self-directed, and different preferences should be considered regarding style, time, place, and pace of learning. It should also place learning from experience at the core of the learning process [97].

The course presented in this chapter was imbedded in a learning module on Business Information Systems. The learning objectives were clearly communicated and not disguised. Following the objectives of the course a case study evolved around the process related to manufacturing and selling bikes. Special consideration was on raising curiosity and on maintaining students' motivation all through the course. Gamification elements were used to increase engagement (e.g., a roadmap and badges), intended to trigger associations of leisure activities and to bring more ease into the learning process.

The scenario evolved over the years. In 2020, a self-paced e-learning environment was developed to cope with the learning situation during the pandemic. Within an iterative approach, this e-learning environment was improved, and flaws and inconsistencies were reduced. Altogether, the learning setting was perceived well by the students [24] even after the pandemic. Within this course, first-hand experiences in the support of business processes through enterprise resource planning systems (ERP systems) should be gained through hands-on training using the example of SAP S/4 HANA. The SAP S/4 HANA system used by our university is hosted by the SAP Academic Competence Center (SAP ACC) in Munich. The SAP ACC provides customized systems and several well-defined case studies. The case study presented here extends the case studies included in the system by challenges related to activities from procurement, manufacturing, and sales to integrated business processes involving different organizational units. The setting is fictional but authentic and provides the preliminaries of understanding how activities within an organizational unit or poor data quality can have an impact on the activities of another organizational unit of a company. At the end of the course, students should be familiar with business processes and material flows in procurement, manufacturing, and sales, as well as the accompanying financial flows. Students should be aware of the relationship between information and material flows and should realize the importance of data quality. Connected with the business processes, some terms and concepts (e.g., Material Requirements Planning, Calculation of Production Costs, and Target Costing) are introduced to build the foundation for the following courses.

According to the nature of evolutionary approaches, observation of the students within face-to-face courses, communication with students over the learning management system or per email, assessments of the data quality in SAP S/4 HANA, and the regular evaluation of the course revealed issues to be dealt with, that led to requirements for the next iteration, for example:

- Content and information within the e-learning environment were distributed over a mix of various media to avoid monotony and to keep interest high. The content was meant to be complementary with videos explaining the goals of each scenario, screencasts for interacting with the SAP S/4 HANA system, process diagrams following the Business Process Model and Notation (BPMN 2.0), data sheets with a compact summary of the relevant data and the corresponding data fields, audio files with additional information about concepts and definitions, etc. The observation of students revealed that some prioritized certain types of media, for example, screencasts or data sheets, sometimes missing complementary content crucial for a sense of meaning. Providing rich media content stays beneficial for most students, but some redundancy of the content crucial for understanding the process is required.

- Screencasts came with thorough explanations of the process but without subtitles. This is an issue for students with impaired hearing and for those students who muted the videos when in the classroom. Subtitles must therefore be included.

- The scenarios should leave more room for students' decision making, giving students a stronger sense of control.

- Some screencasts provided too detailed descriptions, leaving too little room for students' decision making. Too simple challenges or over-explanation lowers the intensity of attention [55] and reduces the number of solution attempts [100]. Screencasts should thus be less detailed. This will lead to increased numbers of mistakes but also to challenges that should be perceived as more rewarding.

- Already established communication processes for constructive feedback and troubleshooting [25] should be expanded to cover a broader range of possible mistakes.

- The case study is about business processes. Following these processes, the students interact with the SAP S/4 HANA system. They maintain master data, insert data representing, for example, purchase orders or invoices, and extract information about material requirements or unpaid invoices. The SAP S/4 HANA system notifies students about inconsistencies (e.g., missing data or conflicts with certain rules). Most students get along well, but some students were so focused on flawlessly entering the data into the system, that they lost the awareness of the activities behind it and how they relate to the process. The story behind the processes should therefore become more meaningful and intriguing and supported by visual clues, for example, 3D representations of elements to enhance the persuasion of the story.

Grounded on the options previously explored (**Table 1**), the design parameters for digital storytelling in this iteration of a self-paced e-learning environment evolved (**Table 2**) as a subset of the solution space.

Students should get a business-oriented process understanding supported and enabled by the SAP S/4 HANA system. Some basic terms are introduced along the process, with content adjusted to the events and activities. Messages, information, and content are more likely to be persuasive when they find fertile ground (receptive audience) and are delivered at the right time and place [101]. Connecting information about, for example, bill explosion or target costing with events and problems along the story connects the information with activities in realistic learning settings, thus adding meaning to each learning element. The story driving these processes is simplified but leans on real-life situations. Conferring the responsibility for the business processes to the students increases their sense of control. The option for failure will be broadened by decision making, without leaving students alone.

Mistakes can and will happen in any scenario and will have an influence on other activities; thus, they must be dealt with. The mistakes can be related to data (e.g., missing data and wrong data) or to activities (e.g., wrong activity, wrong sequence, and missing out activities). These mistakes have an impact on the chain of events and prepare students for similar situations in real life [25]. The option for decision-making will be expanded within this new line of story and, consequently, the option to fail

Criteria	Design parameters	
Audience	Adults	The audience is mostly undergraduate students of Business Administration and Business Law.
Narrator	Teacher	The story is predefined by the lecturer.
Degree of Activity	Interactive	Events and activities along the business processes are represented by data. The representation of this data is maintained by the SAP S/4 HANA system. The students interact with this SAP S/4 HANA system and take decisions, thus taking control over the business process.
Situation	Blended Learning	Even though the learning environment is accessible from anywhere, experiences from previous years and students' observations showed that face-to-face courses are not obsolete but still necessary in this concept.
Degree of collaboration	Individual	The story is predefined, and students can change the turn of events with the choices they make, which are limited by the logic of the plot.
Characteristics	Stories related to a particular concept or practice	The story spins around the manufacturing and sales processes of bikes. These business processes are the concept of interest for this story. The sequence of events of the story corresponds with the sequence of events and activities in the business processes.
Perspective	Plot-based	The plot spins around a bike company.
Approach	Problem-based learning	Several events/problems occur along the business process that requires students to make decisions.
Realism	Fictional	The plot is fictional, leaning on real-life business processes, but simplified for the purpose of learning.
Medium	Rich media	A variety of media is combined: videos, texts, audio files, animations, and 3D objects.
3D Visualization	Scenes and Concepts	The bike and the scenes are visualized in 3D to take the students deeper into the story.

Table 2.
Design parameters for the next iteration.

and learn from failure and mistakes. The trouble-shooting routines already established will be broadened to assist and support face-to-face and remote. Instantaneous feedback keeps the interest of learners alive [33].

Following the customizing of the SAP S/4 HANA system with some minor adjustments, the story deals with the production of bikes, leading the students through the business processes step-by-step. Students are assigned an active role in a story, a role similar to a role they might have in the near future (scenario-based learning) [102]. This concept will be expanded toward intensified storytelling supported by visual clues. Problem-based learning will be supported by events that cause problems, problems students must deal with along the line of events. 3D elements provide visual clues to convey core elements of the story: 3D models of the bike and its parts (Software: Gravity Sketch) and several simple scenes (Software: Adobe Substance 3D Stager), for example, a showroom, a storage room, production planning, accounting. To relate the story to the SAP S/4 HANA system supporting the process, a PC or Laptop with a screenshot of the SAP Fiori Interface of SAP S/4 HANA is placed within each room (**Figure 1**), indicating the option to jump into the system along the chain of events.

Figure 1.
Visual embedding of the SAP S/4 HANA system into the story.

The learning objectives of this course are related to business processes. Business processes can be described as a sequence of activities, each related to business goals and triggered by events. Business processes are therefore almost predestinated for storytelling, as events are also building blocks of a story.

Within this case study, events are characterized by a description, a problem, and learning goals, triggering students' activities. Each activity causes new events, triggering the next activities. A selection of events should show the pattern behind them.

5.1 Example event: new bike is designed

The organizational unit "Research and Development" came up with the concept of a brand-new bike (**Figure 2**). The Marketing department already confirmed that the bike could be sold at 999€ per piece.

Figure 2.
3D scene of a research and design-department showing the bill of material of a new bike pinned to the wall and a visual embedding of the SAP S/4 HANA system on the desktop.

Problem:

How can this new bike be added to the system?

Learning goal:

Students get familiar with multilevel parts lists (Bill of Material), work schedules, and how the list of parts can be linked to an operation. Each operation is assigned to a working place and requires planning set-up times, machine times, and labor times, introducing students to terms like cost categories, cost centers, and activity types.

5.2 Example event: proof of concept is necessary

To prove the concept, a certain number of bikes must be manufactured.

Problem:

None of the raw materials required to build a bike are in stock (**Figure 3**).

Learning objective:

Students get familiar with the term Material Requirements Planning (MRP) before the purchasing process is discussed, and the students jump into the SAP S/4 HANA system.

5.3 Example event: price calculation is necessary

A customer has seen an advertisement for the new bike and requests the prices for the bike.

Problem:

Prices should be above the production cost, but production costs have not been calculated yet.

Learning goal:

Students get familiar with the calculation of manufacturing costs based on the costs derived from the working schedule, the bill of material (**Figure 4**), and the

Figure 3.
3D scene of an empty storage room with a visual embedding of the SAP S/4 HANA system as a visual clue pointing toward the corresponding interactions related to purchasing processes in SAP S/4 HANA.

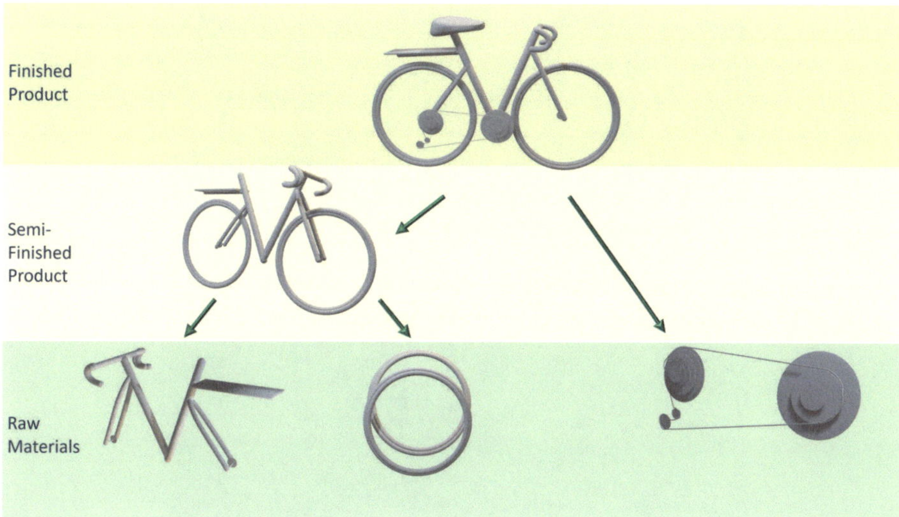

Figure 4.
Bill of material of the bike (simplified).

process paid for the raw materials in the previous step. The students get familiar with sales processes in the ERP system. They understand terms like profit margins and the limits of sales discounts.

5.4 Example event: price reduction is requested

The customer is a wholesaler interested in buying more bikes, but not for 999$ per piece. A price reduction is requested.

Problem:

The production costs will be too high to lower the price as requested by the customer.

Learning goals:

Students get familiar with the term "Target Costing" and evaluate options to lower production costs before they go into SAP S/4 HANA to place several purchase requests, to lower the prices for raw materials and/or to adjust the working schedule. After the stock was replenished, the production costs should be calculated again, making students familiar with moving average prices.

5.5 Example event: order exceeds stock

The wholesaler orders a significant number of bikes.

Problem:

The bikes in stock will not cover the demand.

Learning goal:

Already familiar with material requirements planning, the student can do the MRP Run in SAP S/4 HANA, replenish raw materials (**Figure 5**), and produce semi-finished and finished products as required. After that the order of the customer can be shipped, and the financial flow settled.

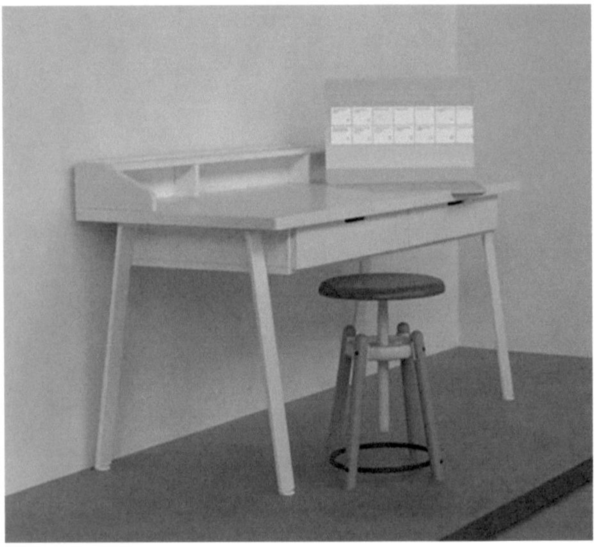

Figure 5.
3D scene of the storage room with a visual embedding of the SAP S/4 HANA system as a visual clue pointing toward the corresponding interactions in SAP S/4 HANA.

6. Conclusion

To get an overview of digital storytelling's state of the art and collect concepts and ideas suitable for this context, a solution space was presented in this chapter as a morphological box fueled by key literature. This chapter contributes to the body of knowledge by putting the solution space of these design parameters up for discussion. This is relevant by informing further research and by accelerating the creative process of storytelling for teachers and designers of gamified e-learning environments. This solution space was constructed to inform a specific context and is thus incomplete. A more thorough literature review would be required to cover all configurations in the field and to explore relationships between design elements in depth.

This chapter contributes to the body of knowledge by providing an iterative approach toward gamified self-paced e-learning about business information systems at a university. The core of the concept has proven itself within the last semesters but must evolve into another iteration. A more intriguing story should improve this iteration meant to take students deeper into the business processes and to endorse a higher sense of meaning. The story is the backbone of gamification [84]. It plays with the content of the course, digitalizes business processes, and transfers the experience toward the digitalization of learning processes. The concept is designed for a specific audience, content, and teaching style; thus, it will not be representative on a broader scale.

The story should be supported by visual clues to become more convincing and to make sure that the process dominates the data instead of the other way around. The design decisions for enriching the learning environment presented in this chapter with digital storytelling were extracted from the solution space of design parameters for digital storytelling. This more sophisticated 3D-based storytelling puts the process stronger in focus but has yet to prove itself in a real-life situation in the next semester and will have to be evaluated properly.

The concept presented in this chapter is student-centered, self-directed, and problem-oriented. It follows the concept of learning from experience and integrates failures and mistakes into the didactic concept of the course. It provides an example of additional values of active learning, self-determined, and directed toward meaningful learning for the target group of adult learners.

Failure is paramount in gamification: challenge comes with the option of failure. Accepting a challenge involves accepting potential failure and getting ready to grow in the process. The option of failure is essential for the learning process, as well as the ambition to master a challenge, a strong intrinsic motivation, and a strong driver to keep going: an interactive learning strategy should empower learners to apply what they learned in the real world [33]. The option of failure makes learning more realistic. It prepares for real life, where failure can have serious consequences. As there is still a paucity of research on learning from failure, from experience, or from mistakes in e-learning, this case study contributes to the body of knowledge but also invites further research.

Author details

Anke Schüll
School of Economic Disciplines, University of Siegen, Siegen, Germany

*Address all correspondence to: anke.schuell@uni-siegen.de

References

[1] Khan RMI, Ali A, Alourani A. Investigating learners' experience of autonomous learning in e-learning context. International Journal of Emerging Technologies in Learning. 2022;**17**(08):4-17. DOI: 10.3991/ijet.v17i08.29885

[2] Lazorak O, Belkina O, Yaroslavova E. Changes in student autonomy via e-learning courses. International Journal of Emerging Technologies in Learning (iJET). 2021;**16**(17):209-225

[3] Rivera ES, Garden CLP. Gamification for student engagement: A framework. Journal of Further and Higher Education. 2021;**45**(7):999-1012. DOI: 10.1080/0309877X.2021.1875201

[4] Maheu-Cadotte M-A, Dubé V, Lavoie P. Development and contribution of a serious game to improve nursing students' clinical reasoning in acute heart failure: A multimethod study. Computers, Informatics, Nursing. 2023;**41**(6):410-420. DOI: 10.1097/CIN.0000000000000966

[5] Luis RMMF, Llamas-Nistal M, Iglesias MJF. On the introduction of intelligent alerting systems to reduce e-learning dropout: A case study. Smart Learning Environments. 2022;**9**(1). DOI: 10.1186/s40561-022-00210-0

[6] Zhou Y, Zhao J, Zhang J. Prediction of learners' dropout in e-learning based on the unusual behaviors. Interactive Learning Environments. 2023;**31**(3):1796-1820. DOI: 10.1080/10494820.2020.1857788

[7] Saleem AN, Noori NM, Ozdamli F. Gamification applications in e-learning: A literature review. Technology, Knowledge and Learning. 2022;**27**(1):139-159. DOI: 10.1007/s10758-020-09487-x

[8] Dicheva D, Dichev C, Agre G, Angelova G. Gamification in education: A systematic mapping study. Educational Technology and Society. 2015;**18**(3):75-88

[9] Aguiar-Castillo L, Clavijo-Rodriguez A, Hernández-López L, de Saa-Pérez P, Pérez-Jiménez R. Gamification and deep learning approaches in higher education. Journal of Hospitality, Leisure, Sport and Tourism Education. 2021;**29**:100290. DOI: 10.1016/j.jhlste.2020.100290

[10] Bruckman A. Can education be fun? In: 1999 Game Developers Conference Proceedings, San Jose, CA, San Francisco: Miller Freeman; 1999. pp. 75-79

[11] DiSalvo B. Pink boxes and chocolate-dipped broccoli: Bad game design providing justifications for reluctant learners. In: Proceedings of 11th Games + Learning + Society Conference, Madison, WI, USA. Pittsburgh: Carnegie Mellon ETC Press; 2015

[12] Camps-Ortueta I, González-Calero PA, Quiroga MA, Gómez-Martín PP. Measuring preferences in game mechanics: Towards personalized chocolate-covered broccoli. In: van der Spek E, Göbel S, Do EY-L, Clua E, Baalsrud Hauge J, editors. Entertainment Computing and Serious Games. Cham: Springer International Publishing; 2019. pp. 15-27

[13] Luo Z. Educational gamification from 1995 to 2020: A bibliometric analysis. In: Educational Gamification from 1995 to 2020: A Bibliometric Analysis. New York, NY: ACM; 2021. pp. 140-145

[14] Buchem I, Carlino C, Amenduni F, Poce A. Meaningful gamification in MOOCS. Designing and examining learner engagement in the open virtual mobility learning hub. In: Gómez Chova L, López Martínez A, Candel Torres I, editors. Proceedings of the 14th International Technology, Education and Development Conference (INTED 2020). Valencia: IATED Academy; 2020. pp. 9529-9534

[15] Wu J, Chen D-TV. A systematic review of educational digital storytelling. Computers and Education. 2020;**147**:103786. DOI: 10.1016/j.compedu.2019.103786

[16] Calvert J, Hume M. Improving student learning outcomes using narrative virtual reality as pre-training. Virtual Reality. (London: Springer Nature). 2023;**27**(3):2633-2648. DOI: 10.1007/s10055-023-00830-y

[17] Vargas-Murillo AR, La Nadia Monica de Asuncion Pari-Bedoya I, Delgado-Chávez CA, Menacho Taipe E, Reyes Cuba CK, Paul Morales Cauti G. Crowdlaw: Application of Emerging Technologies and Collective Intelligence in Law and Policy Making. In: International Conference on Inventive Computation Technologies (ICICT 2024). New York, NY: IEEE; 2024. pp. 288-293

[18] Wang N, Stern RJ, Waite L. Workflow for designing instructional videos to support place-based geoscience education for geoscience majors. Journal of Geoscience Education. 2023;**71**(1):107-125. DOI: 10.1080/10899995.2022.2093543

[19] Monreal JB, Palaoag T. Unveiling effective design elements and features for implementing augmented reality in bicol mythical creatures: Teachers' perspective. Nano-NTP. 2024;**20**(S3):316-330. DOI: 10.62441/nano-ntp.v20iS3.24

[20] Cardinal T, Stavrou S, Murphy MS, Huber J. Ethical relationality, TribalCrit, and autobiographical narrative inquiry: Imagining coming alongside indigenous children. Frontiers in Education. 2023;**7**. DOI: 10.3389/feduc.2022.1051339

[21] Lukey A, Mackay M, Hasan K, Rush KL. Clinical perspectives on the development of a gamified heart failure patient education web site. Computers, Informatics, Nursing. 2023;**41**(8):615-620. DOI: 10.1097/CIN.0000000000000983

[22] Zimmerman HT, Land SM, Faimon L, Chiu Y-C. Mobile augmented reality supporting families' immersive collaborative learning: Learning-on-the-move for place-based geoscience sense-making. International Journal of Computer-Supported Collaborative Learning. 2023;**18**(2):291-322. DOI: 10.1007/s11412-023-09399-9

[23] Veldkamp A, Rebecca Niese J, Heuvelmans M, Knippels M-CPJ, van Joolingen WR. You escaped! How did you learn during gameplay? British Journal of Educational Technology. 2022;**53**(5):1430-1458. DOI: 10.1111/bjet.13194

[24] Schüll A, Brocksieper L. Distance digital learning for adult learners: Self-paced e-learning on business information systems. In: Filipe J, Śmiałek M, Brodsky A, Hammoudi S, editors. Enterprise Information Systems. Cham: Springer Nature Switzerland; 2023. pp. 313-337

[25] Schüll A, Brocksieper L. Gamified self-paced e-learning: Two iterations of an educational design experiment. In: Samarati P, van Sinderen M, Di Vimercati SDC, Wijnhoven F, editors. E-Business and Telecommunications.

Cham: Springer Nature Switzerland; 2023. pp. 84-102

[26] Khaldi A, Bouzidi R, Nader F. Gamification of e-learning in higher education: A systematic literature review. Smart Learning Environments. 2023;**10**(1). DOI: 10.1186/s40561-023-00227-z

[27] McKenney S, Reeves TC. Educational design research. In: Spector JM, Merrill MD, Elen J, Bishop MJ, editors. Handbook of Research on Educational Communications and Technology. New York, NY: Springer New York; 2014. pp. 131-140

[28] Akkerman SF, Bronkhorst LH, Zitter I. The complexity of educational design research. Quality and Quantity. 2013;**47**(1):421-439. DOI: 10.1007/s11135-011-9527-9

[29] Hannemyr G. The internet as hyperbole: A critical examination of adoption rates. The Information Society. 2003;**19**(2):111-121. DOI: 10.1080/01972240309459

[30] Heiskanen E, Hyvönen K, Niva M, Pantzar M, Timonen P, Varjonen J. User involvement in radical innovation: Are consumers conservative? European Journal of Innovation Management. 2007;**10**(4):489-509. DOI: 10.1108/14601060710828790

[31] Volery T, Lord D. Critical success factors in online education. The International Journal of Educational Management. 2000;**14**(5):216-223

[32] Choi DH, Kim J, Kim SH. ERP training with a web-based electronic learning system: The flow theory perspective. International Journal of Human-Computer Studies. 2007;**65**(3):223-243. DOI: 10.1016/j.ijhcs.2006.10.002

[33] Sridharan B, Deng H, Corbitt B. Critical success factors in e-learning ecosystems: A qualitative study. Journal of Systems and Information Technology. 2010;**12**(4):263-288. DOI: 10.1108/13287261011095798

[34] McPherson MA, Nunes JM. Critical issues for e-learning delivery: What may seem obvious is not always put into practice. Journal of Computer Assisted Learning. 2008;**24**(5):433-445. DOI: 10.1111/j.1365-2729.2008.00281.x

[35] Theelen H, van Breukelen DHJ. The didactic and pedagogical design of e-learning in higher education: A systematic literature review. Journal of Computer Assisted Learning. 2022;**38**(5):1286-1303. DOI: 10.1111/jcal.12705

[36] Clark D. Psychological myths in e-learning. Medical Teacher. 2002;**24**(6):598-604. DOI: 10.1080/0142159021000063916

[37] Csikszentmihalyi M. Flow: The Psychology of Optimal Experience/ Mihaly Csikszentmihalyi. 1st ed. New York: Harper and Row; 1990

[38] Admiraal W, Huizenga J, Akkerman S, Ten DG. The concept of flow in collaborative game-based learning. Computers in Human Behavior. 2011;**27**(3):1185-1194. DOI: 10.1016/j.chb.2010.12.013

[39] Treiblmaier H, Putz L-M, Lowry PB. Research commentary: Setting a definition, context, and theory-based research agenda for the gamification of non-gaming applications. AIS Transactions on Human-Computer Interaction. 2018;**10**(3):129-163. DOI: 10.17705/1thci.00107

[40] Csikszentmihalyi M, LeFevre J. Optimal experience in work and leisure.

Journal of Personality and Social Psychology. 1989;**56**(5):815-822. DOI: 10.1037/0022-3514.56.5.815

[41] Heutte J, Fenouillet F, Martin-Krumm C, et al. Optimal experience in adult learning: Conception and validation of the flow in education scale (EduFlow-2). Frontiers in Psychology. 2021;**12**:828027. DOI: 10.3389/fpsyg.2021.828027

[42] O'Keefe DJ. Theories of persuasion. In: Nabi RL, Oliver MB, editors. The SAGE Handbook of Media Processes and Effects. London: Sage; 2009. pp. 269-282

[43] Fogg BJ. Persuasive technology. Ubiquity. 2002;**2002**(December):2. DOI: 10.1145/764008.763957

[44] Behringer R, Soosay M, Gram-Hansen SB, Øhrstrøm P. Persuasive technology for learning and teaching—The EuroPLOT project. In: Proceedings of the International Workshop on EuroPLOT Persuasive Technology for Learning, Education and Teaching (IWEPLET 2013). Research Triangle: Lulu; 2013. pp. 3-7

[45] Behringer R, Sinclair G, editors. Proceedings of the International Workshop on EuroPLOT Persuasive Technology for Learning, Education and Teaching (IWEPLET 2013). Research Triangle: Lulu; 2013

[46] Fogg BJ. Creating persuasive technologies. In: Chatterjee S, Dev P, editors. Creating Persuasive Technologies. New York, NY: ACM; 2009. pp. 1-6

[47] Deterding S, Dixon D, Khaled R, Nacke L. From game design elements to gamefulness: defining "gamification" In: Lugmayr A, Franssila H, Safran C, Hammouda I, editors. Proceedings of the 15th International Academic MindTrek Conference: Envisioning Future Media Environments. New York, NY: ACM; 2011. pp. 9-15

[48] Llagostera E. On Gamification and Persuasion. In: Proceedings of the Brazilian Symposium of Games and Digital Entertainment (SBGames 2021). Rio de Janeiro, Brazil: SBC; 2012. pp. 12-21

[49] Liu Y, Alexandrova T, Nakajima T. Gamifying intelligent environments. In: AAN S, Albayrak HS, Yassine A, editors. Gamifying Intelligent Environments. New York, NY, USA: ACM; 2011. pp. 7-12

[50] Marache-Francisco C, Brangier E. Perception of gamification: Between graphical design and persuasive design. In: Hutchison D, Kanade T, Kittler J, et al, editors. Design, User Experience, and Usability. Health, Learning, Playing, Cultural, and Cross-Cultural User Experience. Berlin, Heidelberg: Springer Berlin Heidelberg; 2013. pp. 558-567

[51] Antonaci A, Klemke R, Kreijns K, Specht M. Get gamification of MOOC right! IJSG. 2018;**5**(3):61-78. DOI: 10.17083/ijsg.v5i3.255

[52] Morschheuser B, Hamari J, Werder K, Abe J. How to gamify? A method for designing gamification. In: Hawaii International Conference on System Sciences. Atlanta: Association for Information Systems (AIS); 2017

[53] Nørgård RT, Toft-Nielsen C, Whitton N. Playful learning in higher education: Developing a signature pedagogy. International Journal of Play. 2017;**6**(3):272-282. DOI: 10.1080/21594937.2017.1382997

[54] Krath J, Von Korflesch HFO. Designing gamification and persuasive systems: A systematic literature review. In: Proceedings of the 5th International GamiFIN Conference (GamiFIN 2021).

Aachen: CEUR/RWTH; 2021. pp. 100-109

[55] Jackson A, Godwin A, Bartholomew S, Mentzer N. Learning from failure: A systematized review. International Journal of Technology and Design Education. 2022;**32**(3):1853-1873. DOI: 10.1007/s10798-021-09661-x

[56] Subhash S, Cudney EA. Gamified learning in higher education: A systematic review of the literature. Computers in Human Behavior. 2018;**87**:192-206. DOI: 10.1016/j.chb.2018.05.028

[57] Hassell M, Goyal S, Limayem M, Boughzala I. Effects of presence, copresence, and flow on learning outcomes in 3D learning spaces. AIJ. 2012;**2**(1):62-73. DOI: 10.5929/2011.2.1.4

[58] Kontogiorgakis E, Zidianakis E, Kontaki E, et al. Gamified VR storytelling for cultural tourism using 3D reconstructions, virtual humans, and 360° videos. Technologies. 2024;**12**(6):73. DOI: 10.3390/technologies12060073

[59] Sánchez-Rivas E, Ramos Núñez MF, Ramos Navas-Parejo M, La Cruz-Campos JC d. Narrative-based learning using mobile devices. ET. 2023;**65**(2):284-297. DOI: 10.1108/ET-06-2022-0244

[60] Koivula M, Turja L, Laakso M-L. Using the storytelling method to hear children's perspectives and promote their social-emotional competence. Journal of Early Intervention. 2020;**42**(2):163-181. DOI: 10.1177/1053815119880599

[61] Zarei N, Chu SL, Quek F, Rao N, Brown SA. Investigating the effects of self-avatars and story-relevant avatars on children's creative storytelling. In: Bernhaupt R, Mueller F, Verweij D, et al, editors. Proceedings of the 2020 CHI Conference on Human Factors in Computing Systems. New York, NY: ACM; 2020. pp. 1-11

[62] Liu C-C, Liu K-P, Wang P-H, Chen G-D, Su M-C. Applying tangible story avatars to enhance children's collaborative storytelling. British Journal of Educational Technology. 2012;**43**(1):39-51. DOI: 10.1111/j.1467-8535.2010.01146.x

[63] Shofiyyah NA, Muharam A, Susanti I, Nurdiana A. Exploring the power of storytelling: Enhancing engagement and learning outcomes among adolescents. IMEIJ. 2024;**5**(1):990-1006. DOI: 10.54373/imeij.v5i1.847

[64] Lim NZL, Zakaria A, Aryadoust V. A systematic review of digital storytelling in language learning in adolescents and adults. Education and Information Technologies. 2022;**27**(5):6125-6155. DOI: 10.1007/s10639-021-10861-0

[65] Caminotti E, Gray J. The effectiveness of storytelling on adult learning. Journal of Workplace Learning. 2012;**24**(6):430-438. DOI: 10.1108/13665621211250333

[66] Anderson K. Speaking from the heart: Everyday storytelling and adult learning. In: Canadian Journal of Native Education. Edmonton: Intercultural Program, Department of Educational Foundations. 2004;**28**(1+2):123-129. DOI: 10.14288/cjne.v28i1-2.196363

[67] Clark MC, Rossiter M. "Now the pieces are in place ...": Learning through personal storytelling in the adult classroom. New Horizons in Adult Education and Human Resource Development. 2006;**20**(3):19-33. DOI: 10.1002/nha3.10258

[68] Shank MJ. Teacher storytelling: A means for creating and learning within a collaborative space. Teaching and Teacher Education. 2006;**22**(6):711-721. DOI: 10.1016/j.tate.2006.03.002

[69] Savvidou C. Storytelling as dialogue: How teachers construct professional knowledge. Teachers and Teaching. 2010;**16**(6):649-664. DOI: 10.1080/13540602.2010.517682

[70] Khoshnoodifar M, Ashouri A, Taheri M. Effectiveness of gamification in enhancing learning and attitudes: A study of statistics education for health school students. Journal of Advances in Medical Education and Professionalism. 2023;**11**(4):230-239. DOI: 10.30476/jamp.2023.98953.1817

[71] Poonsawad A, Srisomphan J, Sanrach C. Synthesis of problem-based interactive digital storytelling learning model under gamification environment promotes students' problem-solving skills. International Journal of Emerging Technology in Learning. 2022;**17**(5):103-119

[72] Cardona-Rivera RE, Sullivan A, Young RM, editors. Interactive Storytelling. Cham: Springer International Publishing; 2019

[73] Cai Y, Miao C, Tan A-H, Shen Z. A hybrid of plot-based and character-based interactive storytelling. In: Hui K, Pan Z, Chung RC, et al, editors. Technologies for E-Learning and Digital Entertainment. Berlin, Heidelberg: Springer Berlin Heidelberg; 2007. pp. 260-273

[74] A'rachman FR, Setiawan C, Hardi OS, et al. Designing effective educational storymaps for flood disaster mitigation in the Ciliwung River Basin: An empirical study. IOP Conference Series: Earth and Environmental Science. 2024;**1314**(1):12082. DOI: 10.1088/1755-1315/1314/1/012082

[75] Meri-Yilan S. Task-based language learning through digital storytelling in a blended learning environment. Education Research International. 2020;**4**:37-43

[76] Neal L. Storytelling at a distance. eLearn. 2001;**2001**(5):4. DOI: 10.1145/566970.566979

[77] Baim SA. Digital storytelling: Conveying the essence of a face-to-face lecture in an online learning environment. Journal of Effective Teaching. 2015;**15**(1):47-58

[78] Uslu A, Uslu NA. Improving primary school students' creative writing and social-emotional learning skills through collaborative digital storytelling. Acta Educationis Generalis. 2021;**11**(2):1-18. DOI: 10.2478/atd-2021-0009

[79] Knorr C, Zinn B. Design and development of a collaborative serious game to promote professional knowledge acquisition of prospective teachers. In: Auer ME, Hortsch H, Michler O, Köhler T, editors. Mobility for Smart Cities and Regional Development—Challenges for Higher Education. Cham: Springer International Publishing; 2022. pp. 890-901

[80] Robin B. The educational uses of digital storytelling. In: Society for information technology & teacher education international conference. Waynesville: Association for the Advancement of Computing in Education (AACE); 2006. pp. 709-716

[81] Fehn BR, Schul JE. Teaching and learning competent historical documentary making: Lessons from national history day winners. The History Teacher. 2011;**45**(1):25-43

[82] Chennamaneni S, Pradhan P, Chebolu V, Vejendla M, Kannaiah SK, Aravinth SS. Designing Cybersecurity AI Based Awareness Games for Citizens: Best Practices and Future Directions. New York, NY: IEEE; 2023. pp. 407-412

[83] Peppler K, Keune A, Dahn M, Bennett D, Letourneau SM. Designing for others: The roles of narrative and empathy in supporting girls' engineering engagement. ILS. 2022;**123**(3/4):129-153. DOI: 10.1108/ILS-07-2021-0061

[84] Bhalerao D, Bagul D, Kesapure N, et al. Design and Development of Gamification Tool for Teenagers for Selection of Higher Education Path Based on Personality Traits. New York, NY: IEEE; 2021. pp. 1-5

[85] Bernard S. Documentary Storytelling: Creative Nonfiction on Screen. London: Routledge; 2022

[86] LaMarre HL, Landreville KD. When is fiction as good as fact? Comparing the influence of documentary and historical reenactment films on engagement, affect, issue interest, and learning. Mass Communication and Society. 2009;**12**(4):537-555. DOI: 10.1080/15205430903237915

[87] Arnedo-Moreno J, Garcia-Font V. A study on the design and application of fictional storytelling in online learning of computer security. Applied Sciences. 2021;**11**(13):6185. DOI: 10.3390/app11136185

[88] Stoldt F, Brandl LC, Schrader A. Pervasive serious game for exam preparation: Exploring the motivational effects of game narratives. In: Haahr M, Rojas-Salazar A, Göbel S, editors. Serious Games. Cham: Springer Nature Switzerland; 2023. pp. 439-446

[89] Kokkotas P, Rizaki A, Malamitsa K. Storytelling as a strategy for understanding concepts of electricity and electromagnetism. Interchange. 2010;**41**(4):379-405. DOI: 10.1007/s10780-010-9137-9

[90] Ritchey T. MA/start: Specifying training and instruction requirements using morphological analysis. In: International Conference on E-Learning in the Workplace. New York, NY: Kaleidoscope Learning; 2010

[91] Zwicky F. Discovery, Invention, Research through the Morphological Approach. New York, NY: Macmillan; 1969

[92] AlDahdouh A, Osorio A, Caires S. Understanding knowledge network, learning and connectivism. International Journal of Instructional Technology and Distance Learning. 2015;**12**(10)

[93] Biesta G. What is education for? On good education, teacher judgement, and educational professionalism. European Journal of Education. 2015;**50**(1):75-87. DOI: 10.1111/ejed.12109

[94] Bowman RF. Teaching and learning in a storytelling culture. The Clearing House: A Journal of Educational Strategies, Issues and Ideas. 2018;**91**(3):97-102. DOI: 10.1080/00098655.2017.1373547

[95] Abd, El-Sattar HKH. A New Framework for Plot-based Interactive Storytelling Generation. New York, NY: IEEE; 2008. pp. 317-322

[96] Mystakidis S, Filippousis G, Tolis D, Tseregkouni E. Playful metaphors for narrative-driven e-learning. Applied Sciences. 2021;**11**(24):11682. DOI: 10.3390/app112411682

[97] Knowles MS. Andragogy: Adult learning theory in perspective. Community College Review. 1978;**5**(3):9-20. DOI: 10.1177/009155217800500302

[98] Siemens G. Connectivism: A learning theory for the digital age. International Journal of Instructional Technology and Distance. 2005;**2**(1):151-157

[99] Lindeman EC. The Meaning of Adult Education. New York: New Republic, Inc.; 1926

[100] Kapur M. Productive failure in learning math. Cognitive Science. 2014;**38**(5):1008-1022. DOI: 10.1111/cogs.12107

[101] Mintz J, Aagaard M. The application of persuasive technology to educational settings. Educational Technology Research and Development (ETR&D). 2012;**60**(3):483-499. DOI: 10.1007/s11423-012-9232-y

[102] Iverson K, Colky D. Scenario-based e-learning design. Nonprofit Management Leadership. 2004;**43**(1):16-22. DOI: 10.1002/pfi.4140430105

Chapter 4

Digital Teaching and Learning: Trust and Intuition in Universities in Kenya

George Katete

Abstract

This study examines the effects of digital teaching and learning; trust and intention in Universities in Kenya during the upsurge of COVID-19 in the year 2020 and afterward. The chapter addresses the question 'how have lecturers to students' interactions been affected by the changes in teaching and learning in universities in Kenya during the coronavirus pandemic and its aftermath? To what extent do the plural stakeholders in universities trust the use of digital technology in their responsibilities? What role does intuition play in explaining the interactions between people and people as well as people and digital at the university? No studies address the question of digital trust and the role of intuition in understanding digital teaching and learning in Kenyan universities and therefore the present study fills the gap by relying on primary and secondary reviews of diverse sources, including books, governmental documents and journal publications. The findings in the study suggest that though Kenyan universities responded to the need to implore the use of digital Ministry of Education did not support full implementation of this shift. This was consistent with other universities that implored the use of MOOCs. But as the findings in the chapter show, Kenya, like other African economies, is not ready to invest fully in the use of digital technology to facilitate teaching and learning in the institutions of higher learning.

Keywords: digital teaching, digital learning, digital trust, Covid 19/coronavirus pandemic, intuition, online platforms, government policy, Kenyan universities

1. Introduction

Universities in Kenya have over the years maintained traditional pedagogical approaches to teaching and learning, where face-to-face lectures have been the acceptable modes of imparting knowledge, giving assignments, class discussions, delivering practical, examinations, correcting student's work, and grading. This traditional lecture method, which many have observed to be conservative with the advent of technological changes that brought new platforms for education, is still undoubtedly retained but with some disruption. In 2020, with the outbreak and escalation of coronavirus pandemic, a new government policy called for the social distancing of the population in Kenyan societies, in response to health advisory to curtail the spread of coronavirus that affected the normal way of life, and required devising and implementing new methods in the public domain was a life changer. This was more apparent in institutions of higher learning in Kenya, both public and private as demands for teaching, learning and other services including examinations had still to be undertaken on a need basis. Delivery of lectures and learning from students then have to take place via online platforms where the popular ones include Google Classroom, Google Meet, Zoom and locally devised including e-learning and 'MITIHANI'. These platforms partly provided for what scholars have referred to as 'Massive Open Online Courses (MOOCs)', which came in as a solution to deal with the challenges experienced that required learning remotely as reviewed in the next section.

However, as this became the norm, lecturers, students, parents, administrators and government officers in the education sector have experienced trust problems while embracing the use of digital. This raises questions as, why use of digital or what has been extensively covered in literature as MOOCs was not or just embraced hesitantly both by learners and instructors. This is despite the fact that numerous trainings to build capacity of staff to engage students online where lecturers receive endless training notifications that inform them to attend particular training on how to use different online platforms for teaching and examining students.

In the recent past, the training has been about asynchronous learning, where content from teachers is shared to the target group of learners. The teacher creates content and posts them in the platform, so that the interaction may not necessarily be direct and live. Teachers' contents and the platform matter most—many observers have concluded. This change necessitated responses and new requirements, which placed responsibilities on the shoulders of a cross-section of plural stakeholders who are affected by digital processes. Important questions, however, remain unanswered in the face of these developments.

In this chapter, I seek to examine how lecturers to students' interactions were affected by the changes in teaching and learning in universities in Kenya. To what extent do the plural stakeholders in universities trust the use of digital in their responsibilities? What role does intuition play in explaining the interactions between people and people as well as people and digital at the university?

There are no studies that address the question of digital trust and the role of intuition in understanding digital teaching and learning in Kenyan universities. As Marcial and Launer [1] describe the concept of digital trust "....underpins every digital interaction, by measuring and quantifying the expectation that a quantity is who or what it claims to be and that it will behave in an expected manner....it is an outcome that you can influence but not control...and referring to the level of confidence in people, processes and technology to build a secure digital world...". In the next section, I provide a methodology that this paper relied on. The study is an analysis of past data that was collected in 2020–2021 in a larger framework of the study of digital trust at the workplace, hosted by the Ostfalia University in Germany. This is acknowledged in the later part of this work. Further, secondary sources have been reviewed to benefit this study as provided in Section 2, which presents a review of the literature, before turning to Section 4, which presents the key findings of the study.

1.1 Methodological statement

The present study is timely and benefits from studies on intuition and digital trust at the workplace within the project coordinated by Ostfalia University of Applied

Sciences in Germany. Literature within the publications of digital trust and intuition as well as the theoretical framework developed by Marcial and Launer [1], and Svenson et al. [2], who develop their study from convincing assumptions—where decision makers can settle on heuristics where actors use under conditions of uncertainty and that intuitive decision can be greater than rational decisions under complex situation that demand choosing on one—that are of great significance to the present study. Furthermore, empirical data that was collected in 2020 which addresses digital trust at the workplace in the Kenyan context and is in the custody of Ostfalia University are timely data that this study will benefit from given the reliance of the questionnaire and responses from the interviewee on responses about trust. The Kenya case of analysis would take into consideration ethics and control of data where reliability, credibility, transparency, integrity, and security must be safeguarded in the proper examination of the interaction between learners and teachers, as well as the administrators' inputs in the pivotal interactions. At the same time, the theoretical framework on digital trust at the workplace as well presented in Marcial and Launer is applicable. But advancing explanation on the role of intuition, the work by Svenson which focuses on intuition has assumptions that can be borrowed in clarifying how intuition is significant in the understanding of relations between people and people as well as people and use of digital.

In addition, Katete [3] observes that Kenyan citizens increasingly embraced digital in the social, economic and political domains, a development that continues to create optimism in embracing the use of digital in the workplace. However, as I observe, even though people-to-people interaction has been affected by digital life in Kenya, liquid trust and solid trust are crucial dimensions that give a description on the Kenyan situation and overinvestment in technology may not necessarily mean that Kenyans trust the digital given their understanding on how the digital may not be reliable, transparent, and deliver integrity.

The hypothesis that the study tests is that in a digital society such as in the case of universities in Kenya, teaching and learning have progressed due to digital trust but lecturers and students have yet to understand whether they have trust on each other and how stakeholders including administrators and education officials interact in the digital space created by this shift.

It is critical to first give an operational definition of digital literacy to guide our understanding of how knowledge is produced, transferred and consumed as far as teaching and learning using digital tools and devices are concerned. The Government of Republic of Portugal [4], refers to digital literacy as the ability to access digital media and ICTs, understand and critically assess content and communicate effectively. In the next section, I review the literature with a view of establishing scholarly coverage of the MOOCs as a critical component of this study which gives insights into the existence of technological infusion to enable learning to proceed, even during calamities that obstructed physical class attendance by learners and their teachers.

2. Literature review

What are some of the important concepts in MOOCs and how can we explain its evolution? A review of the work by Goncalves and Goncalves [5] in the edited book by Gounder [6] is instructive here.

The letter *M* in the MOOC stands for *M*assive—this is about the scope and geographical breadth that the courses reach. It is understandable that a large number of participants can enroll and then access the program. Letter *O* stands for *O*pen, which means that courses are open to any person thereby representing the democratization of knowledge without restriction for not paying. The next *O* means *O*nline whereby the platform is accessible in real time, 24 hours a day as long as there is connectivity. *C* stands for *C*ourse means specific learning topics for skill development and knowledge. This involves technology, pedagogy, and content, it gives the knowledge platform for people anytime, anywhere one wishes to study from and has influence in educational and technological areas.

As observed by Goncalves and Goncalves [5], MOOCs are a continuation of the trend in innovation, experimentation, and the use of technology initiated by online education to provide learning opportunities on a large scale and an innovation in creating non-traditional textbooks [7]. Moreover, MOOCs require nonentry qualifications and open access, based on the distance education model, promoting large-scale interactive participation and reaching far areas.

There is consensus in the literature that observes that MOOCs are an expanding technology and consist of courses that are open and free of charge allowing many people to become enrolled for diverse courses [7]. This technology contributes to the free acquisition of information and to equality in knowledge granting access to content cheaply or even free, depending on the type of courses taken by a student.

The evolution of MOOCs is traceable to the publication of connectivism and connectivist by George Siemens and Stephen Downes in 2008 [7]. The work was about knowledge as an open online course which enabled connections across. In 2008, the term MOOC was created by Dave Cormier at the University of Prince Edward Island and Bryan Alexander. It was not until 2012 that multiple investments were made in the MOOC projects that allowed the courses to acquire large-scale popularity. This oversaw the appearance of thousands of courses that were supported by different platforms. Thousands of MOOCs are now spread across the world and promoted by various learning institutions, as well as public and private companies. According to the authors, some of the best MOOC platforms include Cognitive class, Coursera, Edx, FutureLearn, Iversity, Khan Academy, Myriad X, Udacity, Udemy and Saylor. The technology differs from one platform to the other. The European Commission launched the first Pan-European University MOOC in 2013 which allowed Universidade Aberta (Portugal) to join it. The university then developed a pedagogical model for massive open online courses and became the first university in the world to develop the iMOOC model. The iMOOC model is patented and composed of a set of standardized pedagogical practices extended to the institution as a whole for specific training levels.

Literature points to the existence of a paradigm shift that was driven by Massive Open Online Courses (MOOC) being a groundbreaking innovation in distance education that enables learners to get courses from universities around the world [8]. This means that MOOC came as a solution to the problem of giving an online platform. During the COVID period, there were other learning modalities that can be explained using online concepts.

The synchronous online classes involve real-time interactions replicating in-person lectures and discussions through platforms like Zoom and Microsoft teams. Asynchronous online learning offers flexibility with self access to materials and assignments. Then there is blended learning which combines traditional classroom sessions with online components. There is Virtual Reality (VR) and Augmented Reality (AR) which create new experiences and hands-on collaboration. Then peer-to-peer learning involves students teaching each other. There is one-on-one tutoring that provides personalized assistance. Gamification integrates game elements into education. Traditional classroom learning maintains its importance [8, 9]. Academic discourse on educational technology offering insights that can inform policy makers, educators and institutions. MOOCs are characterized by their open enrollment, allowing anyone with an internet connection to participate regardless of geographical location or prior educational background [10]. It encompasses video lectures, readings, quizzes, assignments, and discussion forums. It fosters collaboration among learners.

The foundational principle of MOOCs is the open access. The concept of open access embodies the notion that anyone irrespective of their geographic location, prior educational experience or financial resources can engage in learning through MOOCs. Such a process has the potential to break down long-standing barriers that have traditionally hindered access to education, transforming learning into an inclusive and borderless endeavor. Then regardless of financial circumstances, individuals can access course materials, video lectures, quizzes, and assignments without financial barriers [11]. This is a significant departure from traditional educational models that may involve substantial tuition fees that make education inaccessible to many.

Another characteristic has to do with massive enrollment when it comes to MOOC whereby it stands as a testament to the transformative power of technology in reshaping the educational landscape. This is seen as a remarkable feature to accommodate a vast number of participants, known as scalability as observed by Ali et al. [12]. Another characteristic is the diverse course offerings from humanities to sciences, business to technology and even creative arts, MOOC encompass virtually every field of knowledge. The prominence of online format whereby the experience of video lectures transcends traditional classroom settings and brings expertise in instruction is yet another visible characteristic of MOOC.

The work by Gounder has put emphasis on MOOCs as an option widely seen by students as supportive for the acquisition of new skills, development of their careers, and learning new concepts. There are various reasons to back up this observation. Students access MOOCs to get new knowledge or for pleasure and to learn new cultures. This observation is furthered in the work by Victor P. Gil Jimenez et al. [13], who specifically study the influence of MOOCs in telecommunication engineering whereby more than one hundred official MOOCs deal with topics such as digital signal processing, Information Theory, Time and Frequency analysis, Internet of Things (IoT), wireless communications, modulations, signal and systems and programming among others.

MOOCs are mainly hosted by relevant universities and technological research centers [13]. The authors identify gaps that can be filled by the MOOCs, a looming gap between the latest innovative evolutionary technologies and the way current students see the future of networks, especially 5G and technology beyond this. In the other chapter by Bruno F. Goncalves and Vitor Goncalves [5], the authors look into the status of MOOCs a decade later to understand its current situation in teacher education. Thus, MOOCs present themselves as useful and appropriate tools for the training of individuals or groups of learners through development of their knowledge and skills supported by technology. Teachers are one of the targeted groups that continue to benefit from skill development. In this case, it is a continuation of the trend in innovation, experimentation, and use of technology initiated by distance and online education to provide massive learning opportunities. MOOC then means a course that targets large-scale, networked interactive participation. It can be considered to provide open access, based on a distance education model, promoting large-scale interactive participation and thus one of the creative ways to provide quality education for those in far flung areas [5]. MOOCs are free online courses available for anyone to enroll in and give an affordable and flexible way to learn new content and acquire or improve new skills, advance career and gain quality experience.

Given this online experience that has transcended boundaries, I seek to establish specific governmental initiatives to understand whether such online platforms have been anchored in governments' specific policy guides (comparable reviews in Section 3) and from where Kenyan universities and education ministry can tap from for reduction of trust deficit in the use of MOOCs (explained in Section 4).

3. Commonalities in education policies on advancing use of digital technology for teaching and learning from which Kenya can tap from for best practices

Gabriel et al. [14] in their work explore how ten countries around the world have integrated digital technology for teaching and learning. According to the authors, their analyses point at improved teaching and learning, digital maturation, data-driven decision-making, evidence-based education and AI in education.

In their sampled cases of ten countries including Australia, Estonia, Finland, Singapore Germany, New Zealand, Portugal, Slovenia, Ireland and Scotland a number of commonalities with the education policy supporting digital learning were ascertainable. Similarities or commonalities have to do with the governments focusing on teacher's competencies and digital literacy in the utility of digital technology [14]. Governments were running digitalization programs in schools, emphasizing on professional development and establishing communities for practice to promote peer learning. Germany has established since 2016 what is referred to as 'education in the digital world strategy' outlining teacher digital literacies to teach their subjects using technologies in a pedagogically sound manner.

This approach of government support is also seen in Scotland, where digital learning and teaching had a strong focus on teacher training, supported by the national 'Glow Digital platform. The Glow was available to all schools in Scotland, integrating video conferencing functions to reach teachers even in remote and rural areas [14]. In Finland, the Ministry of Higher Education and Culture launched a two-year program in 2017 to develop digital skills for teachers across the country. There was significant improvement in teachers' digital competence but an observation that disparities of lack of integration of digital tools in the classroom (as quoted in Ref. [15]).

In these countries, another commonality is seen with the students digital literacy, where they are prepared with digital knowledge, skills and competencies to live and learn in the digital world [15, 16]. However, there are distinctions between generic skills needed to live in a digital age and specific skills needed to use and apply technology as observed by Van der Vlies [16]. The government of the Republic of Slovenia stated in its 2016 report that only digitally literate or e-competent citizens can fully communicate digitally, use modern ICT, develop new skills, be innovative and creative in the use of ICT, and in-depth understanding of ICT allows them to modify and create new technologies, solutions and ideas of use. Another commonality in line with students' understanding is their ability to identify fake news given the digital literacy component in the curriculum.

With digital literacy, the ability to get prepared for jobs for the future increases. The use of digital learning has merit in supporting a modern workforce who have adequate digital skills. ICT is required for growth and innovation, for business across economic sectors. ICT has now proliferated in our world. Digital skills are thus required for future jobs [16]. Observations about the studies also show that digital maturation is a benefit in digital learning and teaching in schools across the jurisdiction emphasizing their use. This concerns equity and inclusion as key ingredients in assuring students have technologies they need for their progress. Thus, government policies were required to help narrow digital divides.

As these studies demonstrated, such policies should deal with two layers of divides, namely, first digital divide and second digital divide. In this case, the first digital divide refers to the gap between those able to benefit from access to internet and ICT infrastructure and those who cannot. Then, the second digital divide separates people who have the competencies and skills to benefit from computer use from those who do not. The observation here is that only providing access to digital technologies does not necessarily ensure equality and opportunity [16]. There are differences between students in terms of digital skills but also they use technology differently. So the second digital divide is a priority of a large number of countries. The focus is on promoting digital skills and inclusion. Research acknowledges that students will continue to need numeracy and literacy skills, socio-emotional skills, and a positive attitude toward learning [17].

The other commonality has to do with the data driven decision-making and evidence-based education. It is observable that education systems across the world are now using data derived from digital technologies to guide their decisions and to develop policies. Access to high-quality, timely data about students and their schools enables a comprehensive long-range view of education in terms of their grades, standardized test scores, surveys, attendance data among others (e.g., [18]).

AI that is Artificial Intelligence in education is another area that espouses commonalities in the education systems across the world. AI has become an integral part of the education landscape. In many education institutions, AI is used in personalizing learning and learning materials, to identify and support students with special needs and also to make education more and more inclusive (e.g., [19]). AI is also being used to improve student administration and school management processes including automation of common service channels, digitization of paper processes, greater integration of systems and improved user interfaces and workforce support for staff. Countries such as Singapore invested in inputting AI into school curriculum to help develop digital and AI competency for better equipping of students entering sectors that need AI adoption that include cybersecurity, logistics, manufacturing, and financial management [19].

4. Discussion of findings: Trust and mistrust in digital learning in the Kenyan context

In the Kenyan context of digital learning and teaching, trust deficits can be understood to emanate from what can holistically be described as the 'fear of the unknown' that arose from diverse quarters, including the education ministry and its key stakeholders, university management, from professors in the university and students. Various reasons, however, explain this fear of the unknown which are largely related to systemic and structural weaknesses that hitherto are reflective on the Kenyan state and its institutions.

First, the government has not been focused on improving teachers' competencies and digital literacy and in the utilization of digital technology. This is left for individual choice and discretion and is not necessarily a policy directive, unlike what we have seen in the studies by Gabriel et al. [14] in their cross-sectional studies addressing ten cases across European and some Asian countries. There are only piecemeal government programs emanating from the education ministry linked to supporting digital skills for teachers across the country. The main institution that is concerned with teacher recruitment does not necessarily insist on candidates' ability to master the use of MOOC as an option to the existence of traditional methods of knowledge dissemination to match the technological progression that is now available in the education sector.

Second, in the Kenyan situation, students' digital literacy is not necessarily guaranteed. Though training is rolled out before teaching and examinations are undertaken, these are not well-coordinated initiatives that can bring change and integration of literacy into the curriculum. The ventures are meant to enable students to only grasp the basics of the use of digital platforms to attend classes online. Their preparedness for digital knowledge, skills, and competencies is not driven by the desire to be in a digital world, save for garnering bare minimum during knowledge transfer imparted by the teacher. This challenge emanates from the fact that students' entry requirements do not emphasize on knowledge of the MOOCs but the majority of them, especially from schools in rural setups begin to learn for the first time as they join undergraduate classes in institutions for higher learning. Thus, students' mastery of online learning remains slow and they lose trust during the learning process, when taking their assignments and in the main examination, thereby leading to poor performance in some of the subjects they take using online platforms, compared to when they undertake the same through the traditional lecture method.

Third, the divides between students are wide and extreme. In the first case of the divide, it is observable that in Kenyan universities, students' access to ICT infrastructure causes increasing disparities. Only a small proportion have personal equipment in terms of desktops and laptops which are required for digital learning. This deficiency by the majority of students then forces them to get alternative ways at their disposal. It has to do with moving to do their work in cyber cafes, most of which are not conducive to undertaking academic work and discussion. Moreover, such cybercafes charge higher rates to profit from their clients, piling more burden on students who face financial constraints. Although students have ownership of smartphones, these can lead to certain limitations, especially regarding undertaking assignments that require generating qualitative and quantitative data and interpretation in longer essays as required in social sciences and humanities. However, more intriguing of this situation of digital divide is differences in digital skills which shows how those without digital skills are disadvantaged and separated from getting knowledge in subjects they are enrolled for in school.

Fourth, data derived from digital technology is still not embraced more so in learning institutions and larger education systems in Kenya. Therefore, decision making on whether universities can entrust the digital data fully such as quality of student assignments, their surveys, examination scores and even class attendance are distrustful. More so whether the use of AI is to be implored is disputable. AI is still not well understood as technology that can facilitate learning. It is feared as a disrupter of learning and teaching. University teaching staff are pessimistic about students' demands to use the aid of AI for learning. Online classes still require full attendance of course instructors where instruction sources are traditional publications.

5. Conclusion

Though the coronavirus pandemic forced some Kenyan universities to transition from face-to-face teaching and learning, the systemic failures in fully embracing the digital education system necessitated calls for a return to traditional lecture and interaction. This suggests that Kenya, like other African economies, is not ready to invest fully in the use of digital technology to facilitate teaching and learning in institutions of higher learning. The limitations observed above show how government priorities are not directed toward digitizing capacities, which in turn affects knowledge production, knowledge transfer and knowledge consumption. In order to respond to technological demands that are determinant for societal growth, Kenya will need to invest in digital technologies to be used in schools and invest in training learners and teachers for better outcomes. As observed in the literature that I have reviewed in this study and the section on comparative policies on the use of digital processes, online learning should not be viewed as a disruptor of normalcy but as a support required by digital students and teachers and to measure to the digital era that the globe has embraced. There is a need for Kenya and other African states to continue prioritizing the use of these online platforms- the MOOCs in order to democratize learning, to make it open for those yearning for more and to increase enrollment rates, but at the same time put measures for maintenance of quality education.

Acknowledgements

I want to acknowledge Markus Launer and Frithiof Svenson for their input and assurance of support especially in sharing available data that can have profound importance in this study and the analysis. Besides this support, I also acknowledge their vast contributions that go a long way in inspiring the development of this particular work.

Author details

George Katete
University of Nairobi, Nairobi, Kenya

*Address all correspondence to: gkatete@uonbi.ac.ke

References

[1] Marcial DE, Launer MA. Towards the measurement of digital trust in the workplace: A proposed framework. International Journal of Scientific Engineering and Science. 2019;**3**(12):1-7

[2] Svenson F, Ballová Mikušková E, Launer M. Intuition and digital trust at the workplace in Slovakia. In: Paper Presented at the Fourth International Service Management Congress, Ostfalia, November 2020. Ostfalia: Ostfalia University; 2020

[3] Katete G. Digital elections and the problem of liquid trust in the Kenyan Election Management Institution. International Journal of African Renaissance Studies, Multi-Inter and Transdisciplinary. 2021;**16**(1):165-176

[4] Government of the Republic of Portugal. INCoDe2030. In: National Digital Competences Initiative e. 2030. Government of the Republic of Portugal; 2017. Available from: https://www.incode2030.gov.pt/sites/default/files/incode2030_en.pdf

[5] Goncalves F, Goncalves V. Perspective chapter: MOOC - A decade later! What is the current situation in teacher education? In: Gounder S, editor. Massive Open Online Courses - Current Practice and Future Trends. London, UK: Intech Open; 2023. DOI: 10.5772/intechopen.1001518

[6] Gounder S. Massive Open Online Courses - Current Practice and Future Trends. London, UK: Intech Open; 2023. DOI: 10.5772/intechopen.1001518

[7] Siemens G. Learning and Knowing in Networks: Changing Roles for Educators and Designers. ITForum for Discussion, An Open Access and Academic Publisher; 2008. pp. 1-26

[8] Rulinawaty R, Priyanto A, Kuncoro S, Rahmawaty D, Wijaya A. Massive online courses (MOOCs) as catalysts of change in education during unprecedented times: A narrative review. Journal of Research in Science Education. 2023;**9**:53-63

[9] Paul J, Jefferson F. A comprehensive analysis of student performance in an online vs face to face environmental science course from 2009 to 2016. Frontiers in Computer Science. 2019;**1**:7

[10] Mutawa MA. Perspectives chapter: MOOCs at higher education current state and future trends. In: Gounder S, editor. Massive Open Online Courses - Current Practice and Future Trends. London, UK: Intech Open; 2023. DOI: 10.5772/intechopen.1001518

[11] Garlinska M, Osial M, Proniewska K, Pregowska A. The influence of emerging technologies on distance education. Electronics. 2023;**12**(7):150. DOI: 10.3390/electronics12071550

[12] Ali S, Abuhmed T, El-Sappagh S, Muhammad K, Alonso-Moral JM, Confalonieri R, et al. Explainable artificial intelligence (XIA) what we know and what is left to attain trustworthy artificial intelligence. Information Fusion. 2023;**99**:101805

[13] Jimenez V, Villalonga D, Morales M, Seitianitis D, Al-Sakkaf A, Khan B, et al. MOOC as a way of disseminating, training and learning of telecommunication engineering. In: Gounder S, editor. Massive Open Online Courses - Current Practice and Future Trends. London, UK: Intech Open; 2023

[14] Gabriel F, Marronne R, Van Sebille Y, Kovanovic V. Digital education strategies around the world: Practices and policies. Irish Educational Studies. 2022;**41**(1):85-106

[15] Education and Training Monitor. 2019. Available from: https://ec.europa.eu/education/sites/default/files/document-library-docs/et-monitor-report-2019-finland_en.pdf [Accessed: June 1, 2021]

[16] Van der Vlies R. Digital Strategies in Education Across OECD Countries: Exploring Education Policies on Digital Technologies. OECD Education Working Paper No. 226. OECD; 2020

[17] Van Deursen AJ, Helsper EJ. Collateral benefits on internet use: Explaining the diverse outcomes of engaging with the internet. New Media and Society. 2018;**20**(7):2333-2351

[18] Marsh JA, Pane JF, Hamilton LS. Making Sense of Data-Driven Decision Making in Education Evidence: Evidence from Recent RAND Research Occasional Paper. 2006. Available from: https://www.rand.org/content/dam/rand/pubs/occasional_papers/2006/RAND_OP170.pdf

[19] Drigas A, Ioannidou R-E. Artificial intelligence in special education: A decade review. International Journal For Engineering Education, ResearchGate. 2013

Chapter 5

Transition in the Concept of Scaffolding

Soyoung Park

Abstract

Scaffolding, which is actively utilized as one of the support strategies in teaching and learning, was originally provided as face-to-face support for novice by expert. However, as numerous technology-based tools including software systems started to be applied to scaffolding, the scope of interactions in scaffolding has become not only limited to instructors and learners but extended to diverse forms of technology-mediated or technology-driven support. Furthermore, adaptive learning technologies including learning analytics and AI-based technologies have further made more adaptive scaffolding possible with instant diagnosis and feedback. This study explores the transition of scaffolding concepts and draws implications for teaching and learning. The literature review method was used to examine studies on scaffolding.

Keywords: scaffolding, software scaffolding, technology-based scaffolding, adaptive scaffolding, learning analytics, AI-based technology, adaptive learning

1. Introduction

Admitting that the concept of scaffolding was introduced in the 1960s, the interaction between humans was the dominant method of scaffolding in teaching and learning. However, along with technological development, the forms of scaffolding have become more diverse and such advanced technologies have made possible scaffolding more instant and adaptive. As scaffolding realized by enhanced technology sometimes does not reflect the original elements that were emphasized by early scholars [1–3], such as calibrated support and fading, it has often been questioned to be regarded as scaffolding [4].

Nevertheless, it might be right to revise the concept of scaffolding as the teaching and learning environment has already embarked on a series of technologically sweeping changes. There seems to be a need to modify the concept of scaffolding which encompasses the various forms of scaffolding between humans and software, mediated by cutting-edgy technologies [4]. Although Roy Pea [4] has criticized software scaffolding as it lacks the important elements of scaffolding of calibrated support and fading and re-conceptualized scaffolding as a process and a structure, it still does not include the characteristics of today's adaptive and automated scaffolding.

This study intends to lessen any confusion in understanding the concept of scaffolding and promote an expansive understanding of it, by comprehensive examination of scaffolding research. Furthermore, it is expected to contribute to developing and employing more varied and innovative forms of scaffolding which will lead to more effective and efficient support in teaching and learning. This research will go over how scaffolding looked like in traditional terms, how it changed over time with technological advancement, and how it is now with adaptive learning technologies including AI technologies.

Scaffolding refers to one of the supportive strategies in teaching-learning, meaning an adequate level of support provided by a teacher or more knowledgeable peer to help learners complete tasks or solve problems that would otherwise be out of reach on their own [5]. The concept of scaffolding was first introduced by scholars, such as Vygotsky [1, 2] and Wood, Burner, and Ross [3]. Since its introduction, scaffolding has been actively utilized and studied as assistance in learning or problem-solving processes. Research and practical applications of scaffolding have evolved around interactions among humans as well.

However, with technological advancement, various software tools have become more widely used for scaffolding. The meaning of scaffolding is no longer confined to the interactions between humans but to the ones between humans and software, as well as the support unilaterally provided by software. Scaffolding is also used to cover diverse cognitive tools and instructional support, including coaching, modeling, and distributed cognition. In addition, new terms were created such as 'software-realized scaffolding' [6], 'scaffolding in a technologically enhanced learning environment' or 'open learning environment' [7], 'synergistic scaffolding' [8], and so on.

Furthermore, as adaptive technologies have been applied in teaching and learning practices, scaffolding with such technological enhancement made more adaptive learning possible. Learners' readiness and needs can be incessantly diagnosed and appropriate supports can be provided in a timely manner, which could consequently promote more personalized and optimized learning. Although early software scaffoldings were often criticized as having limitations in offering calibrated diagnosis, adaptive support, and fading, adaptive scaffolding is clearly distinctive from those early software scaffoldings or other instructional supports, such as cognitive support, coaching, or modeling [4, 6, 9].

This research aims to examine the transition of the scaffolding concept, from traditional approaches to recent software scaffolding and adaptive scaffolding with technological development. Although there are numerous studies concerning various scaffolding practices, including the concept, principles, and strategies of scaffolding, it is hard to find research dealing with how the scaffolding concept has changed throughout time. It seems necessary to investigate how scaffolding has been changed so far since first introduced as a teaching and learning aid. Such research would help re-establishing the concept of today's scaffolding which utilizes advanced technologies and be able to bring implications on how to design and apply various scaffolding strategies for more adaptive learning.

Research Questions: How the concept of scaffolding has been transited over time?

2. Methods

In this study, a method of literature review was used to examine existing studies on scaffolding theories and practices ranging from traditional approaches to scaffolding to software-based and adaptive ones. Based on such investigation, how the concept of scaffolding has shifted was discussed.

The literature review was conducted through the stages of investigation, selection, analysis, and integration. First, in the investigation stage, research methods were used according to the scope of the topic [10] and types of materials [11]. Relevant topics were subdivided into scaffolding, ZPD, cognitive apprenticeship, software-based and technology-based scaffolding, adaptive scaffolding, learning analytics, and AI-based scaffolding. A search was conducted through books, research papers, institutional research reports, academic conference papers, and so on, using thematic keywords via Google Scholar Search, Wikipedia, ERIC, Springerlink, Jstore, and ScienceDirect, etc. Furthermore, to ensure the continuity of precedent studies, Google Scholar Search Alerts (http://scholar.google.co.kr) was used to receive information on relevant topics and materials and to check out the latest research. Second, in the selection stage of the precedent literature, the precedent studies were reviewed based on Hart's [12] criteria on authority, seminality, and relevance, and then suitable studies for this paper were extracted. In addition, references were tracked, which were cited by the selected literatures, and additional literatures were chosen which were continuously mentioned among other related papers. Third, in the stages of analysis of precedent studies and integration, the selected research was classified by the relevant domains, and the main contents of each research were summarized. After analyzing the main concept and elements, scaffolding-related contents and implications were categorized and restructured according to certain criteria.

3. Traditional approaches on scaffolding

The term scaffolding was originally used in architecture, which means a temporary construction that is installed as support for buildings, a path for workers, and a foothold for construction works, and then is removed when the construction is completed and the support is no longer needed.

The use of the term scaffolding as a concept of teaching and learning originated from the study of the development of Vygotsky [1, 2] and Wood et al. [3]. In the socio-cultural developmental theory, Vygotsky [1] sees that children develop through social interactions with adults or with other intellectually mature people. This idea of human development into higher mental processes appears in the concept of the Zone of Proximal Development (ZPD). According to him, humans can develop by solving problems that cannot be achieved by themselves, through interactions with those more knowledgeable others.

Although the concept of scaffolding in teaching and learning context is rooted in the theory of Vygotsky [1, 2], the term was used already in Wood et al.'s [3] research. They used the term 'scaffolding' as a metaphor for the interactions between tutor and children during the course of problem solving aimed at completing the pyramid puzzle, where the meaning of the scaffolding was in line with the assistance by adults in the ZDP of children explained by Vygotsky [2].

Scaffolding has become a more concrete concept that refers to the words and behaviors of instructors and other kinds of support in the context of teaching and learning, enabling learners to accomplish tasks that cannot be achieved alone [13]. Through this scaffolding strategy, instructors can focus on keeping learners interested and engaged, allowing them to gradually take responsibility and control over tasks [14]. At the beginning of the task, the instructors take the initiative and actively support the problems that are difficult to solve independently but they hand over the initiative to learners so that learners become self-contained and self-regulatory problem solvers, which is the purpose of scaffolding [15].

The cognitive apprenticeship model of Collins, Brown, and Newman [16] is a traditional approach in which scaffolding is embodied as a strategy in the teaching and learning environment. In their theory, where learners are guided by an instructor or an expert, scaffolding is conceptualized as one of the important teaching methods along with coaching, modeling, and fading. The core of scaffolding from this model is also rooted in Vygotsky's [2] ZPD concept. By providing scaffolding and fading as teaching strategies in the context of problem solving, learners can gradually complete their tasks that are difficult to solve on their own. Internalization of various learning strategies was used as goals of the cognitive apprenticeship learning including the following: heuristic strategies, which are related to the process or method of progressing the learning as well as knowledge about the contents, and cognitive and meta-cognitive strategies including the use of specific intellectual functions and reflection during the learning process [16, 17].

Concerning these traditional approaches, Pea [4] stated that the nature of scaffolding was mainly based on the work of Vygotsky [1, 2] and Wood et al. [3] as a 'structure' as a noun and a 'process' as a verb. In terms of structure, scaffolding means a kind of 'structured context,' allowing the tutor to limit and structure the problem-solving context through tacit, detailed measurement and evaluation of the children's ability or need. The provision of this structure or form helps children solve problems or tasks that cannot be accomplished by themselves. Scaffolding as a verb would refer to a process, as many types and aspects of activities are frequently supported as scaffolding until the children are able to work out problems independently. In addition, these scaffolding strategies are based on the concept of the ZPD by Vygotsky [1, 2] meaning that learners can achieve their own goals through the assistance from instructors and others.

In such traditional approaches to scaffolding, early studies focus on the interactions between parents or adults and children [18, 19]. Studies in the 1980s show that with the ZPD as a key component, more intellectually mature people support those less mature to elevate their knowledge and skills to a higher level [20]. In the study of 'Dynamic Assessment' by Campione and colleagues [21, 22], a series of step-by-step hints are provided during the course of completing assignments, which allows to consistently measure and assess the level of help needed for learners. Scaffolding has also been actively examined as a strategy to support reading and writing activities. In the research of 'Reciprocal Teaching' by [23] and 'Procedural Facilitation' by Scardamalia and Bereiter [24, 25], scaffolding and fading are utilized in addition to coaching and modeling to serve as structuring devices for reading and writing activities for learners. Learners are provided with necessary strategies for these activities through a demonstration by an expert, or with a dialog or clue card for guidance on the necessary thinking methods at each stage [26]. It has been reported that learners are expected to engage in reflective thinking and inquiry during the learning process and to develop cognitive and meta-cognitive skills and abilities through such supports [27].

4. Scaffolding mediated by enhanced technology

In addition to such a cognitive approach to scaffolding, the meaning, forms, and methods of scaffolding have changed as well with technological development

[28–30]. The meaning of scaffolding has been extended to the interactions between humans mediated by technology, or even into the interactions between technology and humans [30, 31]. That is, scaffolding has transformed into a form of mediation that takes place when learners are immersed in a 'technologically enhanced learning environment' or 'open learning environment' [7, 32, 33].

This 'mediating' scaffolding assists learners in many ways. It focuses on supporting learners by clearly presenting basic procedures and structures for complex tasks and reproducing support information in different forms [7]. For example, if learners perform a complicated assignment, the instructor would provide necessary menu labels through the software, a visual representation of the process activities, or prompts through which they can check whether they are performing well, how far they have completed so far, and which process they are at the moment. Scaffolding is provided in a way that helps learners to fulfill the task more effectively and efficiently [34]. In addition, such technology-based presentation styles and methods of scaffolding can be implemented in the most effective way for each learning phase, which is different from traditional scaffolding provided by instructors [7, 35]. To illustrate, if learners ask for a structured summary of learning progress up to a certain point, scaffolding can help with such organization. If they prefer visual representation, scaffolding can visually reproduce the contents using the advanced technology that learners have chosen as well. In particular, software systems that provide prompts in many ways including face-to-face prompts of instructors, are also called 'distributed scaffolding' [35]. It has been further reviewed that scaffolding is mediated by various contextual factors such as instructors, peer learners, software, curriculum, and teaching-learning contexts with many elements being used as resources for learning, thereby creating learning synergies [8, 31, 35].

Scaffolding provided via technology can be utilized in a way that promotes meta-cognition as follows: helping to understand the concept of the task or grasp its macroscopic process or structure, and strategically assisting in learners' problem-solving or in reflective thinking, monitoring, and decision-making [36, 37].

First, scaffolding that facilitates conceptual understanding aims for 'sense making,' and thus supports learners in many ways: visual representation, diagrams by the visual concept organizer, guidance and advice from experts, inquiry prompts to facilitate understanding or tools for learners to visualize the contents by themselves. Studies [38–40] on scaffolding that facilitates conceptual understanding provide diagrams of the visual concept organizer or network, or different versions of visual materials related to the contents to improve learners' understanding. In the study on Animal Landlord [41] and Galapagos Finches [5, 42], structured space and analysis tools are provided to learners as a means to analyze and explore the learning contents.

Scaffolding, which helps to identify the procedure or structure of the task, visualizes these through a diagram and provides a modeling of the instructor's solution as well as information and resources available to the learners at each stage. Examples of this scaffolding include 'Model-It study' [39] and the 'Training Wheels' study [43]. According to these studies, learners are provided with structures of the activities selected by themselves among the complex task structures, thus scaffolding is offered in a way that enables learners to navigate through complicated tasks without difficulty. 'The KIE' [44] and 'Symphony system' [45] display expert's advice as a rationale as to why learners should go through each step when pressing a particular button. In Galapagos Finches [5], Geometer's Sketchpad [46], and 'TableTop' system [47], graphical visualization is immediately offered for convenient learning at each stage when learners analyze the formula or manipulate specific data. The Symphony system [45] provides a navigation as scaffolding, allowing learners to easily move forward using the tapped interface.

Scaffolding provides meta-intelligent support: It helps learners strategically solve tasks by arranging a pool of problems in which they often have difficulty and by storing expert's guidance or advice in the pool. It encourages learners with a reflective question prompt, collectively records and structures the learning process, and shows a hint to support and elicit sophisticated thinking [7, 31, 36, 37]. Scaffolding that supports meta-cognition shows that the Symphony system [45] guides learners regarding problem-solving procedures, allowing them to identify available action plans at each stage, and to freely drag and drop, where they can design a tailored learning stage. In the studies of KIE & WISE [48, 49] the prompts including 'Checking our understanding' are provided to learners to reflect on and monitor their learning stages. The Geometry Tutor [50] visualizes what learners have performed so far and what they need to do in the future. In addition, in the EEPS study [36], strategic scaffolding is provided by creating a pool of questions in which learners have difficulties to give the expert's advice or clues.

On the other hand, software scaffolding seems to blur the distinction between scaffolding and cognitive supports. That is because, such scaffoldings have limitations in accurately diagnosing the levels and needs of learners and prescribing adaptive supports accordingly, compared to what human-to-human interactions can do [51, 52]. Many software scaffoldings seem to have conceptualized scaffolding in a much larger sense compared to the traditional meaning. It is notable that fading and calibrated support which were the inherent characteristics of scaffolding distinguishing itself from other instructional support were not considered as an integral part of software scaffoldings. Scaffolding mediated and driven only by technology would be far from the adaptive support. In this respect, software scaffoldings would be regarded as distributed cognition, lacking in the elements of fading as well as adaptive, calibrated diagnosis and support [4].

5. Adaptive scaffolding

With rapid advancement in adaptive learning and AI-based technology, traditional personalized learning has further developed in a way that could provide learners with optimal learning support [53]. Bernacki et al. [54] have researched efficient personalized learning and reported that analysis and prescription in accordance with learners' prior knowledge and readiness would be the key factors for the success of adaptive scaffolding. Recent studies [55, 56] on adaptive scaffolding focus on calibrating learners' knowledge levels and needs and supporting them with tailored help, and reporting its effect on learning performance and engagement, self-regulation, metacognition, and so on.

Adaptive scaffolding can be effectively delivered by analyzing and predicting learners' activities using data gathered from learning analytics [57, 58]. Learning analytics aims to better understand and optimize learning and its environment by measuring, collecting, analyzing, and reporting the relevant data on the nature and performances of learners [59, 60]. Research on adaptive scaffolding based on learning analytics sheds light on a way to optimize learning. Pardo et al.'s [61] research on personalized feedback messages in a university course shows the effect of personalized feedback on students' academic achievement and learning satisfaction levels. Lim, Gentili, et al.'s [62] study on the effect of personalized feedback based on learner trace data in the learning management system also implies the positive influence of adaptive scaffolding on students' regular studying and higher grades. Moreover, Lim et al. [56] examined the effects of real-time analytics-based adaptive scaffolding on students' self-regulated learning and argued that analytics-based scaffolding using trace data can support in real time, inducing metacognitive activities. According to them, learner data can be dynamically analyzed and provide at scale support tailored to learners' immediate needs.

Adaptive scaffolding is known to be highly beneficial especially for supporting students' self-regulated learning, and encouraging their metacognition as it intends to diagnose their emerging understanding and provide timely support as well [63, 64]. In order to support learners' conceptual understanding effectively, scaffolding needs to enable learners to understand the contexts and what they are learning, which is why it is important to accurately diagnose learners' current levels of knowledge and to provide immediate and adaptive support according to their levels. In addition, fading, which means gradually withdraw support as learners' understanding improves, would be helpful in that learners can become more self-regulated and self-directed. In terms of support for the task process, adaptive scaffolding can provide the rationale to learners as to why they should undergo a particular stage or activity. Not only that, adaptive scaffolding can furnish guidance and hints in advance if learners request effective learning strategies. In this manner, adaptive scaffolding would facilitate learning a great deal through the mechanism of channeling, focusing, and modeling as traditional scaffolding functions.

Adaptive scaffolding further progresses toward delivering tailored support to individual learners, even in one-to-many learning contexts as well. One instructor cannot provide support to a large number of learners on as-needed basis and the level and degree of support vary depending on individual learners [65]. However, AI-based adaptive scaffolding would have the advantage of providing adaptive support in a one-to-many context, which is called 'automated adaptive guidance' [55]. The automated adaptive guidance would be able to concentrate on assisting the self-regulation of learners, thereby enabling them to reflect on their performance up to date and to achieve tasks more effectively in the future [66].

Azevedo et al. [63] investigated the role of different scaffolding conditions in understanding ecological systems for secondary school students and reported that adaptive scaffolding would be highly effective. According to them, students could more easily shift their mental model when needed and perform better self-regulated learning through adaptive scaffolding. Ritter and Fancsali [67] at Carnegie Mellon University have developed MATHia, an adaptive 1-on-1 math learning platform for secondary students which mirrors a human coach with more complexity and precision. Math problems are known to be rigorous and usually involve multiple ways to model thinking. So, their learning platform mirrors a human tutor and provides AI-based adaptive scaffolding at the very moment students need it in order to help students work to master the lesson standards. Another example is 'Third space learning', a personalized online tutoring program built for schools by math experts, utilized in 3398 primary schools in the UK since 2013. In this program, AI and a real tutor work together to simultaneously analyze what learners have not well understood or learning loss, and accordingly support tutors to understand learners and provide optimized learning. Not only that, a learning platform called 'Knock knock! Math explorers' [68] provides adaptive scaffolding in math learning using AI technology for primary low-graders. Other studies [69–72] have also reported that adaptive scaffolding led to promote students' understanding in geography, algebra, statistics, etc. Such studies also maintain that adaptive scaffolding facilitates students learning by supporting students' self-regulatory behavior and more efficient and effective conceptual understanding.

6. Discussion

Although the transition has been made in the form of scaffolding from traditional face-to-face interaction between novice and expert to adaptive technological support based on recent learning technologies, it is evident that different and diverse types of scaffolding still seek to abide by its original elements and the basic mechanism of scaffolding.

The elements of scaffolding are known to be (1) establishing a shared goal, (2) active diagnosis of learners' understanding and needs, (3) providing tailored assistance, (4) maintaining pursuit of the goal, (5) giving feedback, (6) controlling of frustration and risk, (7) assisting internalization and independence, (8) generalization in other contexts [3, 72–75]. As these elements make scaffolding different from other learning aids, they would still be crucial in terms of distinguishing scaffolding from other supports. To be specific, establishing a shared goal in task completion becomes a priority when providing scaffolding, as any type of learning basically has its purpose of enhancing 'specific performances' [6]. As implied in the concept of the ZPD by Vygotsky [2] and the concept of scaffolding by Wood et al. [3], if scaffolding is to be provided as a strategic support, it must have a clear goal for learners to achieve. Next, active diagnosis of learners' understanding and needs and providing tailored assistance mean that learners' current level and needs are to be frequently measured in specific learning contexts, and based on these measurements, adaptive and calibrated support is to be provided to individual learners. When learners cannot solve the problems by themselves, it is critical to provide them with sufficient assistance to help them find out solutions on their own [76]. Therefore, accurately diagnosing learners' conditions and providing corresponding assistance would be key characteristics when designing and applying scaffolding. Furthermore, maintaining the pursuit of the goal, giving feedback, and controlling frustration and risk are essential in any type of scaffolding. Such function would encourage learners who need to solve problems that cannot be solved independently, to understand the tasks and problem more deeply, make strategic decisions, and exert on achieving their goal, relieving their potential anxiety or fear Through such a process, learners can gain independence, and further be able to apply and generalize the problem-solving techniques in other contexts. In other words, learners gradually internalize problem-solving skills through scaffolding, and even when this is slowly removed, they can manage the task independently. Learners then finally become completely self-reliant, where they can apply the problem-solving skills in other contexts as well. These elements would be able to define scaffolding as 'a social process and a structure' that enables learners to develop independent learning skills by providing adaptive and continuous diagnosis and support [4]. Although the degree of each element may differ in accordance with diverse scaffolding types and methods, these basic elements seem to remain pivotal.

Next, most scaffoldings seem to have things in common in terms of its basic mechanism which was argued by Wood et al. [3]. Pea [4] explained such mechanism of scaffolding connoted in the study of Wood et al. [3] as channeling, focusing, and modeling. To begin with, channeling refers to the provision of a sort of 'pathway' for learners to effectively perform tasks, thus limiting their autonomy so that they can productively cope with complexities occurring in the course of problem solving [4]. In other words, scaffolding is intended to provide learners with step-by-step directions and guidance to follow, thus minimizing uncertainty, chaos, and frustration, eventually enabling them to achieve a more successful task resolution [3, 26, 77–79]. Then, focusing is to help learners maintain attention and concentration by emphasizing the contents related to each stage of the task, so learners can stay focused on their goal [4]. By clearly presenting and highlighting the final goal and underlining relevant contents and activities in various representational forms, learners are encouraged to carry out complex activities with plans, purposes, and directions [3, 26, 30, 77, 79]. Last but not least, modeling is to demonstrate the ideal problem-solving processes and outcomes by experts [4]. Providing learners with expert's approaches and solutions to the current assignment would encourage them to develop their performance by comparing to and reflecting on the expert's one. Scaffolding practices apparently try following this mechanism to provide learners with the momentum for better thinking, understanding, and insight to reach a more efficient and effective solution by inducing and sustaining learners' attention, structuring tasks, emphasizing key contents, and providing emotional support [77–80].

7. Conclusion

In order for technology-based scaffolding to fully maximize the potential of scaffolding, the key would be to carefully diagnose learners, assist them instantly, and deliver adaptive guidance which is to discontinue support little by little as learners' problem-solving ability improves [55]. Although technology has not been developed enough to replace human thinking and decision-making, it can be achieved through more research on further areas such as more automated and adaptive scaffolding with the integration of learning analytics and AI-based technologies.

Not only that, scaffolding that properly utilizes technology needs to be developed to the extent that it can fully function as an 'intelligence amplifier'. Pea [4] mentioned Engelbart's [81] framework for the 'Relationship between Computing and Human Thinking and Activities', suggesting that technology should be exploited to further increase human intelligence. According to Engelbart [81], symbols can be arranged and reproduced already within a very short time through technology tools before humans can see, act, store, recall, or manipulate them. This can be realized by advanced technologies, including computing devices. Technology has evolved beyond imagination, providing a very sophisticated visual image for humans to communicate more easily and quickly, to reproduce information and knowledge, and to achieve various tasks. Therefore, technology is likely to be used as a medium to amplify human intelligence, enabling effective learning when it is possible to accurately provide adaptive help.

Author details

Soyoung Park
Education Research Institute of Seoul National University, Seoul, South Korea

*Address all correspondence to: mellowmarie@snu.ac.kr

References

[1] Vygotsky LS. Thought and Language. Cambridge, MA: MIT Press; 1962

[2] Vygotsky LS. Mind in Society. Cambridge MA: MIT Press; 1978

[3] Wood D, Bruner JS, Ross G. The role of tutoring in problem solving. The Journal of Child Psychology and Psychiatry. 1976;**17**(2):89-12

[4] Pea RD. Scaffolding. 1st ed. England, UK: Psychology Press; 2018. 423 p

[5] Reiser BJ, Tabak I, Sandoval WA, Smith BK, Steinmuller F, Leone AJ. BGuILE: Strategic and conceptual scaffolds for scientific inquiry in biology classrooms. In: Carver SM, Klahr D, editors. Cognition and Instruction: Twenty-Five Years of Progress. 1st ed. Mahwah, NJ: Lawrence Erlbaum Associates; 2002. p. 263

[6] Guzdial M. Software-realized scaffolding to facilitate programming for science learning. Interactive Learning Environments. 1994;**4**(1):1-44

[7] Sharma P, Hannafin MJ. Scaffolding in technology-enhanced learning environments. Interactive Learning Environments. 2007;**15**(1):27-46

[8] Tabak I. Synergy: A complement to emerging patterns of distributed scaffolding. The journal of the Learning Sciences. 2004;**13**(3):305-335

[9] Jonassen DH, Hung W. Learning to troubleshoot: A new theory-based design architecture. Educational Psychology Review. 2006;**18**(1):77-114

[10] Bidwell S, Jensen MF. Using a search protocol to identify sources of information: The COSI model. In: Etext on Health Technology Assessment (HTA) Information Resources. Bethesda, MD: National Information Center on Health Services Research and Health Care Technology (NICHSR); 2004

[11] Gall MD, Borg WR, Gall JP. Educational Research: An Introduction. England: Longman Publishing; 1996

[12] Hart C. Doing a Literature Review: Releasing the Research Imagination. London: Sage Publication; 2018. 352 p

[13] Pearson PD, Fielding L. Comprehension instruction. In: Barr R, Kamil JL, Mosenthal P, Pearson PD, editors. Handbook of Reading Research. 1st ed. New York: Longman; 1991, 815 p

[14] Hogan KE, Pressley ME. Scaffolding Student Learning: Instructional Approaches and Issues. 1st ed. Cambridge, MA: Brookline Books; 1997

[15] Hartman H. Human Learning and Instruction. New York: City College of City University of New York; 2002

[16] Collins A, Brown JS, Newman SE. Cognitive apprenticeship: Teaching the crafts of reading, writing, and mathematics. In: Resnick LB, editor. Knowing, Learning, and Instruction: Essays in Honor of Robert Glaser. 1st ed. Hillsdale, NJ: Lawrence Erlbaum; 1989. pp. 453-494

[17] Lave J, Wenger E. Situated Learning: Legitimate Peripheral Participation. 2nd ed. NY: Cambridge University Press; 1991

[18] Wertsch JV. The zone of proximal development: Some conceptual issues. New Directions for Child Development. 1984;**23**:7-18. DOI: 10.1002/cd.23219842303

[19] Saxe GB, Gearhart M, Guberman SR. The social organization of early number development. New Directions for Child and Adolescent Development. 1984;**23**:19-30

[20] Rogoff B. Apprenticeship in Thinking: Cognitive Development in Social Context. 1st ed. NY: Oxford University Press; 1990

[21] Campione JC. Assisted assessment: A taxonomy of approaches and an outline of strengths and weaknesses. Journal of Learning Disabilities. 1989;**22**(3):151-165

[22] Campione JC, Brown AL, Ferrara RA, Bryant NR. The zone of proximal development: Implications for individual differences and learning. New Directions for Child and Adolescent Development. 1984;**23**:77-91

[23] Palinscar AS, Brown AL. Reciprocal teaching of comprehension-fostering and comprehension-monitoring activities. Cognition and Instruction. 1984;**1**(2):117-175

[24] Scardamalia M, Bereiter C. Child as co-investigator: Helping children gain insight into their own mental processes. In: Paris S, Olson G, Stevenson H, editors. Learning and Motivation in the Classroom. 1st ed. Hillsdale, NJ: Erlbaum; 1983. pp. 61-82

[25] Scardamalia M, Bereiter C. Fostering the development of self-regulation in children's knowledge processing. In: Chipman SF, Segal JW, Glaser R, editors. Thinking and Learning Skills: Research and Open Question. 1st ed. Hillsdale, NJ: Erlbaum; 1983. pp. 563-577

[26] Rha I, Park S. The effect of visual and verbal scaffoldings on web-based problem solving performance. Educational Technology International. 2010;**11**(2):97-114

[27] Kim Y. Analysis of Cognitive Apprenticeship Learning Based on Constructivism. [thesis]. Seoul, Korea: Seoul National University; 2002

[28] Van Haneghan JP. The impact of technology on assessment and evaluation in higher education. In: Surry DW, Gray R, Stefurak J, editors. Technology Integration in Higher Education: Social and Organizational Aspects. 1st ed. Hershey, PA: IGI Global; 2011. pp. 222-235

[29] Kolodner JL. The learning sciences: Past, present, future. Educational Technology. 2004;**44**(3):34-40

[30] Park S. An exploratory study on the meaning of visual scaffolding in teaching and learning contexts. Educational Technology International. 2017;**18**(2):215-247

[31] Quintana C, Reiser BJ, Davis EA, Krajcik J, Fretz E, Duncan RG, et al. A scaffolding design framework for software to support science inquiry. The Journal of Learning Sciences. 2004;**13**(3):337-386

[32] Hannafin M, Land S, Oliver K. Open learning environments: Foundations, methods, and models. In: Reigeluth CM, editor. Instructional Design Theories and Models: A New Paradigm of Instructional Theory. 2nd ed. Mahwah, NJ: Lawrence Erlbaum; 1999. pp. 115-140

[33] Linn MC. Designing computer learning environments for engineering and computer science: The scaffolded knowledge integration framework. Journal of Science Education and Technology. 1995;**4**:103-126

[34] Tabak I, Kyza EA. Research on scaffolding in the learning sciences: A methodological perspective. In: Fischer F, Hmelo-Silver CE,

Goldman SR, Reiman P, editors. International Handbook of the Learning Sciences. NY: Routledge; 2018. pp. 191-200. DOI: 10.4324/9781315617572

[35] Puntambekar S, Hubscher R. Tools for scaffolding students in a complex learning environment: What have we gained and what have we missed? Educational Psychologist. 2005;**40**(1):1-2

[36] Hannafin M, McCarthy J, Hannafin K, Radtke P. Scaffolding Performance in EPSSs: Bridging Theory and Practice. Association for the Advancement of Computing in Education (AACE); 2001

[37] Hannafin MJ, Hill J. Teaching and learning in digital environments: The resurgence of resource-based learning. Educational Technology Research and Development. 2001;**49**(3):37-52

[38] Edelson DC, Gordin D, Pea R. Addressing the challenges of inquiry-based learning through technology and curriculum design. The Journal of the Learning Sciences. 1999;**8**:391-450

[39] Metcalf SJ, Krajcik J, Soloway E. Model-it: A design retrospective. In: Jacobson MJ, Kozma RB, editors. Innovations in Science and Mathematics Education. 1st ed. Mahwah, NJ: Lawrence Erlbaum; 2000. pp. 77-115

[40] Dimitrov DM, McGee S, Howard BC. Changes in students' science ability produced by multimedia learning environments: Application of the linear logistic model for change. School Science and Mathematics. 2002;**102**:15-24

[41] Smith BK, Reiser BJ. National Geographic unplugged: Classroom-centered design of interactive nature films. In: Proceedings of CHI 98 Conference on Human Factors in Computing Systems; 18-23 April 1998; Los Angeles. CA. 1998. pp. 424-431

[42] Tabak I. Unraveling the Development of Scientific Literacy: Domain-Specific Inquiry Support in a System of Cognitive and Social Interactions. [thesis]. Evanston, IL: Northwestern University; 1999

[43] Carroll JM, Carrithers C. Blocking learner error states in a training-wheels system. Human Factors. 1984;**26**(4):377-389

[44] Davis EA, Bell P. Design principles for scaffolding students' reflection and argumentation in science. In: Annual Meeting of the American Educational Research Association, Seattle, WA. Apr 2001

[45] Quintana C. Symphony: A Case Study for Exploring and Describing Design Methods and Guidelines for Learner-Centered Design. [thesis]. Ann Arbor, MI: University of Michigan; 2001

[46] Jackiw N. The Geometer's Sketchpad [Computer Software]. Berkeley, CA: Key Curriculum; 1991

[47] Hancock C, Kaput JJ, Goldsmith LT. Authentic inquiry with data: Critical barriers to classroom implementation. Educational Psychologist. 1992;**27**:337-364

[48] Davis EA. Prompting middle school science students for productive reflection: Generic and directed prompts. The Journal of the Learning Sciences. 2003;**12**:91-142

[49] Davis EA, Linn MC. Scaffolding students' knowledge integration: Prompts for reflection in KIE. International Journal of Science Education. 2000;**22**:819-837

[50] Anderson JR, Boyle CF, Yost G. The geometry tutor. Journal of Mathematical Behavior. 1986;**5**:5-19

[51] McManus TF. Individualizing instruction in a web-based hypermedia learning environment: Nonlinearity, advance organizers, and self-regulated learners. Journal of Interactive Learning Research. 2000;**11**(2):219-251

[52] Saye JW, Brush T. Scaffolding critical reasoning about history and social issues in multimedia-supported learning environments. Educational Technology Research and Development. 2002;**50**(3):77-96

[53] Lee D, Huh Y, Lin CY, Reigeluth CM. Technology functions for personalized learning in learner-centered schools. Educational Technology Research and Development. 2018;**66**:1269-1302

[54] Bernacki ML, Greene MJ, Lobczowski NG. A systematic review of research on personalized learning: Personalized by whom, to what, how, and for what purpose (s)? Educational Psychology Review. 2021;**33**(4): 1675-1715

[55] Gerard L, Matuk C, McElhaney K, Linn MC. Automated, adaptive guidance for K-12 education. Educational Research Review. 2015;**15**:41-58

[56] Lim L, Bannert M, van der Graaf J, Singh S, Fan Y, Surendrannair S, et al. Effects of real-time analytics-based personalized scaffolds on students' self-regulated learning. Computers in Human Behavior. 2023;**139**:107547

[57] Graesser AC, Fiore SM, Greiff S, Andrews-Todd J, Foltz PW, Hesse FW. Advancing the science of collaborative problem solving. Psychological Science in the Public Interest. 2018;**19**(2):59-92

[58] Roll I, Winne PH. Understanding, evaluating, and supporting self-regulated learning using learning analytics. Journal of Learning Analytics. 2015;**2**(1):7-12

[59] Knight S, Shum SB, Littleton K. Epistemology, assessment, pedagogy: Where learning meets analytics in the middle space. Journal of Learning Analytics. 2014;**1**(2):23-47

[60] Papamitsiou Z, Economides AA. Learning analytics and educational data mining in practice: A systematic literature review of empirical evidence. Journal of Educational Technology & Society. 2014;**17**(4):49-64

[61] Pardo A, Jovanovic J, Dawson S, Gašević D, Mirriahi N. Using learning analytics to scale the provision of personalised feedback. British Journal of Educational Technology. 2019;**50**(1):128-138

[62] Lim LA, Gentili S, Pardo A, Kovanović V, Whitelock-Wainwright A, Gašević D, et al. What changes, and for whom? A study of the impact of learning analytics-based process feedback in a large course. Learning and Instruction. 2021;**72**:101202

[63] Azevedo R, Cromley JG, Seibert D. Does adaptive scaffolding facilitate students' ability to regulate their learning with hypermedia? Contemporary Educational Psychology. 2004;**29**(3):344-370

[64] Merrill DC, Reiser BJ, Merrill SK, Landes S. Tutoring: Guided learning by doing. Cognition and Instruction. 1995;**13**(3):315-372

[65] Herrenkohl LR, Palincsar AS, DeWater LS, Kawasaki K. Developing scientific communities in classrooms: A socio-cognitive approach. Journal of the Learning Sciences. 1999;**8**(3-4):451-493

[66] Bell BS, Kozlowski SW. A typology of virtual teams: Implications for effective leadership. Group & Organization Management. 2002;**27**(1):14-49

[67] Ritter S, Fancsali S. MATHia X: The next generation cognitive tutor. In: Proccedings of the 9th International Conference on Educational Data Mining(EDM); 29 Jun–2 July 2016. Raleigh, NC, USA: EDM; 2016. pp. 624-625

[68] Jang H, Nam J. The use of artificial intelligence in elementary mathematics education – Focusing on the math class support system "Knock-knock! Math expedition". Korean Elementary Education. 2021;**31**:105-123

[69] Biemans HJ, Simons PR. How to use preconceptions? The contact strategy dismantled. European Journal of Psychology of Education. 1995;**10**:243-259

[70] Kao MT, Lehman J. Scaffolding in a computer-constructivist environment for teaching statistics to college learners. In: Paper Presented at the Annual Meeting of the American Educational Research Association. Chicago, IL; 1997

[71] Kramarski B, Hirsch C. Effects of computer algebra system (CAS) with metacognitive training on mathematical reasoning. Educational Media International. 2003;**40**(3-4):249-257

[72] Applebee AN, Langer JA. Instructional scaffolding: Reading and writing as natural language activities. Language Arts. 1983;**60**(2):168-175

[73] Burns-Hoffman R. Scaffolding children's informal expository discourse skills. In: Paper Presented at the Biennial Meeting of the Society for Research in Child Development ED362292 (60th, New Orleans, LA, March 25-28, 1993)

[74] Langer JA. Literary Understanding and Literature Instruction. Center for the Learning and Teaching of Literature. NY: University of New York; 1991. Available from: https://eric.ed.gov/?id=ED333469

[75] Tharp RG, Gallimore R. Rousing Minds to Life: Teaching, Learning and Schooling in Social Context. Cambridge: Cambridge University Press; 1988, 317 p

[76] Brown AS, Palinscar AS. Guided, cooperative learning and individual knowledge acquisition. In: Resnick LB, editor. Knowing, Learning, and Instruction: Essays in Honor of Robert Glaser. Hillsdate, NJ: Lawrence Erlbaum; 1989. pp. 393-444

[77] Park S. A study on visual scaffolding design principles in web-based learning environments. The Electronic Journal of e-Learning. 2022;**20**(2):180-200

[78] Bull R, Johnston RS, Roy JA. Exploring the roles of the visual-spatial sketch pad and central executive in children's arithmetical skills: Views from cognition and developmental neuropsychology. Developmental Neuropsychology. 1999;**15**(3):421-442

[79] McKenzie J. Scaffolding for success. The Educational Technology Journal. 1999;**9**(4):12

[80] Gaskins IW, Rauch S, Gensemer E, Cunicelli E, O'Hara C, Six L, et al. Scaffolding the development of intelligence among children who are delayed in learning to read. In: Hogan K, Pressly M, editors. Scaffolding Student Learning. 1st ed. Cambridge, MA: Brookline Books; 1997

[81] Engelbart DC. Augmenting human intellect: A conceptual framework. In: Augmented Education in the Global Age. Routledge; 2023. 17 p

Chapter 6

E-Learning in Morocco: Definitions and Leading Approaches for Assessing the Success of Information Systems

Abdelaziz Ouajdouni

Abstract

E-learning continues to grow increasingly crucial in Moroccan educational contexts as well as those throughout the world. This theoretical chapter examines Morocco's e-learning environment with an emphasis on terminology and the primary methods for assessing information systems' efficacy. Comprehending these mechanisms is imperative in augmenting the efficacy of e-learning endeavors. Using a variety of models and theories, including the Technology Acceptance Model (TAM), user satisfaction, e-learning quality, and DeLone and McLean's Information Systems Success Model, we provide a theoretical foundation for future studies and real-world e-learning applications in Morocco. Additionally, this chapter explores the factors that may influence the success of an e-learning system. This chapter offers insightful information that will help educators and policymakers in Morocco to enhance their e-learning methods.

Keywords: higher education, COVID-19, Morocco, e-learning, information systems, success, platforms, technology acceptance model, information system success model

1. Introduction

Information Technology (IT) has transformed many facets of modern life, and education is no different. The rapid advancement of e-learning platforms has fundamentally changed how students are provided with educational materials. They remove geographical and temporal barriers from instructional resources, making them more interactive, effective, and accessible to students [1]. Nowadays, the majority of educational institutions use e-learning platforms to provide their courses [2]. These institutions have had to switch from in-person to online education as a way to resume students' learning, particularly in the last few years due to the COVID-19 issue [3]. Higher education institutions in Morocco and many other nations are incorporating these technologies more and more into their programs to improve student learning and raise educational standards in this quickly changing environment.

According to Favier et al. [4], e-learning is considered as an instrument for managing relational, cultural, and technological knowledge and could drive change within an organization. Certain terms that are indistinguishable such as online learning, remote learning, web-based education, and open learning have been employed interchangeably during the last few years. Overall, this is recognized as a learning method that enables the flexible transfer of abilities and knowledge to an extensive number of beneficiaries at different times and places. Mixing technology and education offers a new approach to learning in the age of information and communication technologies [1].

As previous studies on the use of digital transformation in education have only examined scattered phenomena, e-learning requires further conceptual discussion and improvement. Many fundamental questions, particularly regarding e-learning assessment, are largely ignored in the current literature. For example, how can the success of e-learning systems be measured? What is the actual performance and success of e-learning systems in Moroccan universities? How do the experiences of Moroccan universities differ from those in contexts more familiar with e-learning, and what lessons can be learned? What are the most effective methodological approaches to evaluate the success of e-learning information systems (IS) in the specific context of Moroccan universities? Although the evaluation of IS has been extensively analyzed, with diverse approaches, gaps remain. There is a lack of information concerning the evaluation of e-learning IS success and even less in proposing methodological frameworks for measuring both the processes and the outcomes of e-learning. Delone and McLean [5] assert that IS appraisal encompasses various aspects, both technical and qualitative. Despite this, critical issues related to e-learning evaluation, especially within universities, remain unaddressed. While some scientific articles explore the real impact of e-learning on accessing educational documentation or providing training in digital formats for Moroccan students, comprehensive coverage of its implementation and impact within universities is lacking. Few studies address issues relating to the evaluation of e-learning systems' success in the context of Moroccan universities, constituting a gap in the literature. This chapter aims to explore the e-learning landscape in Morocco, focusing on the definitions and leading approaches for evaluating the success of e-learning systems in Moroccan context.

1.1 Background

Research into the business value of Information Technology (IT) studies the effects of information technology on organizational performance. Researchers have used a multitude of approaches to evaluate and estimate the mechanisms that can contribute to the organizational performance of firms. Prior research has found that IT can contribute to improving organizational performance [6–8]. In a study on the influence of IT on organizational results, Abrego Almazán et al. [9] were able to deduce that companies that devote a lot of time and effort to improving the quality of IS favor their organizational results. According to Martínez-Caro et al. [10], the digitalization of companies can stimulate the development of value-added activities, but organizations will only be able to unlock this potential if they integrate, ceteris paribus, a digital (also called numerically) organizational culture.

According to Shannak [11], without IT, organizational performance is regarded as unrealizable. These changes also have an impact on educational systems. In the field of education, many interested parties are concerned about the digitization of higher education institutions. The primary goal of institutions is now to train future professionals to be capable of handling problems and finding solutions, including digital competency as a critical level of expertise, because ICT (Information and Communication Technology) skills are becoming increasingly important in all contexts, including the workplace [12]. According to a study in Ref. [13], instructional technologists' pedagogical competency in using educational technology is crucial for professionals in teaching, education, and training fields.

The implementation of technology to boost learning in higher education institutions such as universities has become commonplace due to its ability to lower time and space barriers in traditional learning environments [14, 15]. The main time and location constraints in higher education are eliminated by IT, allowing access at any time and from any location [16, 17]. In conjunction with in-person instruction, online learning is becoming more and more common in higher education institutions and allows students to learn in a timely, continuous, and flexible manner [18].

Nowadays, worth billions of dollars, the integration of digital technology into higher education is transforming into a multibillion-dollar industry where global technology companies are increasingly influencing higher education affairs [19]. The education sector is one of those that has been most significantly impacted by the continued development of information technologies due to the rise of learning technologies. In the words of Januszewski and Molenda [20], technology for education is the study and ethical practice that aims to enhance performance while promoting learning through the creation, application, and management of technologically suitable processes and resources.

Furthermore, it is important to remember that the creation of educational materials and teaching strategies has required several adjustments in response to the growing accessibility of electronic resources. These resources, which include electronic books, electronic journals, full-text review databases, and the Internet, have found a home in libraries and have grown to be significant information sources for students, instructors, and librarians [21].

1.2 Motivations

In an increasingly hyper-connected world, the challenge of digital transformation is now a fashionable one for institutions, whether public or private, leading to a reshaping of all aspects of an organization, including those linked to IS. The digitization of procedures is becoming widespread in organizations, and its implementation requires organizations to invest in their efforts to address financial, human, and strategic issues [22]. Digitalization is becoming more than ever a necessity of the first order, in order to streamline certain procedures and improve user access to services and to build a digitalized organization that can promote a new IT generation [23]. Considering the rapid evolution of the use of IS, in particular those related to e-learning, and the interest in evaluating the success of these systems within any organization, we believe that this is a primary motivation for this study. As we previously stated, there is a lack of information on evaluating the success of e-learning IS, and even less in proposing methodological frameworks for measuring both the processes and the outcomes of e-learning, hence the second motivation. The third motivation relates to the benefits that can be derived from this study and provided to practitioners. Such reference is important in shaping the success of the e-learning system, which in turn will generate academic and scholarly value from the information systems. Our chapter provides implications for theory. The theoretical implication of this chapter is to further discuss the various definitions of e-learning platforms and the definitions of IS success and the main approaches to assessing the success of information systems. It also proposes a milestone model, specifically dedicated to the success of e-learning systems in the Moroccan university context, allowing researchers to better understand the key factors that contribute to improving the level of e-learning success.

This chapter aims to explore the e-learning landscape in Morocco, focusing on the definitions and leading approaches for evaluating e-learning success in Moroccan context.

1.3 Problem statement

While emergencies often have an impact on the activities of universities, the major disruption caused by COVID-19 on a global scale presented particular difficulties for academic institutions [24]. Around the world, and especially in Morocco, the COVID-19 pandemic has brought about a drastic change in university operations, with significant ramifications for public authorities in charge of higher education. These have been forced to implement remote learning systems quickly, so that the learning process could continue without any interruption [25], highlighting the critical need to assess the effectiveness of university e-learning systems.

In order to maintain the continuity of instruction offered to the student body, Morocco's higher education sector has been compelled to swiftly transition to this new mode in tandem with the suspension of classes and the closing of Moroccan schools and universities as of March 16, 2020.

While Moroccan universities, accustomed to traditional teaching methods prior to the pandemic, faced significant challenges in making the shift, institutions in other contexts, already acquainted with e-learning practices, were able to adjust more quickly and effectively. This disparity in the experiences of various institutions raises important concerns about the effectiveness and true success of e-learning systems.

The assessment of this success has grown to be a major concern for researchers, especially at this critical period. Therefore, this chapter aims to explore the different approaches to evaluating the success of e-learning IS, with a special focus on the particular context of Moroccan universities.

2. Digital transformation of public services: case of the Moroccan university

The field of information and communication applications has seen a dramatic transformation in recent years due to advancements in computer technology. We live in a time that is characterized by advancements in ICT and potential changes to public service management to meet citizen expectations for real-time, highly valuable digital services [26, 27].

Universities and government agencies similarly must embrace technological advancements by committing to digitization, which will enable the establishment of an organized platform at the organizational level [28]. The use of ICT in the public sector increases accountability in procedures and public administration management, which enhances service effectiveness and transparency [29].

Considering that public universities are also part of the same institutional framework for public management, we can point out, without being thorough, the oversight processes, managerial architectures, and crucial or beneficial elements of the new public management that are implemented in state-run businesses and governments. The goal of the new public management is to foster an atmosphere of leadership in the public sector that emphasizes on results [30]. As it turns out, ICT is one of the most widely used tools for streamlining work processes, boosting efficiency within organizations, and enhancing transparency [31].

As stated by Lytras and de Pablos [32], the growth of a knowledge-based economy requires well-informed and engaged citizens who have a positive attitude and use innovative technologies such e-administration in a practical manner. Since then, Al-Hujran et al. [33] have focused on the positive effects that governments and citizens have had on the advancement of knowledge society as a result of the adoption and use of e-administration and the decentralization of online services.

As an astute visionary, King Mohammed VI introduced ICTs into public administration, where they are now a vital component in enhancing the effectiveness of information, raising the standard of services, and bolstering structural reforms. In his speech, on the eve of the opening of the first session of the first legislative year of the tenth legislature in October 2016, his majesty insisted on the use of e-administration "*[...] In addition, e-government must be generalized using an integrated approach that enables the various departments and services to have common access to information. In fact, the use of new technologies helps to make it easier for citizens to access services as quickly as possible, without having to make frequent trips to the administration, which is the main cause of the spread of corruption and influence peddling*." Mindful of the potential benefits of the digital revolution underway in Morocco's public administration, the sovereign has positioned ICTs at the center of the administrative reform program in a way that is both coherent and practical.

On a global scale, we believe that the contributions of digitalization technologies to Moroccan universities are significant because they enable timely task completion and rapid information use and dissemination among all parties involved in this academic environment. Furthermore, computational technologies offer some rather significant advantages that could alter the organizational and managerial decisions made by public sector organizations, including universities. These adjustments at the choice level are part of a larger effort that seeks to improve administrative operations carried out by government organizations in an effective and efficient manner, with the goal of improving citizen engagement and producing high-quality final products more quickly [34].

3. E-learning within Moroccan universities: current situation

In a world where people are more hyper-connected than ever, the challenge of digital transformation is now in vogue for companies, whether public or private, leading to reshaping of all aspects of an organization, including those linked to IS. The digitization of procedures is becoming widespread in most organizations, even in universities, and its implementation requires investment on the part of all parties in their efforts to address financial, human, and strategic issues [22].

The prodigious technological developments taking place in today's world are giving universities that provide face-to-face training the opportunity to offer new training alternatives, such as e-learning. The introduction of ICTs as a communication tool and as venues for knowledge transmission was the goal of the so-called scattered initiatives that launched Morocco's very small e-learning phase. However, e-learning really took off when international university partnerships like the Institutional Strengthening Program between Canada and Morocco (PRICAM, Programme de Renforcement Institutionnel entre le Canada et le Maroc) were established. This program, which was started in 1997, brought together universities in Canada and Morocco to research innovative teaching methods and enhance the quality of instruction in science and technology faculties [35]. With a focus on nations in the Mediterranean region, The United Nations Educational, Scientific and Cultural Organization (UNESCO) established the AVICENNE virtual science and technology campus in 2003. The project, which is a distance learning initiative spanning 15 nations, including Morocco, has been funded by the European Commission's Euro-Mediterranean Information Society (EUMEDIS) program in addition to receiving 920,000 Euros from a number of partners, chief among them UNESCO[1]. The project's primary goal was to improve the higher education institutions in the area by creating, assessing, approving, and disseminating electronic courses through the online platform. With a platform for the development and sharing of multimedia courses, the goal of the Mediterranean Network of Universities (Med Net'U) project is to establish a distance-learning European Mediterranean University for academic and professional development. The goal of the Med Net'U project is to create a distance learning institution for academic and professional development that spans the Mediterranean and offers a platform for creating and disseminating multimedia courses. By establishing the Moroccan Virtual Campus in 2005, the Ministry of Higher Education put e-learning educational techniques into reality with the goal of creating and gathering pedagogical practices and content related to modules that complement in-person instruction [35]. Pedagogical resource centers were established under this project to assist with the administration and organization of content, assist with the securing of resources, assist with the scripting of content, and serve as a cornerstone for the advancement of e-learning in Morocco [35]. In addition, the company QualiLearning, which suggests using an e-learning management ecosystem, started a North-South collaboration that resulted in the CoseLearn initiative (Swiss cooperation in e-learning). The initiative has contributed to the growth of e-learning in a number of French-speaking African nations, notably Morocco, by gradually assembling a virtual campus comprising multiple partner colleges. Ibn Zohr University led the program with assistance from the Swiss Agency for Development and Cooperation.

Given that the face-to-face mode of learning is currently the most widely used practice in the academic world, e-learning is gradually introducing a new concept to knowledge. Morocco was no exception to the rule. Consequently, it has been imperative to establish a specific legal framework to enshrine this new learning modality. The government authority responsible for education has introduced framework law No. 51–17 on the education, training, and scientific research system, with a view to ensuring greater coherence between the various components of the education system. This framework law considers distance learning as an adjunct to in-person instruction, which is the conventional approach. The government must take all necessary and appropriate steps to enable education, teaching, training, and scientific research establishments in the public and private sectors. The main objective is to develop teaching, learning, and research resources and tools in the education, training, and scientific research system, especially through the following mechanisms as stated in

[1] https://unesdoc.unesco.org/ark:/48223/pf0000129979_fre [Accessed: July 1, 2024]

Article 33 of Dahir No. 1–19-113 of 7 hija 1440 (9 August 2019) promulgating framework law No. 51–17:

- Strengthening the integration of information and communication technologies in promoting the quality of learning and improving its performance;
- Creating innovation and production laboratories for digital resources and training specialists in this area;
- Expanding and enhancing remote learning as an adjunct to in-person instruction;
- Broadening the scope of after-school programs and services;
- Progressively incorporating e-learning in an effort to increase its accessibility, as stated in Article 33 of Dahir No. 1–19-113 of 7 hija 1440 (9 August 2019) promulgating framework law No. 51–17.

At present, however, we are faced with a number of questions about the performance or true success of e-learning. In the following section, we will look at the success of the learning system by reviewing some definitions linked to success, e-learning platforms and the theoretical underpinnings based on the Technology Acceptance Model (TAM), the user satisfaction approach, the e-learning quality approach and the approach of DeLone and McLean, which can be used in the context of evaluating e-learning systems.

4. E-learning system success: definitions, platforms and approaches

Never before has someone wanting to learn more about a certain topic had access to such a vast amount of knowledge. Access is immediate, and the possibilities are endless. As ICT has developed and the learner's surroundings have drastically changed, traditional learning has given way to e-learning. Not only has the learner-instructor relationship became smoother and more productive but also time and space restrictions have been greatly eased. Internet connectivity today ensures that people in industrialized nations can receive top-notch education at a reasonable price, with little to no costs associated with creating and delivering instructional information. However, e-learning techniques have not yet been fully utilized in underdeveloped nations, in part because of the significant upfront expenditures associated with planning and implementing platforms, as well as poor Internet connectivity [36].

Several approaches have been used to assess information systems' success. In the 1980s, implementing a system and concentrating on the technical features of the technology were necessary for success [37]. Others defined success as the user happiness brought about by the efficient use of the system [38]. Some authors examined IS success from the perspectives of system quality, use, user behavior, and satisfaction [39]. Recent research indicates that the following factors determine whether an IS is successful: user satisfaction, perceived advantages or benefits, system, information, and service quality [5, 40–42]. In a post-adoption phase, success is linked to the adoption of the system and its continued use [5]. The IS literature provides several definitions and measures of IS success. Thus, the measurement of IS success has become increasingly complex, yet it remains simple at heart [43]. There are nearly as many measures as there are studies, as stated by DeLone and McLean [5]. For a number of reasons, however, definitions and metrics of IS success continue to be challenging [42]. The first justification is that an IS combines social and technical components [44]. Alter [45] offers a second justification, stating that it is now challenging to discern the unique contributions that IT and work practices make to success due to their increasing interdependence. Some writers blame methodical techniques to measuring IS achievement for the challenge of defining IS success. They contend that it is extremely challenging to identify a dependent variable due to the numerous theoretical and methodological problems associated with assessing IS performance [46]. Seddon et al. [42] claim that the definition of IS success is still ambiguous and varies based on the stakeholders and kinds of IT.

According to Grover et al. [47], every stakeholder group that assesses the effectiveness of an IS in an organization has a distinct definition. A successful IS, in the perspective of a designer or developer, is one that is finished on schedule, stays under budget, has a feature set that complies with requirements, and operates as intended. When an IS improves a user's performance or job happiness, the user can consider it successful. From an organizational perspective, an effective IS boosts revenue or gives the business a competitive edge. However, the type of system assessed affects the success of the IS [42]. It should be mentioned that some writers interchangeably refer to IS success and effectiveness. Others use the term "individual impact" and "organizational impact" [5] or "net benefits" [41] to allude to the ideas behind IS effectiveness.

For the purposes of this chapter, we will refer to what DeLone and McLean clearly define as the entire spectrum of measurements recommended in their models when we use the term IS success. **Table 1** demonstrates the range of definitions of IS success as depicted across earlier publications concerned with IS success.

Like other organizations, higher education institutions must seize the competitive advantage, whether on a national or international scale, by creating a presence in distance learning in order to meet the needs of the student community [58]. This distance learning takes place via e-learning systems, which are seen as essential new tools to help universities gain this competitive advantage [59]. Many higher education institutions have already begun setting up the infrastructure needed to deliver their programs online [60].

With the growth of the Internet and the establishment of e-learning institutions, however, pedagogical content that satisfies learners' needs and instructors' overall goals must be created using appropriate platforms and clearly defined learning principles and theories in order for e-learning to be effective and for online programs to meet the quality requirements of the e-learning student community. The purpose of these e-learning platforms is to offer a uniform and unified user interface for every facet of a course [61]. They are deemed essential for the implementation of e-learning systems.

It should be mentioned that the literature review uncovered that earlier researches have examined the impact of the SARS-CoV-2 (COVID-19) on various e-learning educational platforms. These platforms were operative during the spread of the pandemic and provided an adequate solution to the challenge that arose during the health crisis of ensuring educational continuity [62, 63] and maintaining direct and indirect means of communication between different participants within academic institutions [64].

These platforms are computer programs that help or encourage online learning. However, there is just as much dispute over the proper terminology for these software programs as there is for the concept of e-learning [61]. Many different names are used to refer to these systems, such as Technology supported Learning Environment (TLE), Virtual Learning Environment (VLE), Managed

Authors	Definitions
([48], p. 530)	"Measuring and analyzing computer user satisfaction is motivated by management's desire to improve the productivity of information systems."
([49], p. 448)	"[...] the effects of IS along a path can lead to better organizational performance, in this case, to a reduction in overall costs."
([50], p. 119)	"If an effective system is defined as one that adds value to the business, any measure of system effectiveness should reflect some positive change in user behavior, such as improved productivity, fewer errors or better decision-making."
([51], p. 213)	"The success of the IS ultimately corresponds to what DeLone and McLean [33] call the individual impact or the organizational impact."
([52], p. 29)	"Due to the extreme difficulty of measuring the success of implementation through cost/benefit studies, another indicator of success is needed. The most attractive indicator for this purpose, from a measurement point of view, is the use of the system."
([53], p. 84)	"An IS must be developed in response to a specific business need, such as the need to be more responsive to changing customer desires, to improve product quality or to improve organizational communications. Systems that do not support business objectives are unlikely to succeed."
([54], p. 248)	"The success of the IS is therefore conceptualized as a value judgment made by an individual, from the point of view of certain stakeholders."
([55], p. 903)	"If the project meets the technical performance specifications and/or achieves its mission, and if there is a high satisfaction with the results among key individuals in the parent organization, the client organization, the project team, and the project's users or customers, the project is considered an overall success."
[56]	"The success of a project is only meaningful if it is considered from two angles: the extent to which the project's technical performance objective has been achieved on time and within budget; and the project's contribution to the company's strategic mission."
[57]	"Major projects are assessed against four success criteria: (1) the project fulfills its functionality; (2) it is delivered to budget, schedule and technical specification; (3) it is commercially profitable for the contractor; and (4) it is terminated reasonably and effectively if it has to be canceled."

Table 1.
Different definitions of IS success.

Learning Environment (MLE), Learning Support System (LSS), Learning Content Management System (LCMS), Course Management System (CMS), and Learning Management System (LMS)[2] [61]. Certain names may be used interchangeably or to refer to distinct kinds of systems. There are many interpretations of what a managed learning environment (MLE) is, from a broad definition to a more focused one that considers it to be a type of improved VLE ([65], p. 1). The terms LMS, CMS, LCMS, MLE, LSS, and learning platform (LP) are other terms for virtual learning environments, according to Stansfield and Connolly ([66], p. 31). VLE is described as "a collection of instructional resources intended to improve student learning through the integration of computers and the Internet into the learning process" by whatis.com[3]. VLE comprises the following primary components: curriculum map-

[2] " Learning Management System (LMS), Learning Content Management System (LCMS), Course Management System (CMS), Virtual Learning Environment (VLE), Managed Learning Environment (MLE), Technology-Enhanced Learning Environment (TELE), or Learning Support System (LSS)".
[3] https://www.techtarget.com/whatis/definition/virtual-learning-environment-VLE-or-managed-learning-environment-MLE [Accessed: July 1, 2024]

ping, which divides the curriculum into sections that can be assigned and assessed; learner tracking; online support for both instructors and students; electronic communication (email, chat, threaded discussions, web publishing); and Internet links to other training resources. In general, users of VLE are given either a learner ID or an instructor ID. The instructor can design or edit program content and keep an eye on the student's progress in addition to seeing what the student does.

A common, accepted definition of an e-learning platform does not exist. Due to the lack of an impartial framework for characterizing, contrasting, and evaluating systems without a clear definition, this presents a challenge for researchers as well as practitioners. We consider it customary in scientific practice to define concepts and provide definitions before advancing further. Researchers' definitions of what constitutes an e-learning platform are summarized in **Table 2**.

Furthermore, there is currently no standard nomenclature for e-learning because it is yet an undefined subject of research ([76], p. 12). Nowadays, there are a lot of phrases and meanings, most of which are only loosely defined and frequently nearly identical, though not quite. Working without independent definitions is especially risky, according to Piotrowski [61], when reviewing systems. In order to facilitate the learning process and maximize the intended learning outcomes, we therefore adopt ([77], p. 3) the definition of an e-learning platform, which is "an operating system and specialized learning management software that allow students and the instructor to plan, organize, monitor, coordinate, and control learning activities."

A higher education institution offering e-learning only requires standard server hardware and Internet connectivity, both of which need to be sized according to

Authors	Definitions
[67], p. 5)	"A software system that combines a number of different tools used to systematically deliver online content and facilitate the learning experience around that content."
([68], p. 35)	"A software system designed to support teaching and learning."
([69], p. 213)	"A computer program used to enhance the teaching of courses via computers and the Internet."
[70]	"A set of teaching and learning tools designed to enhance a student's learning experience by including computers and the Internet in the learning process. This system provides components in which learners and tutors participate in a number of online interactions, including e-learning."
[71]	"A flexible system that makes it possible to work with a large number of students, to process and update teaching material quickly, and to choose the time and place of study. Its requirements are availability of discursive tools (i.e., tools to maintain communication); adaptability (ease with which subject content can be presented across activities); interactivity (ability for students to obtain material, modify and personalize it); reflection (ability to provide feedback from instructors)."
[72]	"A social space, made up of cognitive and social interactions on or around an object of knowledge, in which people interact using hypermedia language for teaching and learning."
[73]	"A socio-technical process in which subjects interact in and through culture and culture is a field of struggle, power, difference and meaning, a space for the construction of knowledge."
([74], p. 78)	"A complete software package that handles some or all aspects of course preparation, presentation and interaction, and allows these aspects to be accessed via a network."
([75], p. 23)	"An integrated combination of web-based tools specifically focused on pedagogical support for content distribution and enabling communication, organization and pedagogical support in courses."

Table 2.
Different definitions of an e-learning platform.

demand, which is determined by factors such as the number of students using the system simultaneously and the type and quantity of media served [61]. The author adds that access to learning content, tests, various communication and collaboration tools for students, as well as course management and assessment possibilities for instructors are typical features of e-learning platforms. These e-learning platforms may also incorporate administrative functions or interfaces with administrative systems related to resource planning and accounting, student admissions and enrollment management, campus management, etc.

There are many online learning platforms available these days. They can be divided into two groups: open-source platforms and commercial virtual marketplaces [59]. Currently, some of the most well-known commercial platforms include Angel, WebCT, Clix, Desire2Learn, Blackboard, and Clix. To name a few examples of open-source learning platforms, there is eFront, Open ELMS e-learning, eXelearning, Sakai, Atutor, Dokeos, Moodle, ILIAS, OLAT, Xerte Online Toolkits (XOT), and Course Builder. All of these platforms enable educators to create educational materials that are tailored to their own teaching and learning methodologies. They provide a fully functional online learning environment in order to produce interactive learning materials [78]. Furthermore, it is simple to export the content created on these to another website or e-learning platform, such as Moodle.

E-learning platforms are becoming a standard in the sphere of education and are emerging as a new phenomenon. As a result, methods for assessing these systems' effectiveness are currently scarce. The path pursued by researchers in their quest to create suitable tools for assessing the effectiveness of e-learning systems has been diverse. Different standards for judging the effectiveness of e-learning systems have emerged as a result of the various interpretations of the word "e-learning" that various writers have used [79]. Studies evaluating the success of IS related to the academic context such as universities and colleges are scarce [80], particularly in the context of Arab countries [81, 82], which poses a problem in terms of proposing a useful evaluation criterion for educational institutions in this setting. In the state of the art, we found that studies on this topic can be based on the TAM, the user satisfaction approach, the e-learning quality approach, and the DeLone and McLean approach that can be used in the context of the evaluation of e-learning systems. Previous works using these approaches are now presented.

4.1 Technology acceptance model (TAM) approach

Within the IS domain, the TAM model is widely accepted as a standard model. The principal objective of using this approach is to evaluate the acceptance and success of the technology. Regarding e-learning systems, some models have been developed to investigate the factors that are considered determinants of the use and intention to use e-learning systems. Studies of the TAM approach to e-learning systems have modified and extended some of the constructs of the model[4].

[4] The use of the TAM model to the acceptance of educational technologies has been demonstrated to offer greater benefits compared to other theoretical models, according to a systematic study conducted by Al-Qaysi et al. [76].

In order to provide an expanded TAM model based on Self-Determination Theory (SDT)[5] for e-learning, Roca and Gagné [83] carried out a study. According to the two authors' concept, perceived autonomy support, perceived competence, and perceived relatedness all have an impact on perceived usefulness, perceived playfulness, and perceived ease of use. One of the first studies to look at how motivational factors affect TAM model constructs was this one. The findings suggest that using SDT to workplace e-learning could be helpful in evaluating learners' intentions to continue with it.

The primary aim of a survey carried out by Al-alak and Alnawas [84] was to assess the level of acceptance and use of mobile learning by academic personnel. The empirical study found that the intention to use e-learning was substantially correlated with perceived utility, perceived simplicity of use, computer literacy, and management support. The intention to accept e-learning was adversely correlated with normative pressure and computer fear.

A model that predicts whether or not a university lecturer would employ e-assessment was proposed by Imtiaz and Maarop [85]. The suggested model expands upon the TAM model by incorporating pertinent ideas from other models of acceptance, including the Unified Theory of Acceptance and Use of Technology (UTAUT), the Theory of Reasoned Action (TRA), the TAM2 model, and the Social Cognitive Theory (SCT).

In order to analyze intentions to pursue e-learning 2.0 in an organizational setting, Wu and Zhang [86] conducted a study. As a result, the authors provide a single model that incorporates social motivation theories, the Information System Success Model (ISSM), and TAM. This survey included 284 participants from Chinese companies. The findings demonstrate that the integrated model offers a more thorough comprehension of the thought processes and actions connected to this context: (1) perceived usefulness was found to be a major mediator of the effects of perceived ease of use, information quality, and social impact on intention to continue; (2) the perceived utility functioned as a significant mediator between the perceived ease of use, the quality of the information, and the social influence on the intention to continue; (3) the perceived ease of use, the information quality, and the social influence all play crucial roles in predicting the intention to continue; (4) the system's quality significantly influenced the perceived ease of use; and (5) unexpectedly, social motivations had no significant impact on attitude.

In a recent study, Riyath et al. [87] analyzed the factors affecting students' attitudes, behavioral intentions and actual use of Zoom for online courses in higher education institutions in Sri Lanka. The authors used the TAM model as a theoretical model which was modified by including computer self-efficacy as an external variable. The authors found that computer self-efficacy affects perceived usefulness and perceived ease of use affects the attitude and behavioral intention and actual use of Zoom in a chain reaction. In addition, perceived ease of use affects perceived usefulness, which in turn affects behavioral intention. Furthermore, the effect size of perceived usefulness on behavioral intention is larger than that of attitude on behavioral intention.

Within the scientific community engaged in Management of Information Systems, there is interest in the subject of acceptability and implementation of e-learning

[5] Self-determination theory is an empirical theory of human motivation and personality in social contexts that differentiates motivation in terms of autonomy and control [77].

systems. To address this issue, a variety of elements and theories have been applied. The field of e-learning systems makes extensive use of the TAM model. The table above illustrates how TAM has been used and expanded in numerous investigations. These additions are primarily meant to encompass a broad spectrum of variables that may affect e-learning system acceptability and to explore the part these variables play in acceptability. Research has indicated that a few key variables significantly affect how well e-learning systems are accepted. To ascertain their significance in the acceptance of e-learning, additional elements must be investigated further.

4.2 The user satisfaction approach

User satisfaction has drawn the attention of IS researchers. The focus has been especially directed toward e-learning systems. An e-learning system's success can be assessed by looking at its user satisfaction rate. With growing utilization of learning systems and the popularity of e-learning, this satisfaction measure is becoming more and more significant. To ensure that their programs are well designed and run smoothly to produce the intended results, academic researchers and decision-makers must determine the elements that affect learners' satisfaction with the e-learning process.

For example, Arbaugh [88, 89], identified three factors affecting student satisfaction: the flexibility of the medium, the ability to develop an interactive course environment, and the ease or frequency of use of the medium.

Lee and Hwang [90] applied a study to explore the factors affecting e-learner satisfaction. The results confirmed that perceived usefulness, perceived ease of use, interaction service quality, self-regulatory learning strategy, and computer self-efficacy affect e-learner satisfaction.

Sun et al. [91] identified six critical dimensions influencing learner satisfaction: learners, instructors, course, technology, design, and environment. About 13 factors were hypothesized within these six dimensions, and of these, computer anxiety, instructor attitude toward e-learning, course quality, flexibility, perceived usefulness, perceived ease of use, and assessment diversity were empirically supported. The results of the study revealed that increasing user satisfaction through these factors promotes the success of an e-learning system.

The Ozkan and Koseler [79] model was another important contribution to the evaluation of the success of e-learning. The researchers developed a hexagonal model based on quality factors (system, information, and service quality) and social issues (support factors, learner perspective, and instructor attitudes). The relationships between the six dimensions and e-learning satisfaction were found to be significant, accounting for 76.9% of the variance in e-learning satisfaction. The researchers concluded that this model should be considered fundamental for evaluating the effectiveness of e-learning and suggested supplementing it with additional dimensions.

Ouajdouni et al. [92] conducted a study that consists of proposing a model specifically dedicated to the success of e-learning systems in the Moroccan University context, allowing for a better understanding of the key factors that contribute to improving the level of e-learning success, which was considered critical in their previous study [93]. The authors found that the use of the e-learning system and the satisfaction of e-learners play a central role in improving the success of the e-learning system. The use of e-learning technology and online learner satisfaction can help students improve their performance in class, enhance their knowledge, and increase their autonomy.

Furthermore, Ouajdouni et al. [92] find a significant relationship between instructor quality and student satisfaction as end users with the e-learning system confirming the results of other previous studies [80, 91].

The user satisfaction approach to evaluating e-learning systems is commonly used by researchers. Most studies have focused on user satisfaction of a single stakeholder, usually students, with little emphasis on other stakeholder groups [94].

4.3 Approach to the quality of e-learning

Quality assessment in higher education institutions is a non-standardized process that varies from one university to another. It has to be said that the quality of traditional teaching in a university is not homogeneous and differs from one subject to another. The quality of e-learning within the same university can also vary [95]. In order to curb this diversity in quality levels, a quality system needs to be put in place to ensure the minimum required level of e-learning quality within a university institution.

The digitalization of education and recent events have led to a considerable increase in the interest and relevance of e-learning in the teaching/learning process, with quality being a fundamental element in its evaluation and improvement. Quality improvement and assurance are essential to the success of higher education institutions involved in e-learning [96, 97]. This process of continuous reflection and refinement of processes toward high levels of quality is now one of the most important roadmaps for any organization or professional involved, and it is here that the intervention of new learning environments and pathways conditions and questions the whole process of achieving quality, its relevance, and its various interpretations [98].

Two strands of literature take a stand on the concept of e-learning quality in the context of the transition to e-learning. Thus, while some scientists believe that it is essential to begin by restructuring and questioning the classic dimensions of quality assessment in the current environment, assessing their relevance and new "dimensionnalisation" for accurate assessment in this field, others believe that assessment should remain the same without changing the "dimensionnalisation" of quality [99].

These transitions, which are currently taking place in most modes of teaching, are essentially based on ICTs, which make it possible to customize teaching processes according to the characteristics of each learner, adapt learning styles, allow greater, faster, and more synchronized interaction, and implement quality models. These models focus not only on the technological variable but also on the didactic, organizational, and pedagogical variables of teaching in its broadest sense [100].

In order to enhance and guarantee the quality of e-learning, a number of models, frameworks, and guidelines have been developed [101–107]. Many of them start from the premise that "the quality principles underpinning successful online teaching and learning are exactly the same as those underpinning successful face-to-face teaching" ([108], p. 87).

Consequently, it should be noted that the applicability of these models in other cultural contexts is questioned [109]. For example, models that have had a significant impact, such as The Institute of Higher Education Policy (IHEP) and The Sloan Consortium Quality Framework (SCQF), are rooted in specific cultural norms and values, in this case Western culture [110]. The IHEP focuses more on educational policy, educational reform, and institutions, while the SCQF provides for guidelines and standards to establish procedures for assessment and quality assurance in online education. Combined, they help guide practices and policies aimed at enhancing effectiveness as well as accessibility of higher education.

That said, in an increasingly globalized environment, and with the attempt to improve the quality assessment of organizations in a cross-cultural context, "e-quality" models should then specifically consider cultural and cultural-pedagogical constructs [111].

Auvinen and Peltonen [112] indicate that the quality of education can be defined from three perspectives: (1) technological; (2) economic; and (3) pedagogical. The pedagogical approach focuses on improving learning processes, including e-learning and the interaction between the learner and the learning environment. Previously, quality standards were associated with specific outcomes. This meant that quality was assessed based on the quality of courses and predefined learning outcomes. This approach has changed in recent years.

Auvinen and Peltonen [112] distinguished three different dimensions: (1) the different understandings of quality within a stakeholder group; (2) the perspectives of different stakeholder groups (e.g., students, instructors, institutions, employers of graduates, governments); and (3) different quality standards may be applied to measure outcomes at different levels. Zhao [113] proposes the following framework for measuring and improving the quality of online higher education:

- Course effectiveness: even the most impressive technology is useless if it does not support content that meets learners' needs;

- Adequacy of access in terms of technological infrastructure: most of the problems faced by online students seem to be caused by deficiencies in technology and access;

- Student satisfaction: student satisfaction relates to course quality, interaction with instructors, collaboration with peers and support services. Interaction between students and instructors, as well as between students, is essential in virtual classrooms and online learning. Studies show that timely feedback and mentor support are essential for successful learning, both from the instructors' and the peers' perspectives;

- Academic satisfaction: academic satisfaction indicates that teaching staff find online teaching effective and professionally rewarding. In many respects, online teaching differs from traditional face-to-face teaching in terms of pedagogical changes and the intensive use of ICT in teaching.

In addition, Zhao [113] recommends that universities implement a quality assurance plan specifically for e-learning programs. In this regard, Oliver [95] points out that there is a rising demand for recognized standards and benchmarks to assess performance as institutions employ e-learning for course delivery more and more and are held accountable for service quality.

In the Moroccan University context, the importance of teaching quality has prompted the Kingdom to create an agency that is subject to state supervision named the National Agency for Evaluation and Quality Assurance of Higher Education and Scientific Research (ANEAQ). The organization in question is a public entity that possesses both financial and legal independence. In order to improve oversight of the quality of the Moroccan university system, ANEAQ's objective is to assess the system of scientific research and higher education on behalf of the Moroccan government. This occurs in the midst of notable developments in the higher education system, most notably the release by the Higher Council for Education, Training, and Scientific Research of its 2015–2030 strategic reform vision and the creation of the corresponding framework law. It should be noted that Dahir No. 1-14-130 of 3 Chaoual 1435 (31 July 2014) regulates this establishment.

However, Law No. 80-12 on the National Agency for Evaluation and Quality Assurance in Higher Education and Scientific Research (ANEAQ) does not explicitly mention the evaluation of the quality of e-learning, since this mode of e-learning only became widespread with the advent of COVID-19, which prompted academic institutions to think about alternative solutions to ensure pedagogical continuity.

The quality of e-learning has gradually become a crucial issue in many higher education institutions. Researchers and institutions have drawn on their efforts to develop models, frameworks, guidelines and criteria for measuring e-learning quality. Two major problems persist in efforts to improve the quality of e-learning. The complexity of the concept of quality is the first problem. It requires a variety of approaches and methodologies to assess this concept [94].

The second issue concerns the different stakeholders involved in e-learning quality, such as students, academic staff, trainers, management and developers. As a result, each stakeholder group focuses on different criteria and characteristics to assess the quality of e-learning. However, despite the two constraints mentioned above, researchers are continuing their research in order to develop the most appropriate measures for assessing and developing the quality of e-learning within universities and colleges.

4.4 DeLone and McLean's approach

DeLone and McLean's [5] model of information system success is considered a highly influential theoretical foundation for predicting and explaining IS use, user satisfaction, and information system success [114–116]. This model can be considered as a basis for evaluating the success of the e-learning system thanks to its solid theoretical basis and the various empirical studies carried out in this area [114].

DeLone and McLean have defined six distinct IS success variables: system quality, information quality, usage, user satisfaction, individual impact, and organizational impact. The quality of the system and the quality of the information have both a separate and a joint effect on the use and satisfaction of users. Furthermore, the degree of use can affect the degree of user satisfaction positively or negatively, and vice versa. Usage and user satisfaction are direct antecedents of individual impact; and finally, individual performance should eventually have some organizational influence [114]. DeLone and McLean [41, 117] proposed an updated IS success model by assessing the rapid evolution of IS, particularly web-based applications. Referring to various previous research studies, they incorporated quality of service and net benefit into their new model. Thus, the updated model included six variables: (1) information quality, (2) system quality, (3) service quality, (4) usage/intention to use, (5) user satisfaction, and (6) net benefits.

Through an examination of the constructs within their new model and their interrelationships, it can be inferred that a system's evaluation can be based on information, system, and service quality. These attributes influence subsequent usage or intention to use, as well as user satisfaction. Certain benefits will be obtained by using the system. The net benefits may (positively or negatively) influence user satisfaction and subsequent use of the IS [118]. The IS success model has been used as a cornerstone for the evaluation of several systems such as e-commerce, e-health, e-justice, e-Gov, ERP systems, and even e-learning [119–126].

In the context of e-learning, learning activities are carried out by students (the end users) via platforms often hosted on the web. The quality of the system and the quality of the information have an impact on system use and user satisfaction, both separately and jointly. In fact, the degree of use of the system can affect the degree of user satisfaction in both directions. Although user usage and satisfaction form the basis of individual effectiveness, it is expected that individual performance will ultimately have some organizational impact [43]. However, referring to our literature review, few manuscripts specified the type of IS or the context of use (i.e., individual vs. organizational/voluntary vs. mandatory), whether the system ranges from hedonic which is developed for pleasure and enjoyment, to utilitarian which has the purpose of improving individual and organizational performance [127].

In summary, a variety of fields have examined and tested DeLone and McLean's model, with different systems and different stakeholders. The model has been used to evaluate the success of e-learning systems. Various methodologies have been used in e-learning systems research. Some studies used the model in part and tested the validity of specific constructs of the model, while others intended to extend the model to identify additional factors influencing the success of e-learning systems.

5. Evaluating e-learning success: a validated model from the Moroccan context

Conducting research requires the use of methodological approaches in order to understand specific phenomena. The research stages must clearly identify the philosophy, approach and method of any study. The aim of the research carried out by Ouajdouni et al. [93] in the Moroccan context was to identify the factors that influence the success of an e-learning system, based on several leading models. To be consistent with a specific paradigm and approach, these factors need to be identified, brought together in a single model, and tested.

The main aim of this research was to develop a model for measuring the success of e-learning systems from different angles in the Moroccan context. The following constructs were chosen for the model to achieve this objective: (1) system quality, (2) instructor quality, (3) e-learning system use, (4) perceived usefulness, (5) learner satisfaction, (6) learner computer anxiety, (7) social influence, and (8) e-learning system success. The importance of these constructs in measuring the success of IS, as well as the literature in the field of IS and e-learning systems, influenced their selection.

These concepts were chosen for our study because of their importance as key measures of e-learning systems. However, there are few studies that combine all of these concepts in a single model, especially in an Arab-African context, and particularly in the Moroccan context. The following **Figure 1** illustrates the model of evaluating e-learning system success.

Various perspectives have been considered for their potential in evaluating e-learning success, including individual factors (such as learner computer anxiety), social factors (social influence, learner quality, and instructor quality); user beliefs (perceptions of satisfaction and usefulness); acceptance (use); and the benefits of using the e-learning system which are considered as a crucial component of e-learning system success.

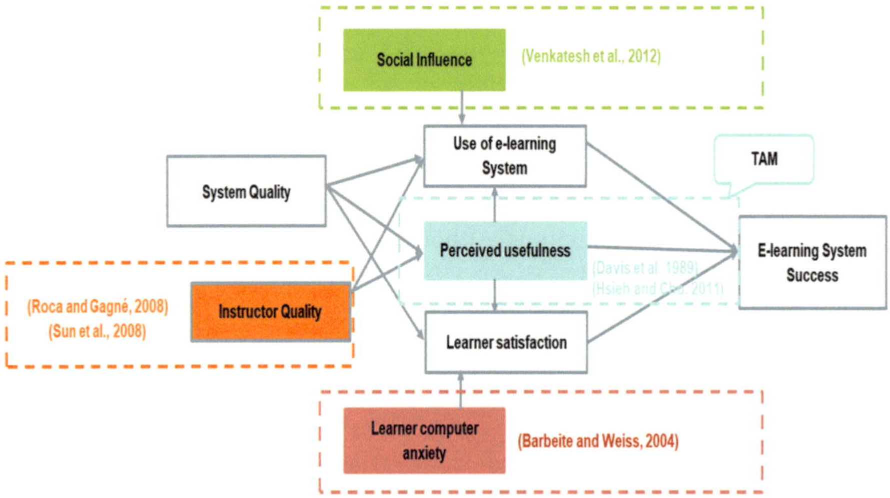

Figure 1.
Assessing e-learning system success. Source: Ouajdouni et al. [93].

This study was designed to meet the following main objectives:

- The first objective was to identify the various determinants having an impact on the success of an e-learning system and to place them in a holistic model. This objective was accomplished based on the theoretical foundations relating to IS and e-learning systems and was supported by the empirical test undertaken on the basis of data collected from the sample targeted by the study, i.e., Moroccan university students.

- The second objective was to test the proposed model by verifying its validity and reliability, and to confirm that the model is likely to measure the success of e-learning systems from the student's point of view. For the model as a whole, the model fit indicators were used to assess the validity of the model. The test results for the measurement model and the structural model show that the model fit indicators met the threshold for these indicators and confirmed the validity of the model.

- The third and final objective was to determine the type and importance of the relationships between these determinants in the context of the proposed model, and to measure the direct and indirect effects between the constructs of the study model. This objective was achieved by means of the structural model, which includes the dependency relationships linking the different constructs of the model [128]. The links between the constructs of the study model were represented by the study hypotheses.

Ultimately, this research offered comprehensive definitions of all concepts related to e-learning success measurement, and the model incorporated the four approaches identified from the literature review above for evaluating e-learning and information systems. Furthermore, this research addressed a very relevant issue in the field of e-learning systems: the success of e-learning systems. The main objectives of this study are to identify the factors that can influence the success of an e-learning system, to situate them in a holistic model, and to subject this model to empirical testing. As a result, a theoretical model was developed and empirically tested with Moroccan university students. The results showed that the model is valid and predictive of the effectiveness of e-learning IS.

Starting from the students' point of view, this study painted a clear picture of the elements that influence the success of e-learning systems. In addition, this unprecedented and original study, set in the specific context of Morocco during the unique circumstances of the COVID-19 crisis, contributes to the theoretical framework and body of knowledge by proposing a valid model for evaluating the success of e-learning systems.

6. Conclusions

The analysis of the digitalization of public services at Moroccan institutions has encompassed an examination of diverse aspects of e-learning and its execution. The state of e-learning at Moroccan institutions today indicates a system under change, motivated by the demand for better accessibility and educational quality as well as technological improvements. Although there are difficulties associated with this change, there are also many opportunities. We have covered a number of important strategies for comprehending and improving e-learning systems in our discussion:

- E-learning System Success: We obtain a thorough grasp of what makes an effective e-learning system by looking at the definitions, platforms, and techniques. Technological efficiency is simply an indicator used to measure success; additional measurements include user performance and satisfaction.

- The TAM offers insights into the adoption and utilization of technology by users. For implementing e-learning systems in Moroccan institutions, it is imperative to comprehend the elements that affect technological acceptability.

- User Satisfaction Approach: User satisfaction remains a critical component of e-learning success. By focusing on the needs and experiences of the users, Moroccan universities can tailor their e-learning systems to better meet educational goals and improve overall satisfaction.

- Quality of E-learning: Ensuring the quality of e-learning involves not just the technological aspects but also didactic, organizational, and pedagogical factors. A holistic approach to quality can lead to more effective and engaging learning experiences.

- The Model of DeLone and McLean: Several factors are taken into consideration when determining the effectiveness of e-learning, such as information quality, system quality, service quality, use, user satisfaction, and net benefits. By using this approach, Moroccan universities can assess the effectiveness of their e-learning programs and find areas for development.

These ideas and frameworks must be included into a comprehensive strategy as Moroccan universities continue to embrace e-learning. By doing this, universities may guarantee that their efforts to transform digitally result in long-lasting and significant advancements in the higher education sector, in addition to improving both the quality and accessibility of education. The development of e-learning at Moroccan universities is still in its earliest stages, but with sustained attention to user satisfaction and quality, there are bright prospects for its advancement in the future.

Acknowledgements

I would like to express my deepest gratitude to Doctor Khalid Chafik (Abdelmalek Essaadi University) for his invaluable guidance, insightful comments, and constructive suggestion throughout this project. Lastly, I appreciate the engagement of the anonymous reviewers for generously dedicating their precious time and mastery to the review process.

Conflict of interest

The authors declare no conflict of interest.

Author details

Abdelaziz Ouajdouni
Management and Information System Research Group, National School of Business and Management, Abdelmalek Essaadi University, Tangier, Morocco

*Address all correspondence to: ouajdouni.abdelaziz@gmail.com

References

[1] Liu M, Yu D. Towards intelligent E-learning systems. Education and Information Technologies. 2023;**28**(7):7845-7876

[2] Khaldi A, Bouzidi R, Nader F. Gamification of e-learning in higher education: A systematic literature review. Smart Learning Environments. 2023;**10**(1):10

[3] Sofiadin A, Azuddin M. An Initial Sustainable E-Learning and Gamification Framework for Higher Education. Lisbon: International Association for Development of the Information Society; 2021

[4] Favier M, Kalika M, Trahand J. E-learning/E-formation : Implications pour les organisations. Systèmes d'Information et Management. 2004;**9**(4):3-10

[5] DeLone WH, McLean ER. Information systems success: The quest for the dependent variable. Information Systems Research. 1992;**3**(1):60-95

[6] Brynjolfsson E, Hitt L. Paradox lost? Firm-level evidence on the returns to information systems spending. Management Science. 1996;**42**(4):541-558

[7] Kohli R, Devaraj S. Measuring information technology payoff: A meta-analysis of structural variables in firm-level empirical research. Information Systems Research. 2003;**14**(2):127-145

[8] Mukhopadhyay T, Kekre S, Kalathur S. Business value of information technology: A study of electronic data interchange. MIS Quarterly. 1995;**19**(2):137-156

[9] Abrego Almazán D, Sánchez Tovar Y, Medina Quintero JM. Influence of information systems on organizational results. Contaduría y Administración. 2017;**62**(2):321-338

[10] Martínez-Caro E, Cegarra-Navarro JG, Alfonso-Ruiz FJ. Digital technologies and firm performance: The role of digital organisational culture. Technological Forecasting and Social Change. 2020;**154**:119962

[11] Shannak RO. An Interpretive Approach to Analysing the Role and Value of Information Systems in Jordanian Financial Organisations. Birmingham: Aston University; 1999

[12] Bond M, Marín VI, Dolch C, Bedenlier S, Zawacki-Richter O. Digital transformation in German higher education: Student and teacher perceptions and usage of digital media. International Journal of Educational Technology in Higher Education. 2018;**15**(1):1-20

[13] OECD. Teaching for the Future: Effective Classroom Practices to Transform Education. Paris: OECD Publishing; 2018

[14] Henrie CR, Halverson LR, Graham CR. Measuring student engagement in technology-mediated learning: A review. Computers & Education. 2015;**90**:36-53

[15] Sweeney MT, Oram I. Information technology for management education: The benefits and barriers. International Journal of Information Management. 1992;**12**(4):294-309

[16] Nayar KB, Kumar V. Cost benefit analysis of cloud computing in education. International Journal

of Business Information Systems. 2018;**27**(2):205-221

[17] Zhang Z, Cao T, Shu J, Liu H. Identifying key factors affecting college students' adoption of the e-learning system in mandatory blended learning environments. Interactive Learning Environments. 2020;**30**(8):1388-1401

[18] Prasad PWC, Maag A, Redestowicz M, Hoe LS. Unfamiliar technology: Reaction of international students to blended learning. Computers & Education. 2018;**122**:92-103

[19] Castañeda L, Selwyn N. More than tools? Making sense of the ongoing digitizations of higher education. International Journal of Educational Technology in Higher Education. 2018;**15**(1):22

[20] Januszewski A, Molenda M. Educational Technology: A Definition with Commentary. New York: Routledge; 2008. 385 p

[21] Johnson K, Magusin E. Exploring the Digital Library: A Guide for Online Teaching and Learning. Vol. 24. Hoboken: John Wiley & Sons; 2009

[22] Ouajdouni A, Chafik K, Boubker O. Transformation Digitale de L'Administration Publique au Maroc: Revue de la littérature et état des lieux. ESJ. 2020;**16**(19):406-432. DOI: 10.19044/esj.2020.v16n19p406

[23] Santiso C, Bernard M. Révolution numérique et transformation de l'action publique. Politique étrangère. 2019;**2**:129-142

[24] Regehr C, Goel V. Managing COVID-19 in a large urban research-intensive university. In: Loss and Trauma in the COVID-19 Era. New York: Routledge; 2024

[25] Aulakh K, Roul RK, Kaushal M. E-learning enhancement through educational data mining with COVID-19 outbreak period in backdrop: A review. International Journal of Educational Development. 2023;**101**:102814

[26] Brown D. Le gouvernement électronique et l'administration publique. Revue Internationale des Sciences Administratives. 2005;**71**(2):251-266

[27] Mergel I, Edelmann N, Haug N. Defining digital transformation: Results from expert interviews. Government Information Quarterly. 2019;**36**(4):101385

[28] Babinet G. Transformation Digitale: L'avènement Des Plateformes. Paris: Le Passeur; 2016

[29] Gupta B, Dasgupta S, Gupta A. Adoption of ICT in a government organization in a developing country: An empirical study. The Journal of Strategic Information Systems. 2008;**17**(2):140-154

[30] Cordella A, Iannacci F. Information systems in the public sector: The e-government enactment framework. The Journal of Strategic Information Systems. 2010;**19**(1):52-66

[31] Saoud H. Les Technologies de L'information et de la Communication Comme Levier de Transformation du Management des Organisations Publiques. Versailles: Université de Versailles-Saint-Quentin-en-Yvelines; 2013

[32] Lytras M, de Pablos PO. Software technologies in knowledge society. Journal of Universal Computer Science. 2011;**17**(9):1219-1221

[33] Al-Hujran O, Al-Debei MM, Chatfield A, Migdadi M. The imperative of influencing citizen attitude toward

e-government adoption and use. Computers in Human Behavior. 2015;**53**:189-203

[34] Bressolles G, Durrieu F, Senecal S. A consumer typology based on e-service quality and e-satisfaction. Journal of Retailing and Consumer Services. 2014;**21**(6):889-896

[35] Ajhoun R, Daoudi N. E-learning in the Middle East and North Africa (MENA) region. In: Weber AS, Hamlaoui S, editors. Cham: Springer International Publishing; 2018. pp. 263-283. DOI: 10.1007/978-3-319-68999-9_12

[36] Ahn JY, Edwin A. An e-learning model for teaching mathematics on an open source learning platform. The International Review of Research in Open and Distributed Learning. 2018;**19**(5):255-267. DOI: 10.19173/irrodl.v19i5.3733

[37] Rockart JF. The Changing Role of the Information Systems Executive: A Critical Success Factors Perspective. Cambridge, MA: MIT Sloan School of Management; 1980

[38] Raymond L. Organizational context and information systems success: A contingency approach. Journal of Management Information Systems. 1990;**6**(4):5-20

[39] Ives B, Olson MH. User involvement and MIS success: A review of research. Management Science. 1984;**30**(5):586-603

[40] DeLone WH. Determinants of success for computer usage in small business. MIS Quarterly. 1988;**12**(1):51-61

[41] Delone WH, McLean ER. The DeLone and McLean model of information systems success: A ten-year update. Journal of Management Information Systems. 2003;**19**(4):9-30

[42] Seddon PB, Staples S, Patnayakuni R, Bowtell M. Dimensions of information systems success. Communications of the Association for Information Systems. 1999;**2**(1):20

[43] Petter S, DeLone W, McLean E. The past, present, and future of "IS success". Journal of the Association for Information Systems. 2012;**13**(5):341-362

[44] Kanellis P, Lycett M, Paul RJ. An interpretive approach to the measurement of information systems success: From concept to practical application. In: Information Systems Success Measurement. Hershey, PA: IGI Global; 1998. pp. 133-151

[45] Alter N. L'innovation Ordinaire. 1st ed. Paris: Presses Universitaires de France; 2000. 278 p. (Sociologies)

[46] Garrity EJ, Sanders GL. Information Systems Success Measurement. Hershey, PA: IGI Global; 1998

[47] Grover V, Jeong SR, Segars AH. Information systems effectiveness: The construct space and patters of application. Information & Management. 1996;**31**(4):177-191

[48] Bailey JE, Pearson SW. Development of a tool for measuring and analyzing computer user satisfaction. Management Science. 1983;**29**(5):530-545

[49] Byrd TA, Thrasher EH, Lang T, Davidson NW. A process-oriented perspective of IS success: Examining the impact of IS on operational cost. Omega. 2006;**34**(5):448-460

[50] Gatian AW. Is user satisfaction a valid measure of system effectiveness? Information & Management. 1994;**26**(3):119-131

[51] Goodhue DL, Thompson RL. Task-technology fit and individual performance. MIS Quarterly. 1995;**19**(2):213-236

[52] Lucas HC Jr. Empirical evidence for a descriptive model of implementation. MIS Quarterly. 1978;**2**(2):27-42

[53] Rainer RK, Watson HJ. The keys to executive information system success. Journal of Management Information Systems. 1995;**12**(2):83-98

[54] Seddon PB. A respecification and extension of the DeLone and McLean model of IS success. Information Systems Research. 1997;**8**(3):240-253

[55] Baker BN, Murphy DC, Fisher D. Factors affecting project success. In: Project Management Handbook. New York, NY: John Wiley & Sons; 1997. pp. 902-919

[56] Cleland DI. Measuring success: The owner's viewpoint. In: Proceedings of the 18th Annual Seminar/Symposium (Montreal/Canada). Montreal, Canada; 1986. pp. 6-12

[57] Morris PW, Hough GH. The Anatomy of Major Projects: A Study of the Reality of Project Management. Chichester, United Kingdom: John Wiley and Sons; 1987. 326 p

[58] Nixon MA, Leftwich BR. Leading the transition from the traditional classroom to a distance learning environment. T.H.E. Journal. 1998;**26**(1):54-57

[59] Sánchez RA, Hueros AD. Motivational factors that influence the acceptance of Moodle using TAM. Computers in Human Behavior. 2010;**26**(6):1632-1640

[60] Ngai EW, Poon JKL, Chan YH. Empirical examination of the adoption of WebCT using TAM. Computers & Education. 2007;**48**(2):250-267

[61] Piotrowski M. What is an E-learning platform? In: Learning Management System Technologies and Software Solutions for Online Teaching: Tools and Applications. Hershey, PA: IGI Global; 2010. pp. 20-36

[62] Castiblanco Jimenez IA, Cepeda García LC, Violante MG, Marcolin F, Vezzetti E. Commonly used external TAM variables in e-learning, agriculture and virtual reality applications. Future Internet. 2020;**13**(1):7

[63] Pal D, Vanijja V. Perceived usability evaluation of Microsoft teams as an online learning platform during COVID-19 using system usability scale and technology acceptance model in India. Children and Youth Services Review. 2020;**119**:105535

[64] Bhatt V, Chakraborty S, Chakravorty T. Impact of information sharing on adoption and user satisfaction among the wearable device users. International Journal of Control and Automation. 2020;**13**(4):277-289

[65] Holyfield S. Developing a shared understanding of the managed learning environment (MLE)–The role of diagramming and requirements gathering. Retrieved March 2003;**15**:2004

[66] Stansfield M, Connolly T. Institutional Transformation through Best Practices in Virtual Campus Development: Advancing E-Learning Policies. Hershey, PA: IGI Global; 2009

[67] Weller M. Virtual Learning Environments: Using, Choosing and Developing your VLE. Oxford, UK: Routledge; 2007

[68] Martín-Blas T, Serrano-Fernández A. The role of new technologies in the learning process: Moodle as a teaching tool in physics. Computers & Education. 2009;**52**(1):35-44

[69] Boggs S, Shore M, Shore J. Using e-learning platforms for mastery learning in developmental mathematics courses. Mathematics and Computer Education. 2004;**38**(2):213

[70] Silva N, Costa GJM, Rogerson S, Prior M. Knowledge or Content? The Philosophical Boundaries in e-Learning Pedagogical Theories: Research, Reflections and Innovations in Integrating ICT in Education. London: Routledge; 2007

[71] Britain S, Liber O. A framework for pedagogical evaluation of virtual learning environments. In: JISC Technology Applications Programme. UK: Education-line; 1999

[72] Valentini CB, do Sacramento Soares EM. Aprendizagem em ambientes virtuais: Compartilhando idéias e construindo cenários. E-book Aprendizagem em Ambientes Virtuais; 2005. 335 p

[73] Dos Santos EO. Ambientes virtuais de aprendizagem: Por autorias livres, plurais e gratuitas. Educaç ao e Contemporaneidade. 2002;**11**(18):424

[74] Collis B, Moonen J. Flexible learning in a digital world. In: JISC e-Learning Models Desk Study. London: Kogan Page; 2001

[75] de Boer WF. Flexibility Support for a Changing University. Amsterdam, Netherlands: Twenty University Press; 2004

[76] Conole G, Oliver M. Contemporary Perspectives in e-Learning Research. London: Routledge; 2006

[77] Eom S. Effects of self-efficacy and self-regulated learning on LMS user satisfaction and LMS effectiveness. In: Proceedings of the 21st Americas Conference on Information Systems (AMCIS 2015). Fajardo, Puerto Rico; 2015

[78] Yi T, Trevino J. Tools for creating learning environments. In: Proceedings of the International Conference on Computer Supported Education. Lisbon, Portugal; 2015. pp. 31-37

[79] Ozkan S, Koseler R. Multi-dimensional students' evaluation of e-learning systems in the higher education context: An empirical investigation. Computers & Education. 2009;**53**(4):1285-1296

[80] Cidral WA, Oliveira T, Di Felice M, Aparicio M. E-learning success determinants: Brazilian empirical study. Computers & Education. 2018;**122**:273-290

[81] Ameen N, Willis R, Abdullah MN, Shah M. Towards the successful integration of e-learning systems in higher education in Iraq: A student perspective. British Journal of Educational Technology. 2019;**50**(3):1434-1446

[82] Luppicini R, Walabe E. Exploring the socio-cultural aspects of e-learning delivery in Saudi Arabia. Journal of Information, Communication and Ethics in Society. 2021;**19**(4):560-579

[83] Roca JC, Gagné M. Understanding e-learning continuance intention in the workplace: A self-determination theory perspective. Computers in Human Behavior. 2008;**24**(4):1585-1604

[84] Al-alak BA, Alnawas IA. Measuring the acceptance and adoption of e-learning by academic staff. Knowledge

Management & E-Learning: An International Journal. 2011;**3**(2):201-221

[85] Imtiaz MA, Maarop N. Feasibility Study of Lecturer's Acceptance of e-Assessment. Kuala Lumpur, Malaysia: University of Malaya; 2014

[86] Wu B, Zhang C. Empirical study on continuance intentions towards e-learning 2.0 systems. Behaviour and Information Technology. 2014;**33**(10):1027-1038

[87] Mohamed Riyath MI, Muhammed Rijah UL, Rameez A. Students' attitudes on the use of zoom in higher educational institutes of Sri Lanka. Asian Association of Open Universities Journal. 2022;**17**(1):37-52

[88] Arbaugh JB. How classroom environment and student engagement affect learning in internet-based MBA courses. Business Communication Quarterly. 2000;**63**(4):9-26

[89] Arbaugh JB. Virtual classroom characteristics and student satisfaction with internet-based MBA courses. Journal of Management Education. 2000;**24**(1):32-54

[90] Lee JK, Hwang CY. The effects of computer self-efficacy and learning management system quality on e-Learner's satisfaction. In: Proceedings of the 2007 European LAMS Conference: Designing the Future of Learning. Greenwich, UK: LAMS Foundation; 2007. pp. 73-79

[91] Sun PC, Tsai RJ, Finger G, Chen YY, Yeh D. What drives a successful e-learning? An empirical investigation of the critical factors influencing learner satisfaction. Computers & Education. 2008;**50**(4):1183-1202

[92] Ouajdouni A, Chafik K, Boubker O. Evaluation of e-learning system during the COVID-19 pandemic in Morocco: A partial least squares modeling approach. International Journal of Information and Education Technology. 2022;**12**(6):492-499

[93] Ouajdouni A, Chafik K, Boubker O. Measuring e-learning systems success: Data from students of higher education institutions in Morocco. Data in Brief. 2021;**35**:106807

[94] Alsabawy AY, Cater-Steel A, Soar J. IT infrastructure services as a requirement for e-learning system success. Computers & Education. 2013;**69**:431-451

[95] Oliver R. Quality assurance and e-learning: Blue skies and pragmatism. ALT-J: Research in Learning Technology. 2005;**13**(3):173-187

[96] Ehlers UD, Pawlowski JM. Handbook on Quality and Standardisation in E-Learning. Berlin: Springer Science & Business Media; 2006. 572 p

[97] Inglis A. Quality improvement, quality assurance, and benchmarking: Comparing two frameworks for managing quality processes in open and distance learning. The International Review of Research in Open and Distance Learning. 2005;**6**(1):1-13

[98] Ortiz-López A, Olmos-Migueláñez S, Sánchez-Prieto JC. Calidad en e-Learning: Identificación de sus dimensiones, propuesta y validación de un modelo para su evaluación en Educación Superior. RIED Revista Iberoamericana de Educación a Distancia. 2021;**24**(2):225-244

[99] Marciniak R, Sallán JG. Un modelo para la autoevaluación de la calidad de programas de educación universitaria virtual. Revista de Educación a Distancia (RED). 2017;**54**:1-30

[100] Cabero AJ. La calidad educativa en el e. Learning: Sus bases pedagógicas. Educación Médica. 2006;**9**:7-12

[101] Frydenberg J. Quality standards in e-learning: A matrix of analysis. The International Review of Research in Open and Distance Learning. 2002;**3**(2):1-15

[102] Gaytan J. Analyzing online education through the lens of institutional theory and practice: The need for research-based and-validated frameworks for planning, designing, delivering, and assessing online instruction. Delta Pi Epsilon Journal. 2009;**51**(2):62-75

[103] Johnstone SM, Krauth B. Balancing quality and access: Some principles of good practice for the virtual university. Change: The Magazine of Higher Learning. 1996;**28**(2):38-41

[104] Newton J. Feeding the beast or improving quality?: Academics' perceptions of quality assurance and quality monitoring. Quality in Higher Education. 2000;**6**(2):153-163

[105] Phipps R, Merisotis J. What's the Difference?: A Review of Contemporary Research on the Effectiveness of Distance Learning in Higher Education. Washington, DC: The Institute for Higher Education Policy; 1999. 49 p

[106] Shelton K. A review of paradigms for evaluating the quality of online education programs. Online Journal of Distance Learning Administration. 2011;**4**(1):1-11

[107] Watty K. When will academics learn about quality? Quality in Higher Education. 2003;**9**(3):213-221

[108] Oliver R. Exploring benchmarks and standards for assuring quality online teaching and learning in higher education. In: Proceedings of Open and Distance Learning Association of Australia Biennial Forum. Canberra, Australia; 2003. pp. 79-90

[109] Fresen JW, Boyd LG. Caught in the web of quality. International Journal of Educational Development. 2005;**25**(3):317-331

[110] Masoumi D, Lindström B. Quality in e-learning: A framework for promoting and assuring quality in virtual institutions. Journal of Computer Assisted Learning. 2012;**28**(1):27-41

[111] Ehlers UD. Understanding quality culture. Quality Assurance in Education. 2009;**17**(4):343-363

[112] Auvinen L, Peltonen B. Measuring quality in collaborative e-learning. In: EUROCALL 2004 Conference: TELL and CALL in the Third Millennium: Pedagogical Approaches in a Growing EU-Community Conference. Vienna, Austria; 2004

[113] Zhao F. Enhancing the quality of online higher education through measurement. Quality Assurance in Education. 2003;**11**(4):214-221

[114] Freeze RD, Alshare KA, Lane PL, Wen HJ. IS success model in e-learning context based on students' perceptions. Journal of Information Systems Education. 2010;**21**(2):173-184

[115] Guimaraes T, Armstrong CP, Jones BM. A new approach to measuring information systems quality. Quality Management Journal. 2009;**16**(1):42-51

[116] Halawi LA, McCarthy RV, Aronson JE. An empirical investigation of knowledge management systems' success. Journal of Computer Information Systems. 2008;**48**(2):121-135

[117] DeLone WH, McLean ER. Information system success revisited. In: Proceedings of the 35th Hawaii International Conference on System Sciences, Big Island, HI, USA; 2002. pp. 2966-2976

[118] Urbach N, Müller B. The updated DeLone and McLean model of information systems success. In: Dwivedi YK, Wade MR, Schneberger SL, editors. Information Systems Theory: Explaining and Predicting our Digital Society. Vol. 1. New York, NY: Springer; 2012. pp. 1-18. DOI: 10.1007/978-1-4419-6108-2_1

[119] Agrifoglio R, Lepore L, Metallo C. Measuring the success of E-justice. A validation of the DeLone and McLean model. In: Spagnoletti P, editor. Organizational Change and Information Systems. Vol. 2. Berlin, Heidelberg: Springer Berlin Heidelberg; 2013. pp. 83-91. DOI: 10.1007/978-3-642-37228-5_9

[120] Delone WH, Mclean ER. Measuring e-commerce success: Applying the DeLone & McLean information systems success model. International Journal of Electronic Commerce. 2004;**9**(1):31-47

[121] Lin HY, Hsu PY, Ting PH. ERP systems success: An integration of IS success model and balanced scorecard. Journal of Research and Practice in Information Technology. 2006;**38**(3):215

[122] Schaupp LC, Bélanger F, Fan W. Examining the success of websites beyond E-commerce: An extension of the IS success model. Journal of Computer Information Systems. 2009;**49**(4):42-52

[123] Wang WT, Wang CC. An empirical study of instructor adoption of web-based learning systems. Computers & Education. 2009;**53**(3):761-774

[124] Wang YS. Assessing e-commerce systems success: A respecification and validation of the DeLone and McLean model of IS success. Information Systems Journal. 2008;**18**(5):529-557

[125] Wang YS, Wang HY, Shee DY. Measuring e-learning systems success in an organizational context: Scale development and validation. Computers in Human Behavior. 2007;**23**(4):1792-1808

[126] Wang YS, Liao YW. Assessing eGovernment systems success: A validation of the DeLone and McLean model of information systems success. Government Information Quarterly. 2008;**25**(4):717-733

[127] Van der Heijden H. User acceptance of hedonic information systems. MIS Quarterly. 2004;**28**(4):695-704

[128] Hair JF, Black WC, Babin BJ, Anderson RE, Tatham R. Multivariate Data Analysis. 7th ed. Harlow: Pearson Education Limited; 2010

Chapter 7

Influence of Prompts Structure on the Perception and Enhancement of Learning through LLMs in Online Educational Contexts

Silvia Rodriguez-Donaire

Abstract

This research examines how the structure of prompts impacts the perceived depth and accuracy of responses generated by generative Large Language Models (LLMs) in educational settings. It specifically investigates how prompt design influences students' learning experiences. The study involved an experiment with 183 students enrolled in a mandatory Business Administration course at the Universitat Oberta de Catalunya (UOC). Data from the experiment were analyzed using both qualitative and quantitative methods. The results show that well-structured prompts significantly improve students' perception of the depth and accuracy of GenAI-generated responses, leading to a more effective learning process. This underscores the crucial role of prompt design in maximizing the educational effectiveness of GenAI. The findings suggest that thoughtful prompt design can enhance educational outcomes, although the study's limited sample size and context-specific nature may restrict the generalizability of the results. This research contributes to the field by highlighting the importance of prompt structure in harnessing GenAI tools for educational improvement.

Keywords: generative AI, GenAI, engineering prompts, large language model, LLMs, formative assessment, online higher education, prompt structure, educational environment, students' perception, learning process

1. Introduction

Artificial intelligence (AI) tools such as OpenAI's ChatGPT, Google's Gemini, and Microsoft's CoPilot are changing how we perform everyday tasks, from writing emails to creating multimedia content. However, the use of AI in education presents new challenges and opportunities, necessitating a re-evaluation of the current educational model. This study aims two-fold: (1) pinpoint the elements of prompt structure that affect the quality of GenAI-generated responses, and (2) examine how prompt structure relates to the perceived effectiveness of GenAI responses in improving the learning experience in educational environments. It is worth mentioning that the structure of prompts is crucial in determining the quality of AI-generated responses as it directly impacts the model's ability to understand and respond appropriately. For instance, [1] study demonstrated that modifying the queries can enhance the performance of language models by 11.46%, indicating that prompt structure significantly affects response accuracy. In addition, [2] emphasized the effectiveness of ChatGPT in structured tasks, but also pointed out its limitations in more nuanced applications, underscoring the importance of prompt structure in optimizing AI performance.

On the one hand, specific elements of the prompt structure influence the quality of generated responses. Bozkurt [3] underlines the significance of prompt engineering as a form of digital literacy, vital for utilizing AI in education. Liu [4] research has identified crucial components in the generated responses, such as definitions and examples, which are essential for the accuracy and reliability of the information.

On the other hand, prompt engineering can greatly enhance the quality of educational applications [5]. For example, techniques like Chain-of-Thought and Ask-me-Anything have improved the quality of answers in mathematical problem-solving [6]. However, despite these advancements, challenges still exist in effectively implementing and validating AI tools in educational settings. This includes the need for AI literacy and the development of prompt engineering skills [7, 8].

Significant progress has been made in understanding how the structure of a prompt influences the accuracy and quality of AI-generated responses in the educational context. However, there are still research gaps that need to be addressed. While current studies have covered general aspects of prompt engineering, further investigation is necessary to explore the specific elements of prompt structure that affect different types of AI-generated responses in various educational contexts [1, 2]. Additionally, more research is needed to understand how these prompt engineering techniques can be effectively integrated into educational settings to improve the perception and effectiveness of AI in the learning process [5, 6]. Additionally, it is essential to explore the ethical implications and challenges associated with AI implementation in education, particularly in terms of ensuring accuracy and addressing bias [3, 7].

Alternative approaches exist, such as integrating frameworks like the CLEAR Framework (Concise, Logical, Explicit, Adaptive, and Reflective) to optimize interactions with AI language models [9]. Other approaches include implementing active methodologies and providing digital literacy training for educators and students, which could offer additional solutions to improve the effectiveness of AI in education [10, 11].

This study investigates how prompt design can enhance the accuracy and depth of GenAI-generated responses in online educational settings and its impact on students' learning processes. As a result, the research aims to answer the following questions:

1. How does the structure of prompts affect the perceived accuracy of GenAI responses in an educational setting?

2. What specific elements of prompt structure influence the quality of GenAI responses?

3. What is the relationship between the prompt's structure and the AI's perceived effectiveness in enhancing the learning process?

This research will be conducted through an empirical study and data analysis on the prompts created by students and their perceptions of the responses received from GenAI. To achieve this, a methodological approach will be used, including coding the prompts and analyzing student perception through statistical analysis of the resulting database.

The chapter is structured as follows. First, a literature review on using GenAI in higher education is conducted. Next, the methodology used to carry out the empirical study is explained. Then, the activity that takes place within the online course is described. Finally, the main results found in the experiment are presented and discussed, and the study concludes by identifying the limitations and future research areas.

2. Literature review

The history of artificial intelligence can be traced back to 1854 when George Boole developed it. However, the term "artificial intelligence" was first coined by John McCarthy in 1956 during the Dartmouth Conference, which laid the foundation for its development. Machine learning algorithms were advanced during the 1980s and 1990s, allowing AI to learn and improve autonomously. In 1997, IBM's DeepBlue computer defeated world chess champion Garri Kaspàrov, and iRobot launched Roomba, the first autonomous robot vacuum cleaner, which became a commercial success. The 2010s saw the development of deep neural networks, which enabled AI to perform complex tasks such as image recognition and natural language processing. As a result, virtual assistants such as Apple's Siri, Microsoft's Cortana, and Amazon's Alexa were launched, and generative AI capable of creating content such as text, images, and music emerged. This opened up new creative possibilities, leading to the launch of ChatGPT and other applications that consolidated content creation globally by 2022.

A significant amount of research [12–18] highlights the potential of GenAI to enhance learning and teaching in various knowledge disciplines. However, despite the many perceived benefits of AI, its use in higher education requires an exploration of potential ethical challenges and reservations related to academic integrity. In recent years, the higher education sector has faced different challenges, primarily due to the COVID-19 pandemic. The most significant challenge for most universities has been adapting in-person teaching to remote teaching. This situation has led to a reconsideration of how academic programs are delivered and the introduction of more flexible approaches to learning and teaching within universities.

Integrating generative AI[1] in higher education is a challenge that questions universities' traditional role in knowledge production and dissemination. According to [20], universities worldwide have varied responses to this technological advancement. Some institutions prohibit using generative AI tools due to concerns about academic

[1] Generative AI—"*computational systems trained on large data sets to generate human-like responses or outputs*" [19].

integrity and the potential hindrance of independent thinking and creativity among students and faculty. On the other hand, these tools can support the generation of ideas and enrich discussions in the context of teaching and learning.

According to [21], AI has several applications in various sectors, and some of these can also be replicated in the education sector. For instance, chatbots can provide 24/7 assistance to students, optimization algorithms can offer personalized learning that adapts to each student's needs, and automating administrative tasks can allow teachers to focus more on teaching.

Although AI has many potential advantages, such as personalization of content, accessibility of information, and promoting more interactive education with immersive and compelling environments, it also poses risks. These include data protection and bias of AI algorithms [22], dehumanization of education, an increase in the digital divide between students with different access to advanced technologies, and excessive reliance on technologies that limit the development of cognitive and problem-solving skills [23]. AI is another technological revolution, like the appearance of the Internet. That is why we must live with it, learn from it, and transform our educational models by training students to use AI ethically and responsibly.

Interacting with LLMs, such as ChatGPT, Gemini, Copilot, etc., might seem easy initially, but it requires a certain level of digital skills and knowledge to use them effectively. Teaching students how to create clear and concise instructions for LLMs is crucial, as it is usually a trial-and-error process [24]. This is because the quality of the instructions directly affects the results' quality. According to [25], a well-crafted prompt can lead to a precise, accurate, and relevant response from the LLMs, thereby maximizing its performance. Conversely, a poorly structured question can result in an ambiguous, incorrect, or irrelevant answer.

To make the most of the capabilities of LLMs, it is essential to master the art and science of formulating effective prompts, known as "prompt engineering". This requires a combination of domain-specific knowledge, model understanding, and skills that can only be honed through experience and learning. By equipping students with these skills, they can use AI safely, ethically, and effectively, receive more accurate answers, understand the limitations of LLMs, and develop new knowledge and skills to adapt to an ever-changing environment.

3. Methodology

This research is part of a qualitative study that explores the relationship between the effective use of prompts in generative AI and the quality and accuracy of the response obtained in a specific activity. The study also aims to determine if this approach positively impacts the participants' learning process. More specifically, the research focuses on a debate activity that is part of a mandatory subject called "Information Systems" (IS) taught in Catalan and Spanish. The subject is offered as part of the curriculum for the Business Administration and Management (ADE) degree at the Universitat Oberta de Catalunya (UOC). This entirely online university follows an asynchronous educational model.

The study was conducted on 304 students enrolled in four Spanish and two Catalan classrooms. The Spanish classrooms had a maximum capacity of 55 students, while the Catalan classrooms had 43 students. Out of these 304 students, only 194

DOI: http://dx.doi.org/10.5772/intechopen.1006481

participated in the debate activity, where they were required to give feedback to one of their classmates with the help of an LLM. Further analysis revealed that only 182 students had included the prompt used in their debate response and had reflected on the response given to them by the LLMs. These twelve values were discarded in the study. To ensure the confidentiality of the participants, all student data has been anonymized.

In each classroom, the students' responses from a discussion exercise were manually coded into binary variables with the assistance of the generative AI ChatGPT 4.0. One instruction was generated to evaluate the effectiveness of prompts created by students within a debate activity, and a second instruction was used to evaluate the students' perception of the responses generated by the LLMs. Both instructions can be found in an open repository [26].

Before proceeding to the quantitative analysis, the coding carried out by Generative AI is reviewed. It is worth noting that in some cases, the coding is not completely correct, and the study authors make manual modifications. Once the data was reviewed, a combination of quantitative and qualitative analysis was applied to confirm the experimental model.

Table 1 shows the descriptive analysis of the final sample of the present article: The distribution of the categorical variables is shown in **Figure 1a–c**.

Variable	Mean	Median	SD	SE	Kurtosis	Skewness
ROLE	0.4250000	0	0.4964157	0.0453163	1.092072	0.3034330
OBJETIVES	1.0000000	1	0.0000000	0.0000000	NaN	NaN
CONTEXT	1.0000000	1	0.0000000	0.0000000	NaN	NaN
SPECIFIC	1.0000000	1	0.0000000	0.0000000	NaN	NaN
VERACITY	1.0000000	1	0.0000000	0.0000000	NaN	NaN
DEPTH	0.3000000	0	0.4601790	0.0420084	1.761905	0.8728716
LEARNING	0.7416667	1	0.4395535	0.0401256	2.219282	−1.1042112
AI_Mark	7.9333333	9	3.2866763	0.3000311	1.895030	−0.4784266
EFFECTIVENESS	3.4250000	3	0.4964157	0.0453163	1.092072	0.3034330

Table 1.
Descriptive analysis of the study sample.

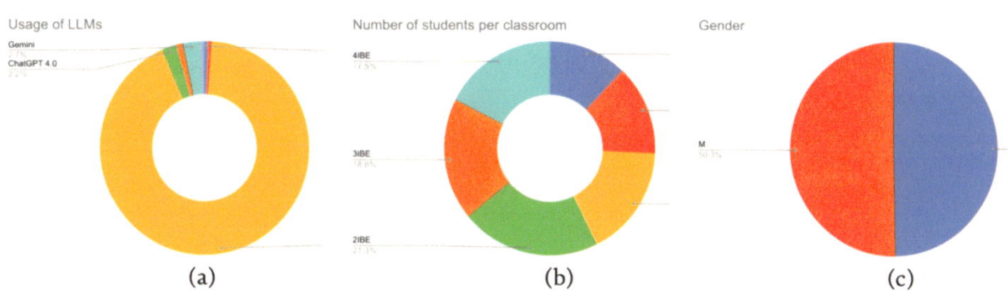

Figure 1.
(a) Typology of LLMs used, (b) number of students per classroom and (c) sample by gender.

4. Experiment design

This project aims to explore using an LLM such as ChatGPT, Gemini, or Copilot as a support tool for students in the virtual classroom. The project proposes that students provide feedback on an initial intervention from one of their peers through the debate area. The UOC's virtual platform, Canvas, assigns this intervention randomly.

As **Figure 2** shows, the activity requires students to write a prompt in a generative AI that identifies the strengths and areas for improvement in the assigned answer, along with recommendations to improve the weaknesses. As part of the exercise, students are expected to verify the accuracy and depth of the AI-generated information vand

Universitat Oberta de Catalunya

Your intermediate intervention in response to the initial intervention of the assigned partner should include the following:

1. The Generative AI used in the exercise.
2. The prompt used (questions you ask within generative AI). Within your prompt, you should include the initial intervention that has been evaluated. To keep your response brief, you can replace this information with the phrase "[Initial intervention of the student's name and last name]
3. The answer that generative AI provides you.
4. Reason truthfulness and depth of the response proposed by the AI.
5. Make a final evaluation of the AI's response according to the following criteria:
   - **Reliability**: the information provided was accurate and free of inconsistencies or errors.
   - **Quality**: the information provided was of high quality.
   - **Completeness**: the information provided was complete.
   - **Originality**: the information provided was original and not copied from other sources.
   - **Creativity**: the information provided showed creativity.
   - **Multiple perspectives**: the information provided contained different points of view that added value.
   - **Coherence**: the information provided was consistent and logical.
   - **Conceptual relevance**: the information provided was related to the concepts discussed.
   - **Suitable examples**: the information provided included appropriate examples.
   - **Improvement**: the AI helped you improve your reflection on critical points.

Figure 2.
Statement of the debate activity—Feedback on an Intervention.

	EXCELLENT (10)	GREAT (9)	GOOD (7)	PASS (5)	FAIL (3)	DEFICIENT (0)
Argumentative intervention Reasoning and reflection of the AI response (20 Points out of 50 points)	Reason and thoroughly reflect on the response provided by the AI in relation to the interventions of classmates, with relevant, well-developed, justified contributions based on concepts studied in modules and/or valuable examples.	Reason and reflect adequately on the responses of the AI provided in relation to the interventions of your peers, making relevant, developed, justified, and concept-based contributions studied in the modules and/or valuable examples.	Reason and minimally reflect on the responses provided by the AI in relation to the interventions of your peers, with sufficient but undeveloped contributions and without examples or with little impact on the concepts of the modules.	Insufficiently reasons and reflects on the responses provided by the AI in relation to the interventions of their peers, with insufficiently argued and/or developed contributions.	Carry out superficial interventions, without exposing the response proposed by the AI, or reasoning or reflecting on the AI's response in relation to the interventions of your peers, and without providing any argumentation.	Does not make argumentative interventions.
Correct use of AI within the argumentative intervention (5 out of 50 points)	Correctly identify the generative AI used, the prompt used in the generative AI, as well as the response proposed by it.		Identify the generative AI used, part of the 'prompt' used in the generative AI, as well as part of the response proposed by it.		The generative AI used, the prompt, and the response proposed by the AI are not identified.	

Figure 3.
Criteria that teachers evaluate on the part of the activity that involves the use of AI.

complement it with their own analysis and perspective. Finally, at the end of the activity, students are asked to evaluate the answer provided by the AI based on various qualitative variables such as reliability, quality, completeness, originality, creativity, and coherence.

After the debate activity was closed, the students' responses were evaluated using a rubric (see **Figure 3**).

Figure 3 presents the two criteria used to evaluate the activity. The first criterion assesses the proper use of AI in the exercise and carries a weight of 5 points out of 50 points. The second criterion evaluates the reasoning and reflection shown in the response provided by AI. It aims to assess the student's development of critical and analytical thinking skills concerning the application of AI and carries a weight of 20 points out of the total 50 points.

The students' prompt design is also evaluated as part of the experiment. This evaluation aims to determine if the prompts are efficient and whether an efficient design impacts the perceived depth and veracity of the answer provided by the AI. It also seeks to understand whether an efficient prompt design has any relationship with students' perception of the usefulness of AI in the learning process.

Therefore, it is crucial that the prompt follows a clear and concrete structure and includes the parts shown in **Figure 4**.

- Indicate the role or character the LLM must adopt in its response (e.g. acts as…);
- Specify the objective/purpose of the expected response;
- Add relevant information about the context and give examples to specify the answers;
- Be explicit in the instructions: the tone and style of the response, the target to whom it is directed, and expectations, among others.

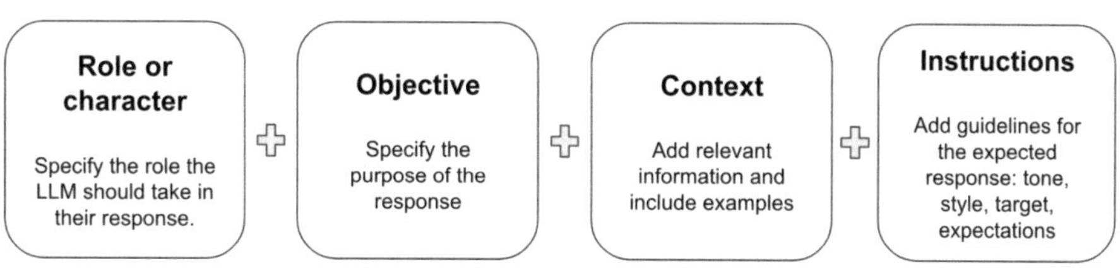

Figure 4.
Parts that an efficient prompt must contain.

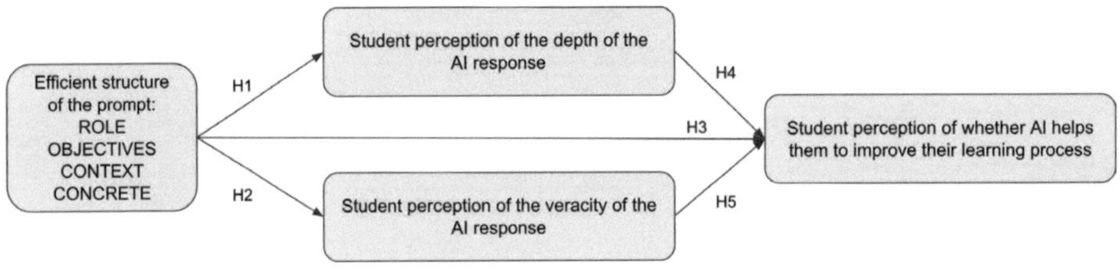

Figure 5.
Experiment model.

A proposed model (**Figure 5**) examines the correlation between the structure of a prompt, the student's perception of depth, the truthfulness of their answers to the LLMs (Learning Module Materials), and their learning progress.

The model's hypotheses (**Figure 5**) aim to help us confirm three things: (1) the relationship between the structure of prompt and student's perception of the answers obtained by the LLMs in terms of depth (H1) and veracity (H2); (2) the relationship between the structure of prompts (H3), students' perception of depth (H4) and veracity (H5) of answers obtained by the LLMs, and the improvement of the student's learning process. The hypotheses are detailed below:

- H1—An effective prompt structure contributes positively to the depth perception of the response obtained by the LLMs used.
- H2—An effective prompt structure contributes positively to the truthfulness perception of the response obtained by the LLMs used.
- H3—An effective prompt structure contributes positively to learning enhancement.
- H4—A student's perception of depth contributes positively to learning improvement.
- H5—A student's perception of truthfulness contributes positively to learning improvement.

5. Results and discussion

The current analysis evaluates how various prompting styles impact the perception of depth, truthfulness, and learning improvement in LLM responses and how these factors differ among different groups of students. The statistical findings of the comparison between GLM and Random Forest models (**Table 2**) and ANOVA (**Table 3**) and the discussion of the results reinforced by qualitative data obtained in the classrooms are presented below.

A comparison of GLM and Random Forest models (**Table 2**) reveals similar accuracy at 77.78% and AUC of 0.82, indicating overall solid performance. However, differences exist in sensitivity and specificity:

- *GLM*: Higher specificity (86.67%), lower sensitivity (33.33%).

Modelo	Accuracy	Sensitivity	Specificity	AUC
GLM	0.7777778	0.3333333	0.8666667	0.8222222
Random Forest	0.7777778	1.0000000	0.7333333	0.8222222

Table 2.
Results of the GLM and Random Forest Models.

Variable	Df	Sum Sq	Mean Sq	F value	Pr(>F)
Gender	1	0.0992029	0.0992029	0.8340435	0.3643806
Classroom	5	7.2374421	1.4474884	12.1696883	0.0000000
AI_Type	5	0.6257711	0.1251542	1.0522281	0.3947219
AI_Mark	9	1.5396431	0.1710715	1.4382749	0.1898325
ROLE	1	0.0744499	0.0744499	0.6259338	0.4316426
DEPTH	1	0.5695996	0.5695996	4.7888811	0.0321349
Gender:Classroom	5	0.7050956	0.1410191	1.1856114	0.3256066
Classroom:AI_Type	1	0.1380074	0.1380074	1.1602907	0.2852685
Residuals	67	7.9691215	0.1189421	NA	NA

Table 3.
ANOVA results.

- *Random Forest*: Higher sensitivity (100%), lower specificity (73.33%).

Both models have strengths depending on the problem context. GLM is better at avoiding false positives, while Random Forest is more effective at identifying all positive cases.

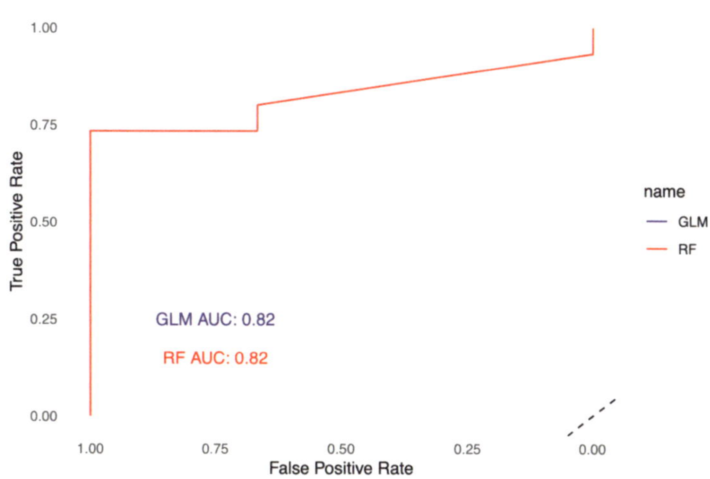

Figure 6.
ROC curves for GLM and Random Forest Models.

Figure 6 shows that both models have the same AUC of 0.82, so they have similar performance in terms of their ability to discriminate between classes.

Additionally, a factor analysis is performed using an ANOVA to understand which factors and combinations of factors significantly affect the dependent variable (LEARNING) and which ones do not have a relevant effect in the study context.

Table 3 shows that Classroom and DEPTH are the only variables that have a significant effect on the dependent variable, with Classroom being highly significant ($p < 0.001$) and DEPTH also significant ($p < 0.05$). This indicates that differences between classrooms and depth have a significant impact on the dependent variable. The rest of the variables and their interactions show no significant effects, suggesting that they do not contribute significantly to the variability observed in the dependent variable. Based on the results of these ANOVA analyses, some hypotheses of the model are supported.

H1: The prompt's effective structure contributes positively to students' depth perception in LLM responses.

Hypothesis H1 has been confirmed. The ANOVA analysis indicates that the variable DEPTH significantly affects LEARNING ($p < 0.05$). This suggests that depth perception influences learning improvement, as seen in **Figure 7**. Qualitative observations from different classrooms further support this finding. Comments such as "*the response is solid, but could be improved with more specific details and concrete examples*" or "*the AI helps better to understand certain aspects, situations, or cases, and can be a good support to expand the basic information*" and "*the AI provides new perspectives that strengthen our initial argument, but we should not use it as the sole source*" reinforce this hypothesis.

Specifically, **Figure 7** shows significant differences in LEARNING variability between the two DEPTH levels. Although the medians are similar, the higher variability at the low DEPTH level could influence LEARNING differently than the high DEPTH level. This information is consistent with the ANOVA results that indicated that DEPTH has a significant effect on LEARNING.

Additionally, **Figure 8** illustrates the significant impact of Classroom variables on learning ($p < 0.001$), indicating variations in learning outcomes across classrooms.

H2: The prompt's effective structure contributes positively to the student's perception of truthfulness in LLM responses.

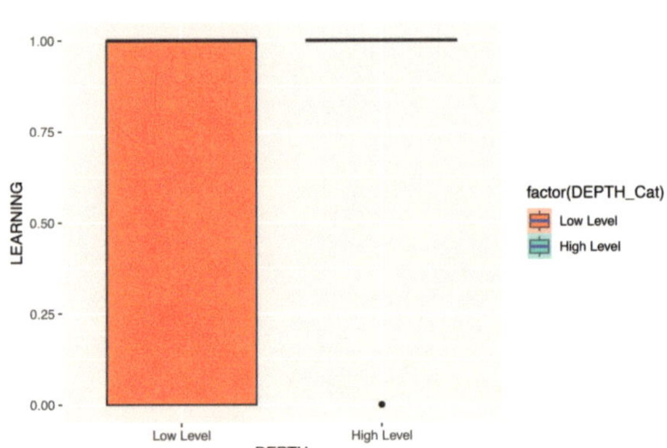

Figure 7.
Boxplot of LEARNING by DEPTH.

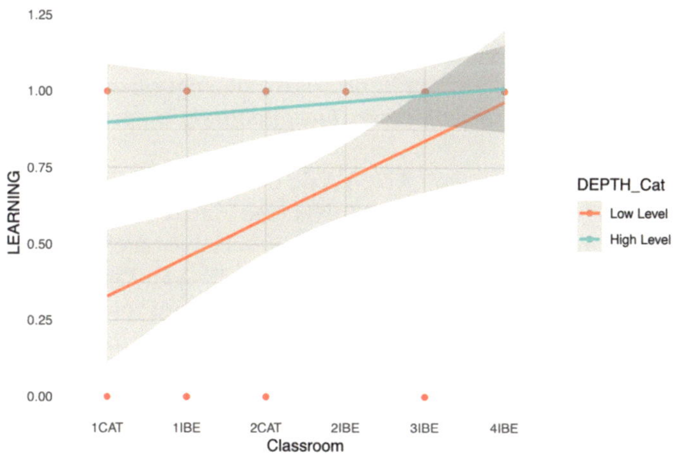

Figure 8.
Interaction between LEARNING and DEPTH depending on Classroom.

The ANOVA results do not allow us to confirm hypothesis H2 due to the elimination of the VERACITY variable from the model because of collinearity. Additionally, the evaluation variable (AI_Mark), which could be indirectly related to perceived truthfulness, does not show a significant impact on the ANOVA results. Qualitative classroom observations note that "*the veracity of the results may also be affected by the quality of the input data and the presence of inherent biases in the data*", suggesting that effective prompt structure and perceived veracity are linked. Qualitative student observations confirm hypothesis H2, indicating that effective prompt structure significantly influences the perceived veracity of responses generated by an LLM. Expressly, in one of the reflections, it is stated, "*By using precise language and providing detailed prompts, it increases the chances of receiving accurate responses that match our needs*". The prompt's precision, specificity, and clarity are determining factors for students to perceive the answers as truthful. Precisely, in another of the reflections, it is mentioned that "*depending on the information you give to the AI and the questions you ask, it will guide us to some answers or others. Therefore, when formulating the questions, you must be very*

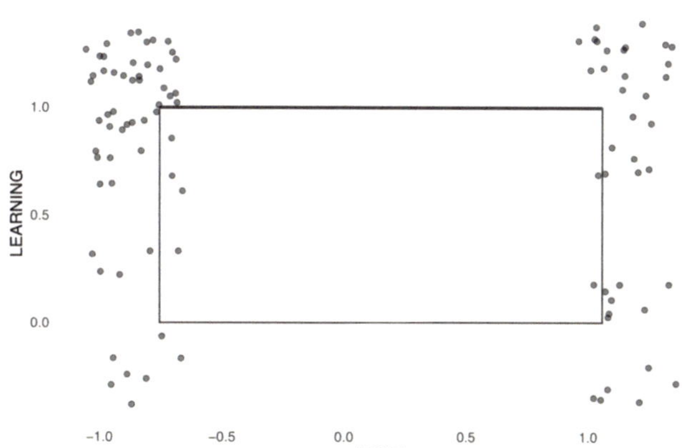

Figure 9.
Distribution of LEARNING by ROLE.

thorough in providing us with the answers we need and following the conversation thread", highlighting that the prompt's quality and specificity affect the response's quality. This implies that a well-structured prompt improves the perception of truthfulness.

H3: The prompt's effective structure contributes positively to students' learning improvement.

The analyses conducted through ANOVA do not support hypothesis H3, as the ROLE does not significantly affect LEARNING (see **Figure 9**). However, it is essential to note that interactions between ROLE and other variables such as Gender, AI_Type, and Classroom could be significant (refer to **Figures 10–12**). **Figure 10** illustrates the variation in LEARNING across different classrooms and roles, indicating that the effectiveness of the prompt can differ significantly depending on the specific classroom and role. **Figure 11** demonstrates the distribution of the ROLE variable across various AI types (AI_Type). Prompt effectiveness generally varies based on the type of AI and the assigned ROLE. **Figure 12** depicts how prompt effectiveness varies

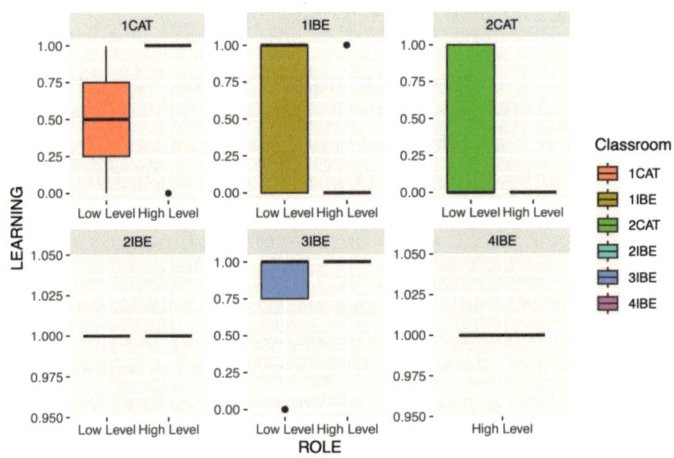

Figure 10.
Distribution of LEARNING by ROLE and Classroom.

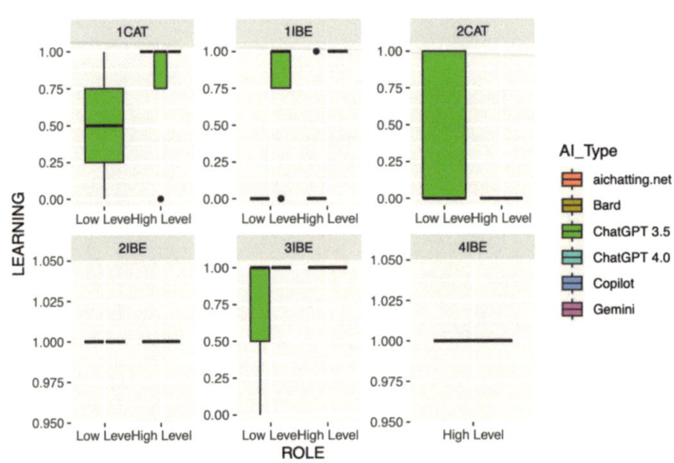

Figure 11.
Distribution of LEARNING by ROLE and AI_Type.

DOI: http://dx.doi.org/10.5772/intechopen.1006481

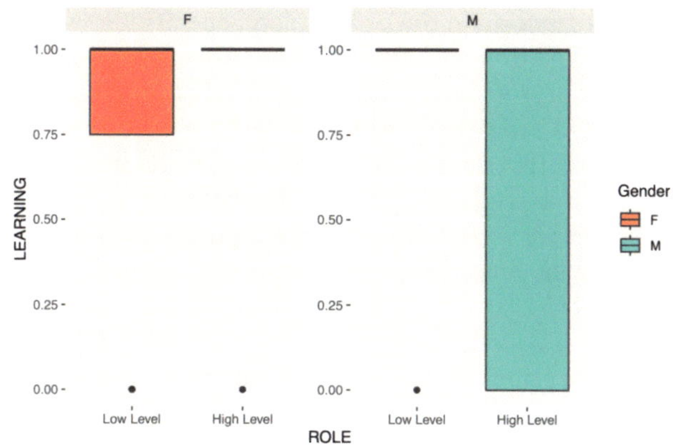

Figure 12.
Distribution of LEARNING by ROLE and Gender.

by gender and assigned ROLE, highlighting notable differences in prompt effectiveness between genders. Classroom reflections reinforce these findings, suggesting that the specificity and clarity of the role in the prompt may influence its perceived effectiveness. One classroom reflection mentioned, "*AI is a very successful tool to help in summaries and generate texts based on very well-worked ideas or prompts, but it lacks reasoning skills*". This indicates that the role's specificity and clarity in the prompt may influence the perception of its effectiveness.

The variables OBJECTIVES, CONTEXT, and SPECIFIC have been removed due to lack of variability and collinearity. However, classroom reflections suggest that a clear objective in the prompt is essential. It was mentioned that providing more information to the AI can make the answer more concrete. Additionally, it was suggested that including more specific details and concrete examples can improve the response. Another reflection emphasized the importance of context provided in the prompt, stating that the quality of the AI response depends on the context provided by the user. Although the ANOVA results did not show variability in these variables, hypothesis H3 can be confirmed as there is an importance of including a clear objective,

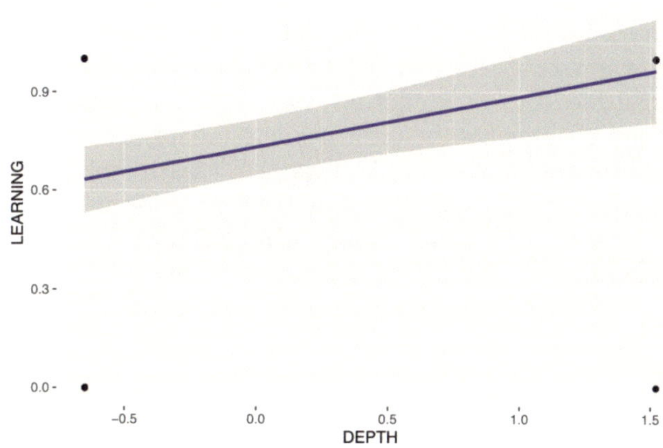

Figure 13.
LEARNING vs. DEPTH scatter plot.

contextualizing the information in the prompt, and specifying what is desired as a result of the question asked to the LLMs.

H4: Student's perception of depth contributes positively to learning improvement.

The hypothesis H4 has been confirmed. The depth of AI responses significantly affects learning, implying that depth perception is essential in improving learning (see **Figure 13**). Qualitative student observations further support hypothesis H4, indicating that depth perception in AI responses significantly influences learning enhancement. For instance, one student's reflection indicates that "*AI contributes to reflecting on critical points by correctly identifying areas for improvement*", suggesting that the adequate depth and structure of the prompt are crucial for learning. Another noteworthy reflection mentions that "*AI helps me to structure the points to comment, to identify key points and concepts, but it does not give me the whole answer. The improvement is due to the ease of use, the structuring of texts, and the summary of concepts, which helps me improve in general*". While AI helps structure and summarize, real learning improvement stems from deeper reflection, partially facilitated by AI, aiding students in enhancing their understanding and learning.

H5: Student's perception of truthfulness contributes positively to learning improvement.

The ANOVA results do not allow us to confirm hypothesis H5 because the variable VERACITY was eliminated from the model due to collinearity. However, the qualitative evidence collected in the classrooms supports this hypothesis, indicating that students' perception of veracity significantly influences their trust in AI responses and their use of AI to enhance their learning process. The evidence suggests that "*Chat GPT 4.0 is a reliable and valuable resource for comparing proposals and facilitating continuous learning in academic settings if used correctly. The quality and reliability of AI responses are crucial for facilitating continuous learning*". Students also mentioned that while AI is useful for obtaining information, it should not be the sole source and should be validated with additional information before making decisions. This statement highlights the importance of perceived veracity in AI responses for effective learning. With these arguments, we can partially confirm hypothesis H5.

The ANOVA model confirmed hypotheses H1 and H4, emphasizing the significance of prompt structure for depth perception and its influence on learning enhancement. However, due to the lack of data on VERACITY and other key variables (OBJECTIVE, CONTEXT, SPECIFIC, and EFFECTIVENESS), we could not fully evaluate hypotheses H2, H3, and H5. Nonetheless, the considerable variability between classrooms suggests the necessity to tailor prompts to specific contexts to maximize their effectiveness. While the ANOVA results did not support hypothesis H3, subgroup analysis revealed trends that were not apparent in the overall analysis. Specifically, interactions between ROLE and other variables such as Gender, AI_Type, and Classroom showed marked differences in prompt effectiveness between genders and how the ROLE variable is distributed across different types of AI (AI_Type) and classrooms. This analysis underscores the complexity of the factors influencing the perception and effectiveness of the responses generated by an LLM, emphasizing the importance of considering multiple variables and interactions to enhance educational outcomes.

6. Conclusions

The study examined how the structure of prompts used in LLM models affects the perception of depth, accuracy, and effectiveness of the student's learning process. The results, obtained through both quantitative and qualitative analyses, confirm several crucial hypotheses regarding the relationship between prompt structure and the perception and effectiveness of AI responses in the learning process.

The main findings of the study indicate that:

1. A well-designed prompt structure contributes positively to the perception of depth and accuracy in LLM responses. This highlights the importance of carefully formulating questions to maximize the usefulness of LLM answers.

2. The positive perception of the depth and accuracy of AI responses significantly improves the student's learning process. This emphasizes the value of comprehensive and truthful responses, not only for user satisfaction but also for long-term educational benefits.

3. The effective structure of the prompt and students' perceptions of accuracy and depth are interrelated, with each enhancing the influence of the other on the perception of the effectiveness of LLM responses.

The results of this study demonstrate the intricate relationship between prompt structure, response perception, and the learning process. By better understanding these dynamics, we can develop strategies to improve prompt design in educational contexts. This will allow us to obtain better responses generated by LLM, ensuring that both prompt effectiveness and students' positive perception of learning are maximized.

However, it is essential to note that the partial significance of the statistical results found in the study has several limitations. Firstly, there was a lack of variability in responses regarding the efficient structure of the prompt and truthfulness of the LLM response, which limited the quantitative analysis and made the results dependent on qualitative data and subjective perceptions. Secondly, the specific use of LLMs for a particular activity means that the results cannot be generalized to all LLM application scenarios or educational disciplines. Finally, although the model was good, a larger sample size could help produce more reliable results.

Below is a set of proposed research ideas that aim to address the limitations observed in the study:

- Expand the database by including a larger and more diverse sample of responses to encompass a broader range of variability in perceived truthfulness and other evaluated metrics.

- Observe whether the type of generative AI used to carry out the activity impacts the confirmation of the hypotheses.

- Conduct experimental studies where the characteristics of the prompts are systematically manipulated to directly evaluate their impact on the quality and perception of AI responses.

- Extend the research to include different educational disciplines and types of questions to explore the applicability and effectiveness of LLMs in various educational contexts.

- Develop analytical tools that enable teachers and developers to evaluate and optimize the structure of prompts in real time.

Acknowledgements

We extend our sincere thanks to all the students who generously volunteered their time and efforts to participate in this study.

Author details

Silvia Rodriguez-Donaire[1,2]

1 Business and Economics Department, Open University of Catalonia (UOC—Universitat Oberta de Catalunya), Barcelona, Spain

2 UPC-BarcelonaTECH, Universitat Politecnica de Catalunya, ESEIAAT, Terrassa, Spain

*Address all correspondence to: srodriguezdon@uoc.edu; silvia.rodriguez-donaire@upc.edu

References

[1] Park D, An G t, Kamyod C, Kim CG. A study on performance improvement of prompt engineering for generative AI with a large language model. Journal of Web Engineering. 2024;**22**(8):1187-1206. DOI: 10.13052/jwe1540-9589.2285

[2] Megahed FM, Chen YJ, Ferris JA, Knoth S, Jones-Farmer LA. How generative AI models such as ChatGPT can be (mis)used in SPC practice, education, and research? An exploratory study. Quality Engineering. 2024;**36**(2):287-315. DOI: 10.1080/08982112.2023.2206479

[3] Bozkurt A. Generative artificial intelligence (AI) powered conversational educational agents: The inevitable paradigm shift. Asian Journal of Distance Education. 2023;**18**(1):198-204. Available from: https://files.eric.ed.gov/fulltext/EJ1389644.pdf

[4] Liu L. Analyzing the text contents produced by ChatGPT: Prompts, feature-components in responses, and a predictive model. Journal of Educational Technology Development and Exchange. 2023;**16**(1):49-70. DOI: 10.18785/jetde.1601.03

[5] Cotroneo P, Hutson J. Generative AI tools in art education: Exploring prompt engineering and iterative processes for enhanced creativity. Metaverse. 2023;**4**(1):14. DOI: 10.54517/m.v4i1.2164

[6] Walter Y. Embracing the future of artificial intelligence in the classroom: The relevance of AI literacy, prompt engineering, and critical thinking in modern education. International Journal of Educational Technology in Higher Education. 2024;**21**(1):15. DOI: 10.1186/s41239-024-00448-3

[7] Schorcht S, Buchholtz N, Baumanns L. Prompt the problem – Investigating the mathematics educational quality of AI-supported problem solving by comparing prompt techniques. Frontiers in Education. 2024;**9**:1386075. DOI: 10.3389/feduc.2024.1386075

[8] Ifenthaler D. Determining the effectiveness of prompts for self-regulated learning in problem-solving scenarios. Journal of Educational Technology & Society. 2012;**15**:38-52. Available from: https://www.semanticscholar.org/paper/Determining-the-effectiveness-of-prompts-for-in-Ifenthaler/55065876334df2698da179898d2f1be7501beca1#paper-topics

[9] Lo LS. The CLEAR path: A framework for enhancing information literacy through prompt engineering. Journal of Academic of Librarianship. 2023;**49**(4):102720. DOI: 10.1016/j.acalib.2023.102720

[10] Santos J, Figueiredo AS, Vieira M. Innovative pedagogical practices in higher education: An integrative literature review. Nurse Education Today. 2019;**72**:12-17. DOI: 10.1016/j.acalib.2023.102720

[11] Falloon G. From digital literacy to digital competence: The teacher digital competency (TDC) framework. Educational Technology Research and Development. 2020;**68**(5):2449-2472. DOI: 10.1007/s11423-020-09767-4

[12] BaiDoo-Anu D, Owusu Ansah L. Education in the era of generative artificial intelligence (AI): Understanding the potential benefits of ChatGPT in promoting teaching and learning. Journal of AI. 2023;**7**(1):52-62. DOI: 10.61969/jai.1337500

[13] Chan CKY, Hu W. Students' voices on generative AI: Perceptions, benefits, and challenges in higher education. International Journal of Educational Technology in Higher Education. 2023;**20**(1):43. DOI: 10.1186/s41239-023-00411-8

[14] Maphoto KB, Sevnarayan K, Mohale NE, Suliman Z, Ntsopi TJ, Mokoena D. Advancing students' academic excellence in distance education: Exploring the potential of generative AI integration to improve academic writing skills. Open Praxis. 2024;**16**(2):142-159. DOI: 10.55982/openpraxis.16.2.649

[15] Michel-Villarreal R, Vilalta-Perdomo E, Salinas-Navarro DE, Thierry-Aguilera R, Gerardou FS. Generative AI for higher education as explained by ChatGPT. Education Sciences. 2023;**13**(9):856. DOI: 10.3390/educsci13090856

[16] Ooi KB, Tan GWH, Al-Emran M, Al-Sharafi MA, Capatina A, Chakraborty A, et al. The potential of generative artificial intelligence across disciplines: Prospects and future directions. Journal of Computer Information Systems. 2023:1-32. DOI: 10.1080/08874417.2023.2261010 [Ahead of print]

[17] Pesovski I, Santos R, Henriques R, Trajkovik V. Generative AI for customizable learning experiences. Sustainability. 2024;**16**(7):3034. DOI: 10.3390/su16073034

[18] Ruiz-Rojas LI, Acosta-Vargas P, De-Moreta-Llovet J, Gonzalez-Rodriguez M. Empowering education with generative artificial intelligence tools: Approach with an instructional design matrix. Sustainability. 2023;**15**(15):11524. DOI: 10.3390/su151511524

[19] OpenAI. ChatGPT (Mar 14 Version) [Large Language Model]. 2023. Available from: https://chat.openai.com/chat [Accessed: July 17, 2024]

[20] Eke DO. ChatGPT and the rise of generative AI: Threat to academic integrity? Journal of Responsible Technology. 2023;**13**:100060. DOI: 10.1016/j.jrt.2023.100060

[21] Ocaña-Fernández Y, Valenzuela-Fernández LA, Garro-Aburto LL. Artificial intelligence and its implications in higher education. Purposes and Representations. 2019;7(2):553-568. DOI: 10.20511/pyr2019.v7n2.274

[22] Samaniego JF. The four great ethical challenges of applying artificial intelligence to online education. The blog of the UOC's computer science. In: Multimedia and Telecommunications Studies. 2022. Available from: https://blogs.uoc.edu/informatica/es/cuatro-retos-eticos-inteligencia-artificial-educacion-online/ [Accessed: July 17, 2024]

[23] UNESCO. Artificial Intelligence in Education. Digital Learning and Education Transformation. 2024. Available from: https://www.unesco.org/es/digital-education/artificial-intelligence [Accessed: July 17, 2024]

[24] Dang H, Mecke L, Lehmann F, Goller S, Buschek D. How to Prompt? Opportunities and Challenges of Zero- and Few-Shot Learning for Human-AI Interaction in Creative Applications of Generative Models. (arXiv:2209.01390). arXiv. 2022. Available from: http://arxiv.org/abs/2209.01390 [Accessed: July 17, 2024]

[25] Lin Z. How to write effective prompts for large language models. Nature

Human Behaviour. 2024;**8**(4):611-615. DOI: 10.1038/s41562-024-01847-2

[26] Rodriguez Donaire S. Engineering prompts for codifying students' prompt structure and understanding their learning perception from receiving feedback on an online activity using AI. CORA, Research Data Repository. 2024;V1:UNF:6:VIaUGgwuP9lPi3I4YBwLZw== [fileUNF]. DOI: 10.34810/data1554

Chapter 8

Intention of Hybrid Learning for Students Deprived of Liberty (Inmates of the San Roque de Sucre Penitentiary)

José Luis Rosales Barrero and María Elena Palma Moreno

Abstract

The intention is to professionalize those deprived of liberty at the San Roque penitentiary center in the city of Sucre by incorporating a hybrid educational model (HL) (online and in-person). For the study, structural equation models were applied, which combine Perceived Social Capacity and Disposition to Online Learning and Perceived Usefulness of Technology in Online Learning, all of these constructs have positive effects to validate the Intention of Online Learning. Of the population of 575 people deprived of liberty, 70 entrepreneurial inmates were considered for the study, who are willing to do hybrid learning to improve their skills. The results show that the inmates accept the use of HL that will be useful in their current and future learning process, improving their social skills and their reintegration into society. The contribution of the study is the combination of the hybrid model, online learning (theory and simulation) complemented with in-person training regarding practices and laboratories. The HL model has not been exhaustively explored in research with students deprived of liberty. Additionally, the findings can help university educators improve curricular designs to incorporate more effective and efficient HL environments that meet the needs of inmates.

Keywords: hybrid learning, perceived social ability, tic, structural equations, PLS-SEM

1. Introduction

Prison education plays a crucial role in the rehabilitation and reintegration of prisoners into society. Worldwide, approximately 11 million people are in penal institutions, and the incarceration rate continues to rise [1]. Despite the difficulties, education is a fundamental human right that should not be denied to prisoners.

In this context, professional education within prisons is of special relevance. Providing inmates with basic skills and vocational training provides them with concrete opportunities. In addition, current regulations allow inmates to obtain Vocational Training degrees and, in some cases, even the Graduate in Compulsory Secondary Education [2].

Education in prison contexts is a crucial and often undervalued topic. As the world moves toward an information and knowledge-based society, it is essential to consider how to provide educational opportunities to those deprived of their liberty. In this context, hybrid education emerges as a relevant alternative [3].

Today's world is experiencing constant changes driven by globalization, which has given rise to a "new society" based on information and knowledge. However, this process has also exacerbated inequalities, increasing the vulnerability of various groups, including people deprived of liberty in penitentiary institutions. Therefore, it is increasingly imperative to rethink established paradigms, review educational communication processes, transform learning scenarios and adapt pedagogical models to address the changing needs of our society [4].

The right to education is intrinsically linked to the idea of universalization. Consequently, ensuring the development of learning skills is directly related to the equity paradigm. Educational equity implies not only equal access to education, but also the creation of opportunities and conditions that allow all individuals to develop their capabilities to the fullest. In this context, ensuring that learning skills are cultivated fairly and without discrimination is essential to achieving a more equal and prosperous society [5].

The development of e-learning environments has been driven by the nature of the context of the international Covid-19 pandemic. Instead of focusing on the consequences of this situation, the research analyzes potential variables that could guide the incorporation of new technologies. Technologies in the academic field in electronic learning environments [6].

Currently, the rapid advance of Information and Communication Technologies (ICT) has led to the emergence of online education as a flexible and accessible alternative in contrast to traditional classroom learning [7]. University institutions have seen a significant boost in the adoption of online learning. This educational modality allows students to access content from anywhere and at any time, promoting self-direction and personalization of learning. Additionally, online interaction with classmates and teachers in forums, chats, and video conferences enriches the educational experience. However, it is essential to address challenges related to equity of access and quality of digital resources to ensure that all students can benefit equally from this modality [8].

Hybrid education is an alternative teaching model that emerged with the advancement of educational technologies, representing a new option for learning: the combination of Distance Education (EAD) and face-to-face meetings [9].

Hybrid teaching models combine face-to-face teaching strategies with distance strategies, through synchronous and/or asynchronous online learning integrating formal and informal presence, applied through various tools such as educational platforms mediated by the Internet [9].

The inclusion of educational programs for prisoners is a common feature in prison systems worldwide [10]. Today, virtually all countries offer some form of education in their prisons, although the diversity of programs available is due to different interpretations of the goals and possibilities of prison education, as well as general societal attitudes toward incarcerated people [11].

The educational profile of prisoners, although it shares some basic characteristics, also presents significant differences. This poses challenges when planning training opportunities for them [12]. Some inmates may have varying educational levels, requiring flexible and personalized approaches to meet their specific needs.

There are multiple reasons that support the provision of education and training in prison contexts. International regulations, conventions and recommendations recognize the right of prisoners to participate in educational activities during their sentence [3, 7]. Prison education is considered a means to benefit prisoners, as they acquire skills and competencies that facilitate their reintegration into society. Additionally, by providing educational opportunities, the social costs associated with recidivism and crime are reduced [10].

Prison education is linked to improving employability among prisoners, an important factor that decreases the likelihood of prisoners reoffending and returning to prison [10].

In Bolivia, the legislation establishes rights: people deprived of liberty have the opportunity to work and study in penitentiary centers and this would help their reintegration into society, a situation that is not fulfilled [13].

Those deprived of liberty in penitentiaries in Bolivia face the problem of accessing education and receiving adequate training in a situation of confinement. These people only think about how to survive and support their families inside and outside the prison and not about individual improvement [14].

In national penitentiary centers there are students enrolled in different levels of learning such as primary, secondary, literacy, and post-literacy education, as well as workshops in technical branches such as hairdressing, tailoring, electricity, gastronomy, computing, among other trades. According to data from the National Institute of Statistics INE, there are 24,824 inmates in the country's prisons, of which 575 correspond to the San Roque de Sucre prison, although its capacity is only for 150 people.

The inmates of the San Roque penitentiary in the city of Sucre, apart from suffering overcrowding and violation of their rights, have the great problem of seeing their aspirations to obtain professional training restricted, due to their status as inmates and not being able to attend in person. to the training centers and if they do, they must be accompanied by a security guard, which is the biggest obstacle because there is not enough of these personnel and it would also represent an additional expense to the State if a greater number were required. of guards, the ideal would be to have a number of inmates predisposed to continue their professionalization, in acceptable technical and infrastructure conditions with access to materials, for whom appropriate training would be planned inside the prison facility.

Hybrid learning, which combines face-to-face and virtual elements, has become a relevant alternative in various educational contexts. In particular, its application in prison settings offers unique opportunities for incarcerated students. In this scientific article, we will explore the intention behind hybrid learning in the San Roque de Sucre penitentiary, considering the challenges and benefits it implies for this population. The combination of in-person and virtual modalities can contribute significantly to social reintegration and the development of skills in these students, who face a particularly complex context. Throughout the article, we will examine how to design effective hybrid learning strategies to maximize their impact on inmates' lives [15].

In the previous context, a hybrid teaching model is seen as an alternative, which combines virtual and in-person education to cover the needs of practices and laboratories [8].

In the study, a sample of 70 inmates has been considered, who are those who showed interest in becoming professional, which allowed the characterization of the learning and professional training needs, from this, the general objective was set: to analyze the theories of the social motivations with the technology acceptance model for the evaluation of the intention of the inmates of San Roque in the city of Sucre to face their professionalization learning online and in person, giving rise to the modality of hybrid learning. It is predicted that perceived social ability will directly influence perceived usefulness and willingness for online learning, and all three variables will have a direct impact on student intention of online learning and face-to-face learning, which will validate the learning model. Hybrid. For this purpose, the state of the art on the constructs related to the topic was analyzed, and a model and a hypothesis have been applied that have been contrasted with the Partial regression technique. Least Squares Path Modeling (PLS) for analysis of results and discussions [16–18].

2. Literature review

This section provides a review of relevant literature related to perceived social capability, technology acceptance models, experience in online learning continuance intention, and cultural context.

2.1 Perceived social capability

Perceived Social Capability is defined as the ability of individuals to form communities of interest in their social context, with the purpose of obtaining benefits [19]. In this sense, it explores how students experience and perceive social interaction while communicating with other members and performing tasks in virtual learning environments. Social competence has been shown to be a significant predictor of online learning acceptance and satisfaction among students [19]. Furthermore, students' participation and interaction are influenced by technological tools, which support their social needs while achieving their learning objectives. Social actions have been studied in online learning environments, focusing on the creation and maintenance of virtual learning communities [20].

Students' ability to participate in discussions [21] is an indicator of their social ability in virtual environments. Research has shown that this skill positively influences online learning outcomes. The construct of Perceived Social Capability (PSC) is defined as an instrument that measures social presence, social exploration, and social connection in virtual learning environments [19]. Social exploration involves being aware of the actions of others as a guide to one's own action. Observing the actions of others before making decisions optimizes the efficiency and effectiveness of online learning, as well as contributing to a greater sense of community [16].

Regarding the sense of community, a moderate and positive relationship has been found between the sense of community in the classroom and the number of messages published in the discussion forums [22]. Student feedback shows that greater interaction and participation fosters a sense of community in online classes. This greater sense of community is attributed to how interaction and participation reduces physical barriers in online class activities. On the other hand, the lack of social interaction decreases the acceptance of online learning [23]. In conclusion, it is essential that students feel involved and develop interactions with both their classmates and their teachers or instructors in virtual environments [24].

2.2 Technology acceptance model

Online education at the basic level is characterized by separation between instructors and students in terms of space and/or time, self-monitoring of learning

DOI: http://dx.doi.org/10.5772/intechopen.1006566

by students rather than direct supervision of the instructor, and communication mediated by technological tools. Between students and instructors. One of the main objectives of online learning systems is to support and improve the learning process of students [16]. In this context, the acceptance and success of online learning are closely related to satisfaction in educational processes [25].

The technology acceptance model suggests that the adoption of a new technology is influenced by the user's beliefs about the consequences of its use [26, 27]. In particular, users adopt a new technology when they perceive it to be easy to use and useful. Students' perceived satisfaction in adopting technology in online classes manifests in better understanding and achievement of their academic goals [28] In addition to perceived ease of use and usefulness, other measures related to the acceptance of online learning systems include perceived satisfaction [29], perceived credibility [30], computer experience, social support, and cognitive absorption.

2.3 Intention of online learning

There is very little research related to the intention of virtual learning, Chiu 's Web-based [31] research identifies four components of subjective task value (achievement, utility, intrinsic and cost) and three dimensions of equity (distributive, procedural and interactional). that affect student satisfaction. This research theorizes the three dimensions of quality (information, system, and service) and the three dimensions of equity that affect student satisfaction. In turn, satisfaction and the three dimensions of equity will influence students' intention to continue training under web-based learning [32].

3. Study methodology

The theories of perceived social capacity and the technology acceptance model define the context of online education and the advantages of its use in different areas of education, such as in the case of students deprived of liberty.

3.1 Model

The proposed model is developed to determine the intention of hybrid learning (HL), proposing eight hypotheses based on: the perceived social capacity (CSP) as an intrinsic motivator, and as extrinsic motivators the disposition for online learning (DAL) and the perceived usefulness. (UP) that determine the intention of online learning (IUAL), directly related to face-to-face learning that covers the needs of direct link between teacher and students in situations of on-site practices and/or laboratories. Given the needs that prisoners have to follow professional training for their reintegration into society as productive and competent citizens who contribute to social needs, with educational processes mediated by online education combined with face-to-face education, the thesis is validated. of the incorporation of hybrid education in prisons as an alternative for professional training, consequently, the hypotheses are raised based on the model called; hybrid learning behavior model presented in **Figure 1**.

3.2 Hypothesis

Based on the model outlined in **Figure 1**, the following hypotheses are proposed:

H1: Perceived social competence (CSP) will have a positive effect on readiness for online learning (DAL).

H2: Perceived social capability (PSC) will have a positive effect on perceived usefulness (UP) toward online learning.

H3: Readiness for online learning (DAL) will have a positive effect on intention to use online learning (IUAL).

H4: Perceived usefulness (UP) will have a positive effect on the intention to use online learning (IUAL).

H5: The intention to use online learning (IUAL) will have a positive effect on face-to-face learning (PR).

H6: Face-to-face learning (PR) will have a complementary positive effect on hybrid learning (HL).

H7: The intention to use online learning (IUAL) will have a positive effect on hybrid learning (HL).

H8: Perceived social capability (CSP) will have a positive effect on the intention to use online learning (IUAL).

However, the previous formulations allow us to demonstrate the general hypothesis of the work in relation to the general objective, formulated as follows: The implementation of a hybrid educational approach (that combines face-to-face and virtual modalities) can improve training and job reintegration opportunities for inmates of the San Roque prison in the city of Sucre.

3.3 Methods, techniques and instruments

This section deals with the methodological design of the research, which includes determining the population and sample.

From 576 inmates of the San Roque prison in the city of Sucre, capital of Bolivia, 70 prisoners who aspire to continue their professional studies were considered. This study adopts a descriptive research design, with the application of the survey technique, for which a structured questionnaire was designed through the forms resource of the Google platform, in such a way that it was answered online by the population. Objective, the scale used to validate the instrument comes from the design

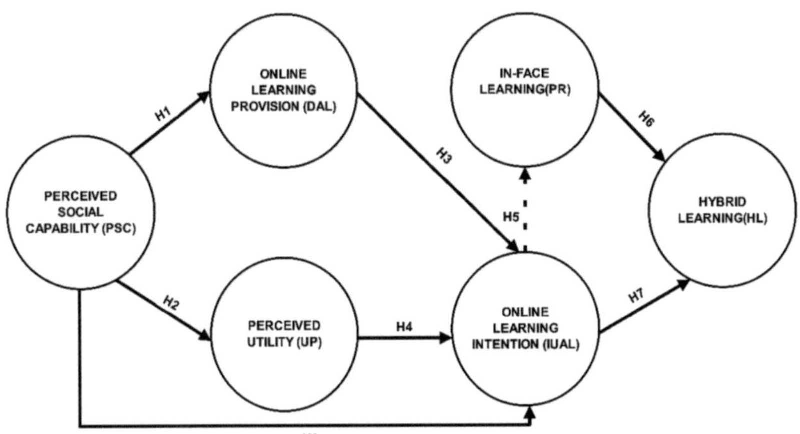

Figure 1.
Hybrid learning model of students deprived of liberty.

of Brahmasrene and Lee [16]. All items were considered on a 5-point Likert scale (**Table 1**).

3.4 Results and validation

Variance-based partial least squares (PLS) structural equation modeling (SEM) approach. For this purpose, Smart-PLS-3.3.3 version was used to perform all empirical calculations related to the evaluation of the structural model.

Table 2 shows the control variable means of access to virtual classes, in which prison inmates would access only through computers provided by the prison in 44%, and in a reduced percentage of 7% through Laptops that were supervised and restricted. For access to different addresses and only to educational and related pages [33].

Survey questions (5-point scale ranging from "Strongly disagree = 1" to "Strongly agree =5")
(CSP): When I take classes online 1. I can have more interaction with my classmates and instructors. 2. I am able to promote social bonding and networking. 3. I can communicate with people to influence the action of others.
(DAL): Regarding your provision for online learning: 1. I am proficient in using the online learning system. 2. I have the necessary knowledge to use the online learning system. 3. I have the ability to acquire skill in using the online learning system. 4. In general, I am ready to use the online learning system.
(UP): When you use online learning it allows you to: 1. It allows me to complete my educational goal more quickly. 2. Improves my ability to perform academic tasks. 3. Increases my productivity in completing academic tasks. 4. Improves my effectiveness in completing academic tasks. 5. I find it useful to complete my study.
(IUAL): intention to continue using online learning 1. If I need to study for advanced degree programs, I hope to use the online learning system. 2. If you ask me, I would probably recommend the online learning system as an ideal learning platform. 3. For future advanced degree programs, I would probably use the online learning system. 4. Overall, I am satisfied with the online learning system.
(PR): What are the advantages of in-person classes? 1. Face-to-face interaction that facilitates relationship building. 2. Practical experiences in real time. 3. Immediate responses to questions or concerns. 4. Structured environment that can improve concentration.
(HL): What are the advantages of Hybrid classes (in-person-virtual)? 1. Personalization of learning. 2. Self-directed learning. 3. Shorten educational gaps. 4. Effective use of digital tools.
How is the quality of your Internet? (5-point scale ranging from "Very poor = 1" to "Excellent = 5"
By what means would you enter Virtual Classes? a. Cell phone b. Computer. c. Laptop
If you wanted to professionalize in, what area would you like to?

Health Sciences (Medicine, dentistry, etc.)
Economic Sciences (Economics, Business Administration, Commercial, Accounting, etc.)
Social Sciences (Law, Communication, Psychology, etc.)
Technological Sciences (Chemistry, food, mechanics, systems, etc.)
agricultural Sciences
Habitat Sciences (Civil Engineering, Architecture)
Postgraduate
What career?
What is your gender?
Women
Man
I prefer not to say
How old are you?
How long are you at the facility?
Less than 1 year
1 to 3 years
4 to 10 years
11 to 15 years
over 15 years
What is your level of training?
Bachelor
Technical
Professional
diplomat
master's degree
Doctorate
Other
Source: Own based on the design of Brahmasrene and Lee [16].

Table 1.
Survey questions.

Regarding the quality of the Internet perceived by the students, it is from good to very good, represented in total by 97%, which is positive for the implementation of hybrid education in the penitentiary, **Table 3**.

In the San Roque prison, in terms of gender, they are similar in their intentions to seek professional training, men represent 53.3% and women 46.7%. The predominant ages are in the range of 30 to 45 years. In the area of training, the area of Economic Sciences is favored with 80%, followed by Social Sciences such as Law with 10%. The inmates who want to follow hybrid learning aimed at having a professional degree are 63.3% high school graduates. The causes for which they are punished are various, with drug trafficking standing out in 27.6%.

Interns who prefer to begin their professional studies in the economic area seek training to direct their small businesses and apply their knowledge in marketing,

Cell phone	**9**	**13%**
Cell Phone, Desktop Computer	0	0%
Cell Phone, Desktop Computer	0	0%
Desktop Computer, Laptop	7	10%
Desktop	44	63%
Laptop	9	13%
	70	**100%**

Table 2.
Means of access to online virtual class.

Bad	5	7%
Regular	0	0%
Good	33	47%
Very good	33	47%
Excellent	0	0%
	70	**100%**

Table 3.
Internet quality.

production and administration. 10% are interested in the study of laws and law, 2% are inclined toward agricultural learning and 1% toward habitat sciences (architecture).

Regarding training, the inmates of the prison are 64% high school graduates, 16% professionals, 13% technicians and 7% other training. And the most enthusiastic to be professionals are women with 54% compared to men with 46%.

Regarding the time spent in the facility, inmates range from 4 to 10 years, which represents 63%, from 1 to 3 years, 20%, from 11 to 15 years, 7%, and more than 15 years, 10%.

Regarding the age of the inmates, the predominant range of 36 to 43 years is 45.8%, in the range of 21 to 42 years of age it is 33.3%, and those over 45 years old represent 20.9%.

3.5 Validity and reliability

The reliability of the model is established by both Cronbach's alpha, rho A and the composite reliability, as the internal variables of the model have values greater than 0.7 [34]; and the convergence validity greater than 0.5 (AVE) [35], as seen in **Table 4**.

Observing the 5 and 95.0% columns (confidence intervals), in **Table 5**, (HTMT criterion), the validity of the discriminant reliability between the constructs is established [36], as they are significantly different from 0.9.

3.6 Structural model evaluation

It can be seen in **Table 6** that all the VIF values related to the collinearity of the model indicators are less than 5, there is an excellent structure, therefore, the

	Cronbach's alpha	rho_A	Composite reliability	Average variance extracted (AVE)
1.(HL)	0.863	0.866	0.908	0.711
2.(PR)	0.866	0.871	0.909	0.713
3.(CSP)	0.805	0.820	0.870	0.627
4.(DAL)	0.814	0.829	0.890	0.729
5.(IUAL)	0.677	0.676	0.823	0.610
6.(UP)	0.786	0.787	0.876	0.702

Table 4.
Reliability and construct validity.

collinearity does not reach critical levels in any of the formative constructs of the model. Model.

In partial least squares structural equation modeling (PLS-SEM) The R2 statistic explains the variance in the endogenous variable explained by the exogenous variables. If R2 is greater than 0.60 it can be considered substantial, 0.19 is weak and 0.33 is moderate.

In the proposed model, the coefficient of determination R2 of the variable Intention for online learning (IUAL) is 0.707, which means that the three latent variables, disposition for online learning (DAL), perceived usefulness (UP) and capacity Perceived social perception (CSP) explain 70.7% of the variance of intention in online learning (IUAL).

Hybrid learning (HL) is explained in 73.5% by the latent variables Face-to-face Learning (PR) with a low explanatory 17.6% and online learning intention (IUAL) with 70.7% which is great importance in the process of accepting hybrid training in prisons. Shown in **Figure 2.**

3.7 Structural path coefficients and hypothesis validation

Bootstrapping technique was used (**Table 7**) to obtain the *t-statistics* and the *p value* of the path coefficient. Face-to-face learning (PR) has a positive influence on hybrid learning (HL) ($t = 3.068$, $p < 0.05$). Perceived social ability has a positive influence on willingness to learn online ($t = 4.001$, $p < 0.05$), perceived social ability

	Original sample (O)	Sample mean (M)	5.0%	95.0%
(PR) - > (HL)	0.396	0.376	0.183	0.608
(CSP) - > (DAL)	0.496	0.546	0.291	0.700
(CSP) - > (IUAL)	0.014	−0.011	−0.312	0.339
(CSP) - > (UP)	0.510	0.517	0.191	0.829
(DAL) - > (IUAL)	−0.053	−0.025	−0.369	0.262
(IUAL) - > (HL)	0.612	0.633	0.445	0.780
(IUAL) - > (PR)	0.419	0.397	0.001	0.837
(UP) - > (IUAL)	0.864	0.841	0.542	0.885

Table 5.
Heterotrait-monotrait radius (HTMT).

(CSP2)	**1496**
(CSP3)	1737
(CSP4)	2079
(DAL1)	1633
(DAL3)	2409
(DAL4)	1912
(HL1)	1636
(HL2)	3343
(HL3)	2762
(HL4)	1833
(IUAL1)	1620
(IUAL3)	1525
(IUAL4)	1166
(PR1)	1797
(PR2)	3131
(PR3)	3187
(PR4)	2024
(UP1)	1427
(UP3)	2199
(UP5)	1897
(CSP1)	1641

Table 6.
VIF collinearity evaluation.

has a direct negative influence on online learning intention ($t = 0.069$, $p = 0.473$), perceived social ability positively influences perceived usefulness ($t = 2.636$, $p < 0.05$), disposition to online learning has the least influence on the intention to follow online learning ($t = 0.277$, $p = 0.391$), the intention to online learning is positive to hybrid learning ($t = 6.016$, $p < 0.05$), the intention to online learning is positive to face-to-face learning ($t = 1.655$, $p < 0.05$) and the perceived usefulness has a positive and direct influence to the intention to continue with online learning ($t = 4.432$, $p < 0.05$).

Those path coefficients (β) were accepted, and by extension, the hypotheses that have a level of significance according to a one-tailed [37]. Student 's t distribution with n-1 degrees of freedom. These values, as [38] should be between the values of 0.2 and ideally exceed the value 0.3, therefore, if $\beta < 0.2$ there is no causality so the hypothesis is rejected, and they also coincide with the Student's t-test.

The tests of hypotheses 1 and 2 indicate that there is a positive relationship between perceived social ability (CSP) and readiness for online learning (DAL) and between (CSP) and perceived usefulness (UP), suggesting that the Perceived social capacity has a positive and significant effect on the perceived usefulness, greater than the willingness for online learning and the intention to continue online learning, the latter not being very significant, as shown in **Figure 2**.

Hypothesis 3 tests the relationship between the disposition for online learning (DAL) and the intention to continue using online learning (IUAL). It is rejected as it is not conclusive, taking into account the inmates who cannot have access to the

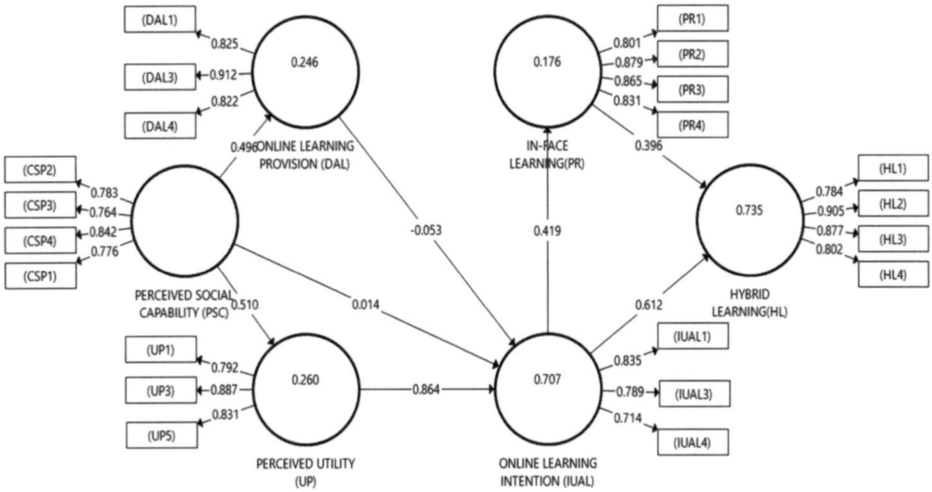

Figure 2.
Test of the integrated model (Source: Own elaboration, –with Smart PLS.

		Path coefficient (β)	t-Statistics	P Values	Decision
H1.	(CSP) - > (DAL)	0.546	4001	0.000	Accepted
H2.	(CSP) - > (UP)	0.517	2636	0.004	Accepted
H3.	(DAL) - > (IUAL)	−0.025	0.277	0.391	Rejected
H4.	(UP) - > (IUAL)	0.864	4432	0.000	Accepted
H5.	(IUAL) - > (PR)	0.397	1655	0.049	Accepted
H6.	(PR) - > (HL)	0.376	3068	0.001	Accepted
H7.	(IUAL) - > (HL)	0.633	6016	0.000	Accepted
H8.	(CSP) - > (IUAL)	−0.011	0.069	0.473	Rejected

Table 7.
Integrated structural adjustment.

technologies. of information for their training freely but monitored and supervised by prison officials.

Hypothesis 4 contrasts between (UP) and (IUAL). Which means that the readiness for online learning and the perceived usefulness directly influence the intention to use virtual online learning.

Hypothesis 5 tests the positive relationship between the intention to use online learning (IUAL) and face-to-face learning (PR), which means that the methodologies of the practices and laboratories that complement the intention of online learning are important.

Hypothesis 6 is positive between face-to-face learning (PR) and hybrid learning (HL), it states that the support of face-to-face classes embodied in practices and laboratories that cannot be taught online is necessary.

Hypothesis 7 is positive and validates the same between the intention to use online learning (IUAL) and hybrid learning (HL), being forceful in its importance and valid for training combining in-person and virtual training [21].

Hypothesis 8 is negative; therefore, it is rejected between perceived social capacity (CSP) and the intention to use online learning (IUAL) and this situation is justified by the need that inmates have for better management of learning technologies. Information for information to the extent that there are prohibitions on the use of cell phones and computers in prisons due to the misuse that inmates could give.

Hypotheses H1, H2, H4, H5, H6, and H7 confirm the general hypothesis "The implementation of a hybrid educational approach (that combines face-to-face and virtual modalities) can improve training and job reintegration opportunities for inmates of the San Juan prison. Roque of the city of Sucre," validating the intention of using hybrid learning with the exception of training in the use of technologies oriented to education and the better availability of access to them by the inmates of the San Roque de Penitentiary, the city of Sucre.

4. Discussions and contributions

The result of the empirical analysis supports all the hypotheses. Theories of perceived social ability are determinants in three directions; first, they support the disposition for online learning by conditioning with the necessary competencies in terms of the development of skills in the use and management of information and communication technologies with their abilities to relate to their peers in the environment. Virtual; second, the perceived usefulness that will provide benefits in your academic training such as the improvement of your capabilities, productivity, effectiveness, and usefulness; and third, the intention to use online learning in situations of deprivation of liberty is conditioned by the social capacity perceived and rejected by society due to the risks involved in the use of ICT in vocational training and the misuse that could give rise to inmates, to commit crimes through these technological means.

The results of this study provide useful information and suggest the following contributions:

First, the results support the existing literature. Perceived social ability contributes to perceived usefulness in online learning. Students with perceived social skills find the online learning system helpful for their hybrid learning.

Second, this study shows that the intention to use online learning depends on the perceived social capacity approved by society and justice administrators, with restricted supervision of the inmate in both his online and in-person learning.

Third, greater perceived social capacity can improve the intention to use online learning and will be decisive in the use of hybrid learning as the main axis supported by face-to-face learning in situations where face-to-face learning is necessary. Therefore, teachers of hybrid education courses or programs should encourage greater use of communication tools in the designs of their teaching plans to increase social capacity among inmates, thus encouraging their participation and interaction in the classrooms. Online classes, the curricular design can include collaborative group work activities, debates, and web surveys, complemented by practices and laboratories that are necessary in person-oriented to area preferences such as economic sciences as an alternative to improve knowledge and strategies to enhance the business initiatives that they have within the penal system of the legal sciences to fully understand the criminal situation of each one. In addition to traditional communication tools such as chat rooms, discussion forums, and blogs, there are other technological features that are also useful in educational environments. For example, support discussions allow students to interact with their peers and teachers to resolve questions and share ideas. Likewise, the personalization of content through adaptive algorithms improves the learning experience by providing relevant material tailored to the individual needs of each student. Considering the age range interested in vocational training, between 21 and 43% stand out, who already have the knowledge and skills that favor the implementation of the hybrid model, reinforced by the training of interns who are mostly high school graduates or professionals.

Fourth, online learning and the usefulness of online classes support existing findings on attitudes toward computer-based learning; however, the tracking of virtual learning through cell phones and the low quality of Internet use [39] are control variables that attenuate the intention to apply online learning and therefore, hybrid learning is conditioned by the permanent accessibility to educational technologies mediated by the Internet and the budget that comes with presence because the intern has to leave the prison facility accompanied by a personal guard which has an impact on the facility's budget. However, the conditions for hybrid training in prisons can be favorable with adequate planning and coordination with training centers and the coherent development of the academic curriculum, which is beneficial for inmates, as well as the provision of supervised computer laboratories and restricted access to pages or social networks that may give rise to cybercrime, that is, they only allow access to educational platforms and virtual libraries.

5. Conclusions

Based on the intention of hybrid training for the professionalization of inmates of the San Roque penitentiary in the city of Sucre, the aim is to analyze the conditions and needs of the use of hybrid learning, confirming the general hypothesis: inmates are willing to be trained with a hybrid education considering that their learning and expertise in the use of information and communication technologies will benefit them in their particular objectives that contribute to their reintegration into society as productive citizens and corrected for their punishable offenses, and in their needs to apply their knowledge as small business entrepreneurs inside the prison, allowing them a wide willingness to learn online and value the usefulness of this teaching-learning modality, by allowing them to improve their productivity and achieve their academic objectives without time and space [21].

To support the general hypothesis, it is important to consider the following points:

Access to education: Hybrid education allows inmates to access educational content both inside and outside the penitentiary. This could increase your access to vocational training and technical skills.

Flexibility: The hybrid modality offers flexibility in study schedules, which could be adapted to the circumstances and limitations of the inmates.

Development of digital skills: Virtual education enriches digital skills, which are increasingly relevant in today's world of work.

Labor reintegration: By acquiring knowledge and skills, inmates could be better prepared to reintegrate into society and find employment after serving their sentence.

Hybrid education could be an effective strategy to improve the training and job prospects of inmates at the San Roque penitentiary. However, further research is required to evaluate its specific impact in this context [40].

DOI: http://dx.doi.org/10.5772/intechopen.1006566

The inmates of the San Roque prison in the city of Sucre have a preference, which is to begin their professional studies in the economic area at 80%, with the purpose of training themselves to direct their small businesses and apply their knowledge in marketing., production and administration. 10% are interested in the study of laws and law, 2% are interested in agricultural learning and 1% in habitat sciences.

Regarding the training of the inmates of the sample studied, high school graduates stand out at 64%, professionals 16%, technicians 13% and other training 7%, with women being the most interested in professionalization with 54% compared to men with 46%.

Among the limitations of the study are the accessibility to educational technologies mediated by the Internet, due to the situation of the inmate who is prohibited from using cell phones or computers inside the prison due to the risk it implies of committing a crime [41], which means that they must adapt the policies and infrastructure regarding computer laboratories in prisons and provide more personnel to accompany the inmate when they have to leave the prison for their in-person classes.

It would be useful for the hybrid learning modality to carry out complementary research regarding the vision and position of educators or teachers and address evaluative and comparative research between different prisons, contrasting with the real needs perceived by inmates not only in professionalization but in all training cycles (primary and secondary), which will surely emerge complementary positions and results for the improvement of the online and in-person teaching and learning process, aimed at a more appropriate hybrid learning in favor of those deprived of liberty [18].

Author details

José Luis Rosales Barrero* and María Elena Palma Moreno
San Francisco Xavier de Chuquisaca, Sucre, Bolivia

*Address all correspondence to: rosales.jose@usfx.bo; joseluisrosalesbarrero@gmail.com

References

[1] UNESCO 2014 [Online]. 2015. Available from: https://unesdoc.unesco.org/ark:/48223/pf0000232432 [Accessed: June 11, 2024]

[2] UNESCO 2014 - UNESCO Digital Library. [Online]. Available from: https://unesdoc.unesco.org/ark:/48223/pf0000232432 [Accessed: June 11, 2024]

[3] Manger T, Eikeland OJ, Asbjørnsen A. Effects of educational motives on prisoners' participation in education and educational desires. European Journal on Criminal Policy and Research. 2013;**19**(3):245-257. DOI: 10.1007/S10610-012-9187-X

[4] McFarlane R, Pike A. From prisoner to student. In: Degrees of Freedom. Cambridge University Press; 2019. pp. 11-32. DOI: 10.51952/9781447353096.CH002

[5] DSNS Ag Isha and SR Mohd. Hashim, Structural equation modeling in investigating the role of academic motivation upon academic achievement, International Journal of Academic Research in Business and Social Sciences, vol. 13, no. 9, 2023, doi: 10.6007/IJARBSS/V13-I9/17853

[6] Wang FH. On the relationships between behaviors and achievement in technology-mediated flipped classrooms: A two-phase online behavioral PLS-SEM model. Computers in Education. 2019;**142**:103653. DOI: 10.1016/J.COMPEDU.2019.103653

[7] Kim RH, Clark D. The effect of prison-based college education programs on recidivism: Propensity score matching approach. Journal of Criminal Justice. 2013;**41**(3):196-204. DOI: 10.1016/J.JCRIMJUS.2013.03.001

[8] Damián Simón J. Hybrid university training: Challenges and opportunities. Investigative News in Education. 2014;**14**(2)

[9] Farliana N, Setiaji K, Rusdarti R, Hardianto H. Behavioral switching model to hybrid learning based on push pull mooring framework. Journal of Education Research and Evaluation. 2023;7(1):129-139. DOI: 10.23887/JERE.V7I1.52169

[10] Vryonides M, Torlone F. Innovative Learning Models for Prisoners. Vol. 70. Firenze University Press; 2016. p. 1-9

[11] Yuebo L, Halili SH, Razak RA. Online learning success model for adults in open and distance education in Western China. PLoS One. 2024;**19**(2):3-4. DOI: 10.1371/JOURNAL.PONE.0297515

[12] Johnson LR. Online teaching and learning in correctional facilities: Opportunities and tensions. Progressio. 2021;**42**. 21 pages. DOI: 10.25159/2663-5895/10556

[13] Esperanza GB. Overcrowding in the San Pedro Penitentiary Center in the city of La Paz violates the Right to Education. 2016 [Online]. Available from: http://repositorio.umsa.bo/xmlui/handle/123456789/12223 [Accessed: March 20, 2024]

[14] Gironda Pablo JC, Need to Include Reforms in the Educational Regime, to Achieve Redemption in the Law of Criminal Execution and Supervision; 2008. pp. 15-45

[15] Iván AV. Implementation of hybrid teaching as a derivation of COVID-19 implementation of hybrid teaching as a derivation of COVID-19.

Revista Docentes 2.0. 2022;**13**(1):5-10. DOI: 10.37843/rted.v.13i1.305

[16] Brahmasrene T, Lee JW. Determinants of intent to continue using online learning: A tale of two universities. Interdisciplinary Journal of Information, Knowledge, and Management. 2012;**7**(January):1-20. DOI: 10.28945/1548

[17] Alvarez-Risco A, Del-Aguila-Arcentales S, Yáñez JA, Rosen MA, Mejia CR. Influence of technostress on academic performance of university medicine students in Peru during the covid-19 pandemic. Sustainability (Switzerland). 2021;**13**(16). DOI: 10.3390/su13168949

[18] Nair PK, Ali F, Lim CL. Interactive technology and smart education article information. Interactive Technology and Smart Education. 2015;**12**(3):183-201

[19] Laffey J, Laffey J, Lin GY, Lin Y. Assessing social ability in online learning environments. Journal of Interactive Learning Research. 2006;**17**(2):163-177

[20] Riva G. Shared hypermedia: Communication and interaction in web-based learning. Environments. 2016;**25**(3):205-226. DOI: 10.2190/KCQW-YN00-6WYR-BVDQ

[21] Orgaz F, Moral S, Domínguez CM. Student attitude and perception with the use of technology in the university. Purposes and Representations. 2018;**6**(2):253. DOI: 10.20511/pyr2018.v6n2.230

[22] Rovai AP, Rovai AP. Building classroom community at a distance: A case study. Educational Technology Research and Development. 2001;**49**(4):33-48

[23] Arbaugh JB. Virtual classroom characteristics and student satisfaction with internet-based MBA courses. Journal of Management Education. 2016;**24**(1):32-54. DOI: 10.1177/105256290002400104

[24] Medina CDA, Duque GAC, Flórez JAF. PLS regression models applied to educational variables. Scientia et technica. 2016;**21**(3):254. DOI: 10.22517/23447214.10311

[25] Terán-Guerrero FN. Acceptance of university students in the use of Moodle e-learning systems from the perspective of the TAM model. Science Unemi. 2019;**12**(29):63-76. DOI: 10.29076/issn.2528-7737vol12iss29.2019pp63-76p

[26] Davis FD. Perceived usefulness, perceived ease of use, and user acceptance of information technology. MIS Quarterly. 1989;**13**(3):319-339. DOI: 10.2307/249008

[27] Siqueira F, Davis JG. Service computing for industry 4.0: State of the art, challenges, and research opportunities. ACM Computing Surveys. 2022;**54**(9). DOI: 10.1145/3478680

[28] Lin Y-M, Understanding Students' Technology Appropriation and Learning Perceptions in Online Learning Environments. 2005. [Online]. Available from: https://mospace.umsystem.edu/xmlui/handle/10355/4130 [Accessed: October 27, 2021]

[29] Lee J, Lim H, Allen J, Choi G. Effects of learning attitudes and COVID-19 risk perception on poor academic performance among middle school students. Sustainability (Switzerland). 2021;**13**(10):1-10. DOI: 10.3390/su13105541

[30] Ong CS, Lai JY, Wang YS. Factors affecting engineers' acceptance of

asynchronous e-learning systems in high-tech companies. Information & Management. 2004;**41**(6):795-804. DOI: 10.1016/J.IM.2003.08.012

[31] Chiu CM, Chiu CS, Chang HC. Examining the integrated influence of fairness and quality on learners' satisfaction and web-based learning continuance intention. Information Systems Journal. 2007;**17**(3):271-287. DOI: 10.1111/J.1365-2575.2007.00238.X

[32] Chasco C, Pumarada M, Contreras J. Role of ICT in academic performance: An application with structural equation models. Research in Economics of Education. 2017;**12**:449-471. [Online]. Available from: https://www.researchgate.net/publication/323542738_Papel_de_las_TIC_en_el_rendimiento_academico_una_aplicacion_con_modelos_de_ecuaciones_estructurales

[33] Rivera SIG. Impact factors in virtual learning in students of the Bolivian Catholic University 'San Pablo' regional Cochabamba. Revista de Propuestas Educativas. 2021;**3**(5):10-42. DOI: 10.33996/proposals.v 3i5.249

[34] Hair JF, Sarstedt M, Ringle Christian M. A First on Partial Least Squares Structural Equation Modeling (PLS-SEM). 3rd ed. New Delhi, India; Singapore: United Kingdom SAGE Publications India Pvt. Ltd. SAGE Publications Asia-Pacific Pte. Ltd; 2021

[35] Hair J, F Jr et al. Advanced Issues in Partial Least Squares Structural Equation Modeling. SAGE Publications; 2018

[36] Hulland J. Use of partial least squares (pls) in strategic management research: A review of four recent studies. Strategic Management Journal. 1999;**20**:195-204. DOI: 10.1002/(SICI)1097-0266(199902)20:2

[37] Roldán JL. Variance-based structural equation modeling: Guidelines for using partial least squares in information systems research. In: Research Methodologies, Innovations and Philosophies in Software Systems Engineering and Information Systems. IGI Global; 2012. pp. 193-221. DOI: 10.4018/978-1-4666-0179-6.ch010

[38] Chin WW. The partial least squares approach to structural equation modeling. In: Marcoulides GA, editor. Modern Methods for Business Research. Mahwah, NJ: Lawrence Erlbaum Associates. References - Scientific Research Publishing. [Online]. Available from: https://www.scirp.org/(S(i43dyn45teexjx455qlt3d2q))/reference/ReferencesPapers.aspx?ReferenceID=534264; 1998. pp. 295-336 [Accessed: April 7, 2022]

[39] Hamdan KM, Al-Basaireh AM, Zahran Z, Al-Daghestani A, AL-Habashneh S, Shaheen AM. University students' interaction, internet self-efficacy, self-regulation and satisfaction with online education during pandemic crises of COVID-19 (SARS-CoV-2). International Journal of Educational Management. 2021;**35**(3):713-725. DOI: 10.1108/IJEM-11-2020-0513/FULL/XML

[40] Pineda Ballesteros E, Dallos ARL, Valencia JAP. Planteamiento del problema de investigación en educación: algunas orientaciones para profesores que investigan en el aula. Plumilla Educativa. 2021;**28**(2):57-79. DOI: 10.30554/pe.2.4300.2021

[41] Ahmad T. Student perceptions on using cell phones as learning tools. PSU Research Review. 2020;**4**(1):25-43. DOI: 10.1108/PRR-03-2018-0007

Chapter 9

Perspective Chapter: New Approaches for Learning Design – Course Architecture and Media Educational Technologies

Veronika Yarnykh

Abstract

The background of this topic is the need to research the current situation in the educational market. The current state of affairs in education implies a shift in approaches to learning design and the architecture of training programs, including Massive Open Online Courses (MOOCs). Research in learning design is both theoretical and practical. An analysis of the current state of the education market, Generation Z's demands, and new requirements for educational processes makes it essential to understand the potential for change in both online and offline learning environments. This creates a new onlife reality and space that is reflected in various ways by MOOC education. In the theoretical analysis of approaches and practices, ADDIE instructional design models, Infosys 4A communication models, concepts of onlife environments as well as approaches to using media educational technologies in MOOCs, were used to understand and implement the proposals. The study identified the main factors influencing the approaches to building the architecture of the course and the learning design of the educational experience and study process. The contribution of this study to the field of knowledge about learning designs for modern MOOCs is to identify new opportunities for designing the architecture of a MOOC course, form motivational focuses for MOOC participants, and create conditions and environments within the MOOC for learning.

Keywords: learning design, instructional design, Gen Z, media educational technologies, course architecture, educational space, E-mentoring, interactive communication, MOOC

1. Introduction

The learning process has not just changed today. It is constantly changing. Many factors affect the focus of learning, how it is structured, the use of educational technology, etc. As we have already noted, today there are many factors that have a significant impact on this process. Thanks to the development of media and digital technology, the format of education is changing. MOOCs have become one of the most popular formats. They are training courses with mass interactive participation, using e-learning technology and open access through the Internet.

MOOC is a form of distance learning that is highly sought after today. The demand for distance education in both the educational and corporate sectors is conditioned by a change in the learning paradigm due to the fundamental change of generations. Within the framework of the theory of generations, Generation Y is the basis of the education market in the corporate sector, and Generation Z is in the educational sector. Despite the dissimilarities between these generations, they share common features such as a focus on digital learning technologies and distance education (exacerbated by the COVID-19 pandemic), widespread media use in education, and a focus on practical education.

For the corporate sector, MOOCs have significantly optimized training costs and shifted replicated courses with simple and easily replicable skills to a distance learning format. MOOC also provides an opportunity for individuals outside the corporate sector to independently implement the concept of lifelong learning during their lives, acquire new skills and change specializations. Given the pace of scientific and technological advancement and technological changes in both life and business, this is essential for any career path. However, the demand for distance learning forces and is highly attentive to the design of the educational process. Just putting together, a MOOC course as a learning space where all course materials are stored is simply not enough.

It seems necessary to start by understanding and defining what learning design is in modern education. There is no single well-established and established definition yet, despite the fact that the idea itself is quite old. Nevertheless, within the framework of today and the importance of learning or educational design for the education system and for the learning process as a whole, it seems necessary to focus on several definitions. Today, under the learning or instructional design, we understand the following.

First, there is the systematic process of interpretating principles of learning and instruction into plans or specifications for instruction: materials or activities [1].

Also, learning design is a systematic approach to the creation of educational solutions, which uses learning principles and theories to ensure high quality of education [2]. A more modern and voluminous definition is the understanding that learning design is a system of procedures for developing ways to deliver educational content (educational products) to students, created to help them develop the required competencies [3]. An approach that defines two key tasks in the field of modern design of the learning process is also important: combining and "synchronizing" different narrow experts on the same program, organizing their content, and observing all known rules of learning, so that it is optimal for the student [4]. Thus, learning or educational design today is an approach that "assembles" the learning process in particular, or the educational process as a whole, in such a way as to make it as effective and efficient as possible using modern technologies aimed at developing the necessary competencies. With this understanding of learning (educational) design, it becomes extremely important to understand which factors will have the maximum impact on this process.

Educational design is influenced by many factors. These include the demands of the generation, the ability to use media educational technologies, and approaches to course architecture.

Paying attention to learning design, it is also important to note the following. Educational design is of particular importance today for distance education. When in an offline format, the educator has the opportunity to closely monitor not only the progress of the student or course participant. In the offline format, all errors in the acquisition of knowledge can be seen almost in real time. In the online format today, regardless of the type of distance course, such a real-time mode in tracking errors is only possible in real time. Then, you have to resort to the approach that prevails today in corporate mobile learning [5]. M-learning is the short information block of material with instant verification through gadgets [6]. However, this approach does not work in the MOOC course. MOOC courses require more time; they are fundamental, unlike short mobile learning aimed at practicing soft skills, for example. The motivation for this study was the interest in analyzing existing experience and combining it with existing practice to understand what factors and approaches should be taken into account when designing MOOC courses today, maintaining the interest and motivation of participants on the one hand and implementing fundamental learning on the other. The experience of corporate mobile learning turned out to be a motivational trigger for the research.

The main knowledge gap in this area is the imbalance between the new requirements for the educational process of Generation Z and the previous experience of the educational system as a whole. MOOC courses, as part of distance learning and e-learning, are always fundamentally filled in terms of knowledge, but due to the format, they are technologically poor in terms of motivational tools for maintaining interest for long-term course completion [7]. Identifying opportunities and approaches and expanding the framework for finding solutions became a way to fill this gap.

The importance of this study lies in the following fact. Several numbers have important meanings. Worldwide, 49% of students have completed some sort of online learning. The online learning sector will grow to be a $240 billion dollar industry by 2022. More than 200 million learners signed up for at least one massive open online course last year. Only 60% of students are able to complete the course [8]. We see the corporate and university investments in this sphere on the one hand and not so outstanding results for completing the courses on the other one. The second factor which is important in this case. Gen Z is now changing the situation with the education process. Most researchers agree that the clip-like nature of consciousness, focus on the practical application of knowledge, unwillingness to study theoretical approaches, and digitalization of the perception of the world as a whole as factors in the behavior and perception of Generation Z have turned approaches to the learning process upside down [9]. This has become especially noticeable in the situation of traditional offline learning. Here, it was necessary to actively implement digital technologies in order to create familiarity in the educational environment [10]. As for online learning, these factors are, in some way, to some extent facilitating the learning process, but they raise the question of motivation to complete a long course and maintain interest in learning [9]. This theoretical study, supported by experience and the practice of Mongolia International University and Russian State University for Humanities, allows us to implement and offer opportunities and technologies for distance MOOC learning that will be successful in solving the above-mentioned problems.

Generations Y and Z clearly demand different requirements for both learning processes and course materials. All of this must be taken into consideration within the framework of educational design for learning processes. In the current conditions of generational change in the education market and the development of modern technologies, it seems necessary to determine what new approaches, technologies, and opportunities will be appropriate to the prevailing changes. First of all, we need to consider the need to change the learning design paradigm. How should we build educational programs? How can we combine various activities to better assimilate material? Which activities are generally appropriate for Generation Z? These questions force us to rethink the learning paradigm in a different way.

Speaking about the methodology used, it is important to pay attention to the following. Within the framework of this material, an empirical analysis of the problem and the results of the study on it was carried out. The main approaches analyzed in this study were the most famous and used theories in the framework of learning design. First of all, this is the ADDIE model, one of the oldest and most frequently used in learning design to form the learning process and course architecture [11]. Infosys 4A Model (any content anytime, anywhere, and in any device) which is response to the request of Gen Z [12]. Analyzing new approaches in the environment of modern MOOC problems, we can use the ideas of onlife reality, which is important for understanding the profits and possibilities of media technologies use [13]. Building the architecture of the MOOC course and assuming the use of media educational technologies, it is important to note the possibilities of a single educational space [14]. At the same time, speaking about the possibilities of expanding and diversifying the use of media educational technologies in general, it should be noted that it is the approach within the framework of educational design that is able to fully utilize these possibilities. A variety of digital educational technologies today (that is, the use of media space and media within a course) is becoming an everyday reality, responding, among other things, to the demand of Generation Z for new approaches to learning [15]. And finally, one such digital educational technology that is becoming the most widespread within the framework of educational design is E-mentoring [10]. As the examples of using certain models and media educational technologies given below have shown, these technologies really enrich the methodological reality of MOOC courses. Students do not simply perceive them as a familiar reality (of any digital ecosystem or communication tactics), which largely helps to keep attention on the course and ensures the passage of the material. MOOC courses differ significantly from the usual offline standards and examples of training, which also allows you to keep attention due to the novelty of the environment (onlife environment, for example). Such a combination of familiar and long-used methods and approaches of educational design and new media educational technologies, or other additional opportunities from the point of view of teaching methods, creates a new perspective for the development of MOOC courses and distance education in general.

Further, the structure of the material assumes the following division. Further, we are talking about learning design in the modern times. Here, we consider the practices of learning design that exist today and the approaches that are being implemented. We also analyze the factors that influence learning design today, and opportunities for the new approaches and technologies' implementation. Next, the MOOC course architecture in the learning design paradigm is considered. Here, the greatest attention is paid to the essence of the distance nature of MOOC courses and problems with the motivation of participants to complete the course.

The next part of the study is devoted to the influence of Gen Z in the distant learning process. Here, the factors of the educational environment and the educational process that influence the learning process of representatives of Generation Z are considered. This part of the study describes the way in which the influencing factors can be balanced by the architecture of the MOOC course and media educational technologies. Finally, the last part of the study considers and analyzes media education technologies in learning design for MOOC. It is in this part that the practice of using various educational technologies at Mongolia International University and Russian State University for Humanities is presented, and the possibilities of recommendations for the use of the declared and mentioned media educational technologies in the practice of learning design in MOOC courses are studied.

The results of the analysis are given in the conclusion of the presented material.

2. Learning design in the modern times

It is important to pay attention to the change in Generation Z's request for the learning process as a whole. The key principles of learning today are the principles of communication. Modern students (and we are talking about higher education) adhere to the principles of communication in the learning process: simple, understandable, convenient, and familiar [10]. Speaking about educational design, it is important to note the following. Instructional design is a relatively new concept in the modern education system. The need to form high-quality knowledge is constantly growing, while traditional tools are suitable for relatively simple, "linear" training methods. When creating more complex programs, the use of traditional methods leads to a loss of time and resources. As a result, the concept of pedagogical design appeared—a discipline that development teams apply at the stage of designing, creating, and evaluating educational materials. It is based on the systematic use of knowledge about effective work, building an educational process with an "open architecture," and creating a real learning environment. At the same time, the tasks of an educational designer are extensive and very difficult. First of all, this is an analysis of the needs of the target audience, its competencies, and expected learning outcomes. Then, it is necessary to talk about defining the goals and objectives of the educational material. The next stage is the analysis and structuring of materials in accordance with the goals. The choice of means and methods of educational work is also important. A mandatory stage in this case is the development of tests and assignments, control tools, and information collection. Finally, creating a distance course using appropriate tools, or assigning tasks to team members to develop specific elements. Thus, pedagogical design, being a multifaceted concept, is defined in world science on the basis of various aspects and areas of activity (pedagogical design as a science/discipline/process/reality/practice).

An important element of the paradigm is the principles of instructional design. They were developed by Gagne [16]. Among them, the following principles are distinguished. First, this is attracting the attention of students, motivating them to learn, and awakening interest in the topic and methods. The second principle is explaining the goals and objectives of learning. This not only answers the question "why?," but also forms a certain level of expectations from the results of the process itself. The third important principle is the presentation of new material. This is the most difficult part of the process, since the selectivity of perception of any new material is inherent in the human psyche. This means that it is necessary to provide for certain elements in advance that will allow you to keep the student's attention on important points and convey to him the main idea of the project in the most accessible form. An important process within the paradigm is training support. This is the management of students and the semantic formation of the installation for retaining the received material in long-term memory. Practice has also become an important element of the system of principles. It is necessary to quickly, while new knowledge is still fresh, test it in real conditions or simply confirm it with an appropriate experiment, which will clearly and very effectively link the theory and application of knowledge. Considering that communication is very important in training, the importance of feedback was specially noted. Evaluation of the selected teaching method and its effectiveness is impossible without prompt analysis. Therefore, even at the stage of course development, a maximally flexible feedback system should be laid down (the results of the analysis of the target audience and its capabilities will come in handy here). Finally, it is necessary to evaluate the learning outcomes. The last principle was the definition of metrics for assessing the effectiveness of training, which necessarily include an assessment of academic performance and an overall assessment of the effectiveness of the course. Another important component of the paradigm of principles was the translation into the practical plane, helping students retain knowledge and apply it correctly. Unlike the fifth principle, it is important to transfer practical skills to new conditions not specified by the original framework of the course. This will allow you to assess the depth of knowledge acquisition.

An equally important component of the modern paradigm of learning (instructional) design today is the very request of Generation Z for the learning process. First of all, it is important to note that the approach to learning and activity has changed dramatically. Representatives of Generation Z are primarily not focused on the future; for them, the present is much more important [17]. This means that long programs or tasks with a long deadline will not be valid for them; they simply skip deadlines. The second important point in the learning process of Gen Z is a practical approach to learning. For them, practice is much more important than theory. For them, knowledge becomes important for the implementation of practical tasks [18]. Here, the main motivator for learning becomes interest. However, it also does not always work, and everything will not always be interesting in the learning process. An equally important point was the influence of gamification in general on the learning request. It was gamification and a certain type of games popular with this generation that partially predetermined the demand for project work and a project-based approach to learning. This means that working in groups is more than familiar and convenient for representatives of this generation [10]. If we talk about learning habits, then in this context it is necessary to talk about the use of gadgets or, in general, about media technologies in education. In general, the use of media education technologies or media technologies in the learning process has been known for a long time. But, speaking of changing approaches in modern learning design, it is necessary to talk about the possibility of wider inclusion in the learning process of educational platforms for performing tests, tasks in a digital environment, etc.

The paradigm shift in educational design has gone through several stages [19].

1. Multimedia-based learning (1970–1979)

2. Transition from audiovisual to computer-based learning (1980–1989)

3. Distance and interactive learning (1990–1999)

4. Collaborative online learning and ICT in school (2000–2009)

5. Learning analytics and collaborative learning on mobile devices (2010–2018)

These stages were characterized by changes in the educational design paradigm (in the formation of the learning process, changes in the course architecture, and the emergence of media educational technologies in the design of the learning process). For example, the stage of distance and interactive learning in the corporate environment led to the massive development of mobile learning, which in turn has an impact on the educational design paradigm [6].

It is safe to say that in recent years, two factors have had a fundamentally important impact on the educational design paradigm. These are the entry of Generation Z into the educational services market and the emergence of Artificial Intelligence technologies over the last 3 years. These challenges have led to the fact that the educational design paradigm has undergone significant changes. The influence of Gen Z on the educational design paradigm and on the change in course architecture will be discussed further.

The second important factor influencing modern approaches to learning design is artificial intelligence tools. As a MIL Talk Host (as a co-leader of UNESCO's global initiative for the development of media-literate cities, I do webinars and meetings with experts from many countries and continents), I can note that last year the most popular issue, both in demand and in views, was the issue discussing Chat GPT and its role in the development of universities. During the discussion, experts from several countries and Universities (Brazil, Argentina, Mongolia, Kazakhstan) actively discussed both the ethical problems of using Chat GPT in teaching and, in general, the possibilities of using such tools.

Speaking about the development of AI technologies in education in general, it is important to pay attention to the fact that, in general, these technologies have been used for quite a long time. For example, appropriate technologies are used to analyze the behavior of students, personalize the learning process, proctor (control procedure for an online exam or test), check the level of knowledge and work of students, and perform other tasks. Nevertheless, AI technologies in general not only solve some of the problems but also form the whole directions and areas that can be included in the learning process through learning design technologies including them in the process. For example, checking educational assignments. The task of educational design is to form study assignments in such a way that it is possible to organize a quick automatic check. For example, when using MOOC (Massive Open Online Courses), AI can evaluate assignments and answer students' questions automatically, which will save a lot of time and resources. Or Google Classroom has an automatic function for checking the level of the author's text of an essay or written work of a student. For example, I use this tool to pre-check the level of the author's text in writing assignments as a professor at Mongolia International University. This helps to immediately give the student feedback if there are signs of generated text or copying of other works.

AI technologies are also already widely used for data visualization (creating infographics, for example, or bots for interactive learning). For example, bots are widely used at Anna University (Tamil Nadu, India) both for testing knowledge and for the learning process. Also, at Amrita Vishwa Vidyapeetham University (India), faculty uses AI technologies to work with a mobile application for students and University staff. This is the implementation of both informational and educational tasks. Most of the educational and training content is in the mobile application.

Finally, the gamification of the learning process as a whole is quite a popular use of AI technologies in education. Educational games allow students to put their knowledge into practice and receive feedback, which contributes to a deeper understanding of the material and the development of skills. So, at the RSUH Faculty of Journalism, start-ups were launched in the form of a game for the development of literacy and the Russian language for schoolchildren. Moreover, the creators of start-ups are the students themselves.

In short, it is important to note that AI technologies today can not only be used pointwise in the learning process, but occupy an increasingly important place both in the learning process and in the knowledge assessment process. This is important to note, because from the point of view of learning or educational design, it is necessary to include AI technologies on an ongoing basis.

Thus, for the development of the paradigm of learning design in combination with AI technologies, it is important to pay attention to the need to understand the change in the request for training from Generation Z, the change in the request for educational activity, the use of media educational technologies in the learning process, and, finally, given the widespread entry of AI technologies into our lives—also including them in the learning process.

3. MOOC course architecture in learning design paradigm

Considering the issue of changing the concept of learning design in the context of digital transformation, it is also important to note that, in today's world, learning designs must take into account several factors. These factors include the use of educational media and digital technologies in education.

The technologies used must meet certain conditions such as convenience and ease of use. We need to discuss the interfaces of these technologies and their simplicity, as well as how easy they are to master if necessary.

There are several models within learning processes and several characteristics that should be present in all of them. First and foremost, the design must be student-centered, with a focus on students' academic performance. This focus is more than just an important factor; it represents a shift in the overall paradigm of learning and the role of teachers. Secondly, learning design is goal-oriented. Clearly defined goals are essential. Thirdly, the focus of learning design is on real-world productivity. It is necessary to create conditions where students must demonstrate the behavior expected of them in real life. This is a fundamental principle that becomes crucial in competency-based learning. Developing project management and communication skills and group work abilities are crucial tasks that learning designers must take into account in the context of digital transformation.

Learning design also focuses on measurable results [3]. Creating reliable and accurate measurement tools is essential. Understanding that pedagogy is an empirical process is another crucial aspect. Data analysis forms the heart of the learning design process, and learning designs often involve teamwork. There are several models of learning design, one of which is the ADDIE model. This model is widely used and consists of five stages: analysis, design, development, implementation, and evaluation [20].

The analysis stage is crucial because it helps to determine the purpose of the course and the desired outcomes. It also helps to identify the gap between the current and desired competencies and the level of development needed to achieve them. This stage forms the basis for the path toward discipline development [20].

A key component of this stage is defining the target audience and understanding their training needs [20]. This information is essential for ensuring the relevance of the content and material in the future and integrating modern education.

Another important stage is designing the course or discipline. This involves creating a plan for teaching and learning that is aligned with the goals and objectives [21]. It also includes choosing appropriate methods and materials to support the learning process. Within the framework of this stage, the format of teaching, the formulation of educational goals, and the choice of theoretical material are determined. Teaching strategies and formats are also chosen. For example, webinars and remote consultations with teachers may be included in the E-mentoring process. Additional formats could include master classes, lectures with group work, case studies, round tables, conferences, and more.

The next stage involves the development and creation of educational materials, such as scripts, assignments, videos, texts, and tests. Next, the actual implementation of the educational process takes place, with necessary adjustments or updates to the materials. I would like to emphasize the importance of being able to update materials during the study of a discipline. It is always necessary to include relevant interviews, links to interviews, or videos, and so on. Finally, there is an evaluation of the results. The assessment provides for the correlation of set goals and training objectives with real indicators after training, which helps to evaluate the effectiveness of training and develop solutions to improve the educational course.

Like design thinking, ADDIE can be considered a model of common sense. It describes a general process that seems obvious and logical. Most models fit within the ADDIE framework to some degree, as they all include analysis, design, development, implementation, and evaluation of results. Within this approach, students can answer questions about their familiarity with media, communication, and ease of interaction in the learning environment. Additionally, an important part of learning design is the verbal involvement of students in learning in a remote format [21]. It is no secret that motivation for learning, especially for active participation in distance learning, is not only an important component, but also a significant factor in success. Several solutions are mentioned below.

4. Gen Z in distant learning process

Gen Z has had a huge impact on the state of educational design today. Its appearance on the educational market and fundamentally new requirements for the learning process have forced educators and methodologists to significantly change the paradigm of educational design.

Motivation in distance learning is a big problem. MOOC courses may have different durations, but the problem of motivating participants is still open. According to statistics, only about 5% of MOOC students complete the course. This is a frighteningly low number. If MOOC platforms are used in hybrid learning, the percentage of students who complete the task will increase significantly. However, as experience has shown, problems with deadlines, sequence, and completion of modules remain relevant. What characteristics of Generation Z shape the specifics of their motivation for learning, and what should be taken into account in the design of distance learning? The difference between Generation Z and previous generations is as follows.

First, they are children of multimedia technology. They cannot imagine life without mobile phones, and are more reliant on digital technologies because they grew up in a digitally-enabled environment, receiving almost all information from the Internet. For them, virtual reality is almost as real as physical reality. Therefore, we can speak of the "onlife reality" in which we all now live [22].

However, Generation Z, along with the mix of Generation Y and Generation Z, has adapted significantly to this online world. They spend more time in virtual worlds, communicating more with computers than with parents or each other. Online communication is becoming increasingly important. That is why, in designing and architecting the learning process, it is worthwhile to pay attention to horizontal connections and the possibility of interaction with other participants [23].

This is a generation of entertainment media, which is why students are very susceptible to gamification elements in the course or learning process. As for the cognitive sphere, Generation Z representatives easily navigate information flows and quickly analyze large volumes of information. At the same time, they have low attention concentration (8 seconds), high task-switching ability, and low attention stability [3]. Generation Z is extremely susceptible to visualized information perception [24].

Representatives of Generation Z focus on practicality, so they have a habit of multitasking, which is practical for performing several activities at once. On the other hand, they focus on the practical value of knowledge. This affects, among other things, the popularity of podcasts, both video and audio. The popularity of these podcasts is growing rapidly worldwide, with over 504.9 million people expected to listen by the end of 2024 [25]. However, clip thinking has become a meme and leads to a lack of systematic perception of information, as well as an inability to think systematically and express thoughts consistently. Imagination, reflection, and understanding of texts and others are weakened [9].

This leads to two major challenges in designing MOOC programs: the problem of lengthy texts in materials and the need to provide more concise and clear content. Course participants simply do not read the materials. We need to revise the theoretical material and use short (no more than 5–7 pages) texts. Another important thing is the use of short videos, such as TikTok videos, in the course [24]. This is consistent with the habits of visual content Generation Z. As noted, members of this generation demonstrate an increased ability for multitasking (opening several bookmarks and files simultaneously, performing several tasks), but they are less likely to be diligent, persistent, and purposeful in their work. This feature prevents many from completing the course, so it is necessary to divide course information not only into modules, but also smaller parts (as described in the course architecture). At the same time, downloading ready-made information discourages interest in independent discovery. Representatives of Generation Z are characterized by poorer memorization (compared to previous generations) and a decline in long-term memory [10]. As part of the learning design process, in order to attract attention, it is important to vividly design and emphasize all the important points in the text, create a dictionary, and so on, that is, to use the same visual aids. Students do not remember information itself, but they remember where it is located. They only recall what is relevant and has practical significance. In terms of changing the approach to learning design, we need to constantly focus on the practical application of the material, or search for and create practical examples. Taking into account all the above, within the framework of educational design, it is necessary to create the following conditions for the learning process:

1. It is necessary to abandon reproductive methods of education.

2. It is important to use media education technologies and interactive teaching methods, such as games, interactive tasks, brainstorming, and problem-solving

lectures with discussion. This should be done in an online format, using synchronous and asynchronous learning formats.

3. We see a change in the role of teachers, who now play unusual roles such as mentor, emotional leader, communicator, and navigator. They organize student interaction and help students to learn.

4. From the perspective of learning design, this involves putting into the learning process activities such as forums and chats for horizontal and vertical E-mentoring, forming project groups, and using interactivity to share knowledge. In order to ensure student independence and preserve interest and motivation, it is necessary to create a unified educational environment and use gamification elements to reward students for their achievements (while avoiding ratings). This system of encouragement allows students to maintain interest and keep moving forward. Generation Z representatives absolutely do not like negativity and only move forward with constant positive motivation [9]. As noted earlier, information should be provided in small amounts, and video materials should be short.

Speaking about the main requirements for a MOOC course from a learning design perspective, it is necessary to mention the following. As Julie Coats noted, it is necessary to structure the learning process well [26]. Modern students want to know exactly what is required of them and within what time frame. It is important to provide constant feedback and praise, even for small achievements. Some kind of allowance for excellent and simply good results works well in practice (moving the deadline depending on the outcome, etc.). This includes an element of competition by avoiding ranking. The maximum amount of time for monotonous activities should be no more than 25–30 minutes, after which the type of activity should be changed. In a synchronous hybrid learning format, a quick survey on a media platform is perfect, allowing you to consolidate material and introduce game elements into the learning experience. Information should not be repetitive. The new generation wants "concentrated" knowledge [26].

It also turned out that modern students from Generation Z cannot work without praise and rewards. The motivational success of learning, as practice shows, also consists in recognition and praise, even for some correct or correct answers during the seminar [18]. As mentioned earlier, long ideas do not work. Long motivation in this case (at least the end of the semester, for example) it is not in demand enough. Dividing the whole process into large parts, tasks become mandatory conditions of the game.

5. Media education technologies in learning design for MOOC

Within the framework of media educational technologies, media is used as a learning tool or the learning process itself takes place in a media environment. In this context, it is important to note that the very use of any media tools (e.g., Google and Moodle) is a form of media education technology.

As noted earlier, when discussing the architecture of a MOOC course, the ecosystem allows you to create a single educational space. The principles for forming a unified educational space fit fully into the modern paradigm of educational design. Given the practicality of representatives of Generation Z and their focus on concise and structured information (brief), it is necessary to structure information very clearly by sections and topics. The architecture of the space in this case may be as follows: The first level of division into studied topics. Further, within each topic, it is possible to divide materials into presentation materials (including mandatory texts from textbooks and mandatory articles for study), video materials (mandatory and optional), project assignments, a link to a final test or other format for assessing knowledge acquisition. Additional materials should be highlighted separately, such as additional videos, articles, blog posts, and so on. Given the difficulties with motivating representatives of Generation Z, it can be recommended to use clear and consistent task guidelines. It is also recommended to immediately post a link to a chat or forum for clarification. At Mongolia International University, students have access to a shared chat with their teacher, which allows them to implement the idea of horizontal E-mentoring. Students themselves answer questions from their classmates. What needs to be controlled, of course, is the quality of the content that is shared in the chat. However, it is important to also pay attention to media education technologies such as E-mentorship and student project work within the Google Classroom ecosystem.

As for E-mentoring, it should be noted that this educational and supportive technology is not new, but it certainly gained a second wind during the pandemic. The development of the mentoring system, especially in the digital environment, was primarily due to the need to implement a supportive learning function within the distance format. E-mentoring (or digital mentoring), as a media-based educational technology, allows you to solve problems both through comments on completed tasks and to support students' project work (from the teacher). However, within a single information and education space, there is also an opportunity to design and implement mentoring opportunities for groups of students. Thus, both horizontal and vertical levels of E-mentoring are implemented [27]. It is the e-format that allows providing support as quickly, comfortably, and fully as possible within the context of correspondence via Google Classroom, for example.

Another important media education technology within the framework of the paradigm shift in learning design is project work in the media space. For example, as part of the discipline "Intercultural Communications in the Media Space," students from the Faculty of Journalism at RSUH created videos about auto- and hetero-stereotypes. This was group project work. All work, discussions, scriptwriting, etc., took place within a unified information and learning environment. The results were published there. This approach allows group work to be converted into a digital format that is convenient and comfortable for Generation Z and the combination of Generations Z and Y. It greatly simplifies student communication, on the one hand, while giving them the opportunity to collaborate in the digital space, receive E-mentor support, and discuss scripting or filming options in a familiar format. Another example of project group work was the preparation of presentations based on the results of a mini-study within the framework of the discipline. The assignment included topics on the use of stereotypes in the modern media environment, as well as recommendations for practical use in the business sphere. The preparation of this assignment involved group work over a period of time. Group project work involves the development of several important types of competencies. These are communication competencies, project work skills, and project management in a digital environment. For Generation Z, it becomes important to adhere to the following principles in communication and pedagogy: convenience, comfort, familiarity, and simplicity. For training, the practicality of the acquired knowledge, skills, and abilities is added.

An important component of the approach to educational design in this case is interactivity with students, both in the traditional learning format and through distance learning. Interactivity also becomes an extremely important aspect in a mixed-mode learning environment, where some students are physically present in the classroom, and others are online for various reasons. In this type of blended learning, it is essential to create an interactive space for collaboration.

Within the framework of educational design, several technologies can be used to facilitate interaction while not interfering with the learning experience. One of the tools for forming and developing collaboration in an interactive environment is the use of an interactive media whiteboard (Jamboard). First of all, such an interactive whiteboard on any media platform allows individuals or groups to work remotely or in a classroom in both individual and group formats. Participants in the process can immediately see the work of the whole group and generate ideas during the process. Feedback and analysis of results is possible not only from teachers but also from the group itself, which is a plus. Students can see the entire landscape of opinions, ideas, and practices at once as a group. Another advantage is that the results of group work can be saved in the educational ecosystem and reused by students if needed. In this case, any MOOC education ecosystem can be used (Moodle, Google, etc.).

The second important point is the possibility of developing communication skills, group work skills, analysis and presentation of results, etc. The second important tool for implementing interactivity in the knowledge control process is rapid surveys (quizzes) on specialized media resources, such as Mentimetr and Ahaslides. A quick survey at the beginning or end of a lesson allows you to quickly assess the group's level of knowledge. This is a traditional approach. Such surveys are an unobtrusive element of edutainment, allowing us to engage participants in the learning process and create a sense of team spirit.

An important media educational technology in the educational design paradigm is the Infosys BMP 4A Model (any content anytime, anywhere, any device) [12]. In short, this model appeared in 2010 [28]. Initially, it was aimed at interacting with clients on social media and included social media content. However, with the expansion of the number of young millennials in the educational market, accustomed to the fact that companies communicate with them anywhere and anytime, the 4A model became popular in the educational space. It was for various types of distance learning (e-learning, MOOC courses, and mobile learning especially) that the model turned out to be most in demand. This media technology solved several problems. First of all, it was aimed at the availability of educational content, which means it methodically ensured the asynchrony and synchrony of learning. This approach also allowed the student to study the course at his or her own pace. And finally, it ensured the convenience of seamless course completion on any device.

Why is it so important to pay attention to this model when designing a MOOC course? First of all, it is necessary to recall the principles of learning for Generation Z—familiar, convenient, comfortable, and simple [10]. Based on these principles, we have to admit that within the framework of a MOOC course on any platform, it is necessary not only to ensure the availability of educational content but also to make it technologically convenient for tablets and mobile devices, for example. A good example is the use of this 4A model in the Duolingo learning process. This content can not only be studied on any type of gadget. Within the media platform, all student achievements and the sequence of the entire course of study are visible. There are elements of competition, and the principles of E-mentoring are implemented. Duolingo has a mobile application and a website. As you can see, a practically completely modern paradigm of educational design has been implemented.

6. Conclusions

In conclusion, the following should be noted. Modern media education is undergoing a major transformation, influenced by new technologies and changes in the education market due to Generation Z. Generation Z has not just brought new demand for structure, dynamics, and tools in the educational process but also fundamental changes in pedagogical approaches to educational programs. First, it is important to understand that the changes in educational space as a whole have been significant. There are two main reasons for this, in my opinion: the dominant role of Generation Z and the mix of Generations Z and Y in the market, with a paradigm shift in training and an increased role of media and technology in learning processes. These factors become key for distance education in MOOC format and carry the greatest risk. The specifics of Generation Z make it necessary to simplify materials, use visualization extensively, and reduce course durations, without relying on long-term motivation. Focusing on simplicity, convenience, and familiarity with the environment forces us to strike a balance between student motivation and methodological learning opportunities. This balance becomes the foundation for the design of educational MOOC programs. The main risk and main challenge of distance education is a change in the learning paradigm. Student-centeredness is not just a demand from a new generation, but it fundamentally changes the role of educators. In this context, it seems necessary to expand tools for educators' new activities—such as mentoring and coaching. This can be done through specially provided consultations on media platforms or MOOC platforms, active promotion of chat use, or built-in group tools, and other opportunities for interactive interaction. Similar consultations can also be provided after the survey results. For example, at Mongolia International University, I have added a link to my email and internal chat to allow students to ask questions. However, it is also important to understand other things. The modern paradigm of education and the student-centered learning process significantly increases the load on educators, both during the preparation of materials and in the learning process. Distance education and its implementation through MOOC platforms do not reduce but significantly increase educators' time employment and involvement. The answer to the need for a new training request, including in a remote format on MOOC platforms, lies in the use of educational media terminology. As has already been noted, media educational technologies include the use of media in the learning process (video, etc.) as well as working in a media environment. For example, working with media platforms (conducting surveys and testing on media platforms). Generation Z is really more comfortable, clear, and familiar with the media environment, which means it is more convenient for this generation to learn and communicate there. In this respect, MOOCs in a distant format really meet demand and partially solve the problem of learning motivation. Also, using a media-rich environment helps solve the problems of long-term learning and achieving results. Breaking down the course into smaller theoretical pieces with immediate feedback, elements of mobile learning allow us to gradually progress toward the goal. At the same time, one of the main media technologies is the creation of a unified educational space in the course. The placement of all the necessary materials, the ability to instantly verify knowledge (slice of knowledge), and the opportunity for an individual student to return to certain materials create a feeling of familiarity. All of this is similar to your favorite media platform, such as Instagram, etc. It creates a familiar environment that works both for motivation and moving forward. Also, it is necessary to remember 3A rule: content must be accessible at anytime, anywhere, and in any form. Everything from the field of Internet marketing is used in distance education, including the use of video materials that are also familiar to students. Finally, interactive surveys and the use of suitable media platforms introduce gamification elements into the learning process. Thus, it is necessary to emphasize once again that a paradigm shift in educational design allows us to solve all the above-mentioned tasks and create a course within the framework of MOOC, which will be equally demanded by students in different forms of tertiary or secondary education.

Author details

Veronika Yarnykh
Mongolia International University, Ulaanbaatar, Mongolia

*Address all correspondence to: vyarnykh@gmail.com

References

[1] Scholes V. Trade-offs in a new instructional design for online distance learning: Home-supported time on task versus autonomy. In: Applied Ethics for Instructional Design and Technology. Open Polytechnic; 2023. p. 105

[2] Stripe K, Simpson-Bergel E. (Re) defining learning design: A framework fit for the twenty-first century. Compass: Journal of Learning and Teaching in Higher Education. 2023;**16**(2):121-136. DOI: 10.21100/compass.v16i2.1435

[3] Turton C. How learning development and learning design can inform each other: Reflections and discussion points. Journal of Learning Development in Higher Education. 2023;**29**:1-6. DOI: 10.47408/jldhe.vi29.1080

[4] Hokanson B, Clinton G, Tracey M. The Design of Learning Experience: Creating the Future of Educational Technology. Springer; 2015. DOI: 10.1007/978-3-319-16504-2

[5] De la Torre S. Mobile Learning and the Corporate Training Revolution, September, 6, 2024—[Electronic access]. 2024. Available from: https://www.iseazy.com/blog/advantages-of-mobile-learning-in-online-education/

[6] Rangel-de Lazaro G, Duart J. Moving learning: A systematic review of mobile learning applications for online higher education. Journal of New Approaches in Educational Research. 2023;**12**(2):198-224. DOI: 10.7821/naer.2023.7.1287

[7] León-Urritia M, Cobos R, Dickens K. MOOCs and their influence on higher education institutions: Perspectives from the insiders. Journal of New Approaches in Educational Research. 2018;7(1):40-45. DOI: 10.7821/naer.2018.1.252

[8] Carlton G. 2024 Online Learning Statistics. Forbes Advisor. August 23, 2024—[Electronic Access]. 2024. Available from: https://www.forbes.com/advisor/education/online-colleges/online-learning-stats/

[9] Elayan MB. The new world of work and digital learning: Millennials and generation Z. Webology. 2022;**19**(2):4593-4603. Available from: https://www.webology.org/. ISSN: 1735-188X

[10] Yarnykh VI. Pedagogical design of the specialization process of students of the journalism faculty of the Russian State University for the Humanities. In: Yarnykh VI, editor. Journalism of the Digital era: Anthropological turn: Collection of Materials of the All-Russian Scientific and Practical Conference with International Participation (Ekaterinburg, April 14-15, 2022). Yekaterinburg: Publishing House of the Ural University; 2022. pp. 99-101

[11] Wasson B, Kirschner PA. Learning design: European approaches. TechTrends. 2020;**64**(815):827

[12] Tucker R, Morris G. Anytime, anywhere, anyplace: Articulating the meaning of flexible delivery in built environment education. British Journal of Educational Technology. 2010;**42**:904-915. DOI: 10.1111/j.1467-8535.2010.01138.x

[13] Floridi L. The Onlife Manifesto: Being Human in a Hyperconnected Era. Springer Open; 2015. 520 p. DOI: 10.1007/978-3-319-04093-6

[14] Papaioannou G, Volakaki M-G, Kokolakis S, Vouyioukas D. Learning spaces in higher education:

A state-of-the-art review. Trends in Higher Education. 2023;**2**(3):526-545. DOI: 10.3390/higheredu2030032

[15] Haleem A, Javaid M, Qadri MA, Suman R. Understanding the role of digital technologies in education: A review. Sustainable Operations and Computers. 2022;**3**:275-285. DOI: 10.1016/j.susoc.2022.05.004. ISSN 2666-4127

[16] Gagne RM, Wager WW, Golas KC, Keller JM. Principles of Instructional Design. Performance Improvement. 2004;**44**(2):44-46. DOI: 10.1002/pfi.4140440211

[17] Kohnová L, Papula J, Salajová N. Generation Z: Education in the World of Digitization for the Future of Organizations. In: INTED2021 Proceedings. 2021. pp. 10199-10208. DOI: 10.21125/inted.2021.2126

[18] Aniella SM, Palvinderjit K. Digitizing the teaching process to best meet the needs of generation Z a study in understanding the importance of digitizing education to match gen Z needs. International Journal of Scientific & Technology Research. 2020;**9**(01):3213-3216

[19] Spatioti AG, Kazanidis I, Pange J. A comparative study of the ADDIE Instructional Design Model in distance education. Information. 2022;**13**(9):402. DOI: 10.3390/info13090402

[20] Tu J-C, Zhang X, Zhang X-Y. Basic courses of design major based on the ADDIE model: Shed light on response to social trends and needs. Sustainability. 2021;**13**:1-22. DOI: 10.3390/su13084414

[21] Murdoch M, Muller T. The Learning Explosion: 9 Rules to Ignite Your Virtual Classrooms. UK: Franklin Covey; 2011. 195 p. ISBN 13: 9781936111213

[22] Yarnykh VI. Modern media education technologies in master's programs in journalism education. Pedagogical Journal. 2021;**11**(6-1):497-503. DOI: 10.34670/AR.2021.38.14.067. EDN TBCWWJ

[23] Shorey S, Chan V, Rajendran P, Ang EN. Learning styles, preferences and needs of generation Z healthcare students: Scoping review. Nurse Education in Practice. 2021;**57**:103247

[24] Veřmiřovský J. The importance of visualisation in education. In: E-learning & Lifelong Learning. Monograph. Sc. Editor Eugenia Smyrnova-Trybulska. Katowice-Cieszyn: Studio Noa for University of Silesia in Katowice; 2013. pp. 453-463. ISBN: 978-83-60071-66-3

[25] Singh S. Podcast Statistics 2024 (Number of Listeners & Trends). DemandSage. July 23, 2024—[Electronic Access]. 2024. Available from: https://www.demandsage.com/podcast-statistics/

[26] Coates J. Generational Learning Styles. UK: LERN Books; 2006. 149 p

[27] Gottlieb M, Fant A, King A, et al. One click away: Digital mentorship in the modern era. Cureus. 2017;**9**(11):e1838. 1-7. DOI: 10.7759/cureus.1838

[28] Onjewu A-KE, Godwin ES, Azizsafaei F, Appiah D. The influence of technology use on learning skills among generation Z: A gender and cross-country analysis. Industry and Higher Education. 2024:1-19. DOI: 10.1177/09504222241263227

Chapter 10

Perspective Chapter: Collaborative Learning Benefits and Its Role in Critical Thinking

Zanub Ansari and Sabila Naseer

Abstract

"Collaborative Learning" is instructional method in which students of diverse performance levels engage and work communally in small groups to achieve common goals or to find collective solution of particular problem. At current time, our education system and learning process are not limited to individualized approach but have extended to collaborative learning, including mutual activities. This chapter highlights different types of collaborative learning, such as Think-Pair-Share, Problem-Based Learning, Guided Designs, Case Studies, Simulations, Peer Teaching, Small Group Discussion, Peer Editing, Jigsaw Strategy, Using Roles in Group Work, Catch Up, Fishbowl Debates, Team-Based Learning, Number Heads Together, and Concept Mapping. Further benefits of collaborative learning have been discussed in learning process, as it is a kind of relationship among students who foster positive interdependence, individual accountability, interpersonal skills, development of higher-level thinking, communication skills, self-management, leadership skills, and most significantly critical thinking. Critical thinking involves asking appropriate questions, gathering and creatively sorting relevant information, relating new information to existing knowledge, reexamining beliefs, reasoning logically, and drawing reliable conclusions. After reviewing scientific papers, importance of collaborative learning is highlighted, so that policymakers can bring fruitful changes to make addition of collaborative projects and activities in education system. Particularly, promotion of student's interaction in groups as well as interaction among students and faculty is increased; this will cause student retention and enhance their self-esteem and responsibility.

Keywords: collaborative learning, types of collaborative learning, benefits of collaborative learning, critical thinking, role of collaborative learning in critical thinking

1. Introduction

Collaboration is one of the requisites for every human being, as humans are social beings, they need to interact with others, support each other, and work together. This is why collaboration is essential in learning activities as well [1]. For learning, whenever students work together they are not just absorbing what the teacher is saying;

rather they are actively participating in the process [2]. In collaborative learning, each individual has a responsibility to hold. They share knowledge, generate ideas more comfortably, and resolve issues together with group members [3, 4]. Individuals depend on each other to gain new knowledge, support each other in learning process, and do not feel isolated [4, 5]. When participants perform tasks in groups, collaborative learning helps to preserve more information and helps them to develop a comprehensive understanding of course material [6]. In collaborative learning, students are not relying merely on ideas or information but they are rather innovating with the help of ideas and information [7]. Hence, group learning becomes more meaningful and productive [8].

Collaborative learning is known by many names i.e. learning in community, team learning, cooperative learning, and others but all of these serve a common goal i.e. working in group [9]. Collaborative learning is a kind of learning and teaching method, which brings together two or more students, with different aptitudes and skills, on a single table to work together and engage in learning [4, 5, 10]. Collaborative learning is a learning strategy in which learners engaged in shared task with similar or dissimilar characteristics to accomplish indirect or definite shared learning objective [11]. In collaborative learning, two or more students in a class work together and divide workload equally to complete the task, which is specifically designed to meet certain learning outcomes [12]. Collaborative learning is one of the learning strategies that put students in learning process as active subjects and they learn as well as teach from one another by group collaboration [13]. Furthermore, collaborative learning is a form of learning in which students work collectively to resolve issue or attain shared goal through dialog, knowledge sharing, and mutual construction [14].

Concluding upon the definitions mentioned above, collaborative learning is an approach to education where students work in groups to accomplish shared objectives, share knowledge, and learn from each other through discussions, debates, cooperation, and interaction.

Social interdependence theory and Vygotsky's sociocultural theory are two major theoretical perspectives that explain the effectiveness of collaborative learning. According to social interdependence theory, when individuals work mutually to get a common goal, they are more likely to achieve that goal rather than working individually. According to social interdependence theory, collaborative learning fosters positive interdependence in group members, which motivates them to work harder and be more committed to learning. Vygotsky's sociocultural theory is another perspective that supports collaborative learning. According to this theory, knowledge is built via social interaction and learning is a cultural and social activity [15].

2. Objectives of the study

Several researches have been carried out to illustrate the various forms of collaborative learning and their numerous advantages for educational institutions as well as students' learning processes. The current chapter devotes a lot of space to discussing collaborative learning, including its main applications and advantages in critical thinking.

This study/chapter's primary goal was determined after examining a number of standard research papers and scientific publications, especially those from the most recent years.

1. To provide more detail on the collaborative learning concept.

2. To assess the various forms of collaborative learning.

3. To look for the advantages of collaborative learning, especially in critical thinking.

3. Method

The 24 most recent studies were chosen for evaluation in order to determine the benefits of collaborative learning and its role in critical learning. The review procedure was directed by a Systematic and Tripartite Approach (STA) [16]. By using content analysis, the data were examined.

4. Results

Collaborative learning is very important in learning process of the students. After reviewing the diverse latest research papers, it has been explored that many forms of collaborative learning are intended to help students develop their communication, critical thinking, and teamwork skills. Each strategy has distinct benefits of its own, and teachers are free to select the one that best suits the needs and learning objectives of their students [15]. After systematically reviewing the empirical research, various forms of collaborative learning and their advantages for the learning process were identified. In particular, the major role that collaborative learning plays in critical thinking was examined in several studies.

4.1 Types of collaborative learning

4.1.1 Think-Pair-Share

The cooperative learning model Think-Pair-Share (TPS) is one of the learning models that best fits the characteristics of the student. This is one cooperative learning model that allows students to learn and work together in cooperative groups. According to Nasution and Surya [17], the Think-Pair-Share method allows students to work both independently and collaboratively. This method works well for assisting students in identifying and comprehending challenging ideas, developing critical thinking abilities, and assisting friends in discussing their issues. Students converse with one another about the answers to questions during Think-Pair-Share. The instructor poses a question to the class and allots a predetermined amount of time for each student to respond. Subsequently, the instructor instructs the pupils to face their neighbor and engage in a conversation about their response [17]. Pupils are given time to talk with their partners about their responses. In the event that the answers differ, one partner will attempt to persuade the other that his response is the right one [18]. Think-Pair-Share is a low-effort, low-stakes method for brief collaboration and active learning. Students are expected to work independently, share their work with peers, think about what their peers have to say, and share in a way that starts to synthesize an exchange. Calling on random pairs indicates that the majority of the pairs should be ready, even though it is unlikely that every pair in the class will get the chance for the final step. In order to participate in Think-Pair-Share, students must do more than just listen.

4.1.2 Problem-based learning

In order to encourage critical thinking and problem-solving in real-world learning environments, problem-based learning, or PBL, has been widely implemented in a variety of fields and educational contexts [19]. PBL, or problem-based learning, presents a particular problem to students over an extended period of time, usually in groups. It demands that they comprehend the problem and start to suggest a response or solution. PBL starts to resemble the kind of work that academics do (consider the "problem" as a type of research question) and the kind of problem-solving that students might have to do in their postsecondary careers [20].

4.1.3 Guided designs

One kind of problem-based learning (PBL) is guided designs, which walk students through an assignment as they work on it. Thus, for example, teams could conduct preliminary research and submit their findings simultaneously, identify stakeholders and submit their findings concurrently, suggest compromises and submit their findings at the same time, and so on [21].

4.1.4 Case studies

Using this method, a group of students is presented with a real-life scenario or problem, and they collaborate to analyze it and come up with potential solutions. This method fosters teamwork and collaboration while assisting students in strengthening their decision-making and problem-solving abilities [15].

4.1.5 Simulations

In simulations, students take on roles and carry out the tasks of a group that solves problems. For instance, in a zoning dispute, students studying politics and government could pretend to be neighborhood activists, city council members, and business owners [22].

4.1.6 Peer teaching

Students can learn new concepts very effectively through peer teaching, both as learners and as teachers. Peer teaching includes things like tutoring or guiding the learning of a less experienced student. An informal discussion in which a student clarifies any misunderstandings or provides an explanation of a concept could serve as this. Supplementary instruction is the extra guidance students receive throughout a course from a secondary source (like a tutor). Students are expected to effectively communicate course material to their peers during presentations. This necessitates going beyond simply restating or summarizing the day's readings [23].

4.1.7 Small group discussion

Small group discussions give students the ability to teach, listen, and engage with peers. Clear instructions and the request for students to present a product—a consensus view with minority report, a summary of the discussion, or even a criticism of the discussion prompt—are the foundation of an effective small group discussion [24].

4.1.8 Peer editing

Students are guided by their peers when they edit each other's written drafts. Both editors (who need to learn how to read critically and communicate criticism) and writers (who need to learn how to take in, assess, and incorporate feedback) can benefit from this foundational knowledge of academic writing craft. Instead of just asking students to read and evaluate writing (e.g., have them identify a thesis statement and assess the strength of the writer's evidence), clearly state expectations when requiring peer editing [25].

4.1.9 Jigsaw strategy

The jigsaw strategy divides tasks into manageable chunks and distributes them to teams so that each one can complete a piece of the puzzle by reporting back. For instance, each student in a group might be given a different article to read about a common subject or problem; each student would then summarize all of the articles by presenting them to the group [26].

4.1.10 Using roles in group work

Group roles can be assigned by instructors to improve organization and student participation in cooperative learning activities. Group responsibilities can help students stay on task and encourage accountability [27]. Below are a few instances of group roles:

4.1.10.1 Manager or facilitator

Oversees the group by assisting in keeping everyone on topic, maintaining focus, and allowing space for everyone to participate in the discussion.

4.1.10.2 Recorder

Maintains a list of everyone who was a part of the group and their roles within it. Important details from the small group discussion are also recorded by the recorder, along with any conclusions or responses.

4.1.10.3 Spokesperson or presenter

Shares the ideas with the class as a whole. The recorder's notes should serve as the spokesperson's guide when preparing their report.

4.1.10.4 Reflector or strategy analyst

Monitors group dynamics and directs the process of reaching a consensus (assists in reaching a shared understanding).

4.1.11 Catch up

When some students in a group find it difficult to follow the material, they can employ this strategy. Pupils who are struggling to catch up can cooperate with those who already understand. This tactic supports more advanced students by reinforcing the material and aiding struggling students [15].

4.1.12 Fishbowl debates

With this method, a small group of students sits in the middle of the classroom and converses or debates while the other students listen. Students will take turns role-playing after a set amount of time so that everyone can contribute to the discussion. This tactic encourages critical thinking and attentive listening [15].

4.1.13 Team-based learning

With this approach, students are divided into teams and given tasks or problems to solve collaboratively. Every team member has distinct duties and responsibilities, and in order to accomplish a common objective, the team must cooperate. This tactic fosters leadership, communication, and critical thinking abilities [15].

4.1.14 Numbered heads together

Members of learning groups, which usually consist of four individuals, note 1, 2, 3, or 4. The teacher poses a question that usually requires some higher-order thinking skills but is truthful in nature. Students discuss the question and confirm that everyone in the group is aware of the agreed-upon solution. The instructor requests a specific number; which is primarily assigned by colleagues who act as group spokespersons during the make-note reaction. Everyone on the team has a stake in knowing the right response because nobody knows the number the teacher will call [28].

4.1.15 Concept mapping

Concept mapping is a cooperative learning approach that allows students to map out the relationships between concepts or terms covered in the course material in groups. The method is as follows:

- Students write terms from the seminar on a large sheet of paper.

- To illustrate the relationships between terms, lines connecting specific terms are drawn. The majority of terms in an idea guide have multiple meanings.

- Students must identify and categorize data and establish significant connections between the disparate pieces of information in order to construct an idea guide [28].

Furthermore, talking chips, send-a-problem, buzz group, note taking pairs, learning cell, drill-review pairs, round table, thinking aloud pair problem-solving, etc., are also some collaborative learning strategies used in classrooms.

5. Benefits of collaborative learning

Collaborative learning can take many forms, such as group projects, discussions, and debates. Individuals are urged to express their ideas, listen to others, and cooperate to achieve a common objective. Additionally, as it improves their capacity for problem-solving, collaboration, and communication, students gain a deep comprehension of the material being studied [15]. Collaborative learning proponents point out that student's interest in learning increases when they actively negotiate, share, and discuss ideas in groups [9]. In contrast to individual learning, collaborative learning enhances student's participation, conceptual understanding, skill development, socialization, and creative problem-solving [29]. In collaborative learning, students collaborate to solve obstacles, interact with peers, develop the responsibility for learning, and exercise reasoning and metacognitive skills [4].

Moreover, collaborative learning promotes peer interactions. For an individual learner, active interaction improves the process of knowledge formation. Active learning happens when students actively contribute to knowledge creation rather than merely receiving information taught by the instructor. Active interactions are done by discussing, debating, inquiring, explaining to one another, and actively engaging in information formation processes [30]. Subsequently, collaborative learning builds important communication and interpersonal skills that assist student's transition into or advance their professional careers [31].

In collaborative learning, thinking process is involved because different members discuss in groups; this encourages them to discover different ideas to gain understanding and to develop higher-order thinking skills [32]. Students who participate in collaborative learning are also better able to settle disputes amicably. They must be instructed in the art of refuting notions and defending opinions without making them seem personal [33]. Previous researchers reported over 50 benefits of collaborative learning [34, 35]; later these benefits were categorized into four categories i.e. social benefits, psychological benefits, academic benefits, and assessment; the detail of each benefit is given below [36]:

5.1 Social benefits

- Learning communities are created through collaborative learning.
- It also helps students create a network of social support.
- It fosters understanding between students and staff.
- It creates a supportive environment for modeling and practicing cooperation.

5.2 Psychological benefits

- Collaborative learning fosters positive attitudes toward teachers;
- Cooperative learning lowers anxiety.
- Student-centered instruction boosts students' self-esteem.

5.3 Academic benefits

- Large lectures can be personalized.
- Collaborative learning models appropriate for student problem-solving techniques.
- It actively involves students in the learning process.
- It improves classroom results.
- It is particularly useful in motivating students in particular curriculum areas.

5.4 Alternate student and teacher assessment techniques

A range of assessments are used in collaborative teaching methods. Subsequent research revealed that students who are able to learn independently are highly motivated and enjoy learning more [37]. This could be the reason why study group participation improves students' self-esteem, self-control, problem-solving, and decision-making skills. They eventually grow to love learning new things and discover what inspires them to keep learning [38, 39]. In light of these advantages, collaborative learning is preferred over competitive and individualistic approaches. It usually leads to increased productivity and achievement as well as more devoted, caring, and supportive relationships as well as improved psychological well-being, social competence, and self-esteem [36].

6. Critical thinking

Critical thinking is a term, which is used not only in learning but also in various situations that involve decision-making, information processing, problem-solving, and learning [9]. Critical thinking is considered as a skill to query, infer, evaluate, reason, and make informed decisions and judgments [4]. Howard et al. [40] described critical thinking is deemed as thinking process of using one's judgments, knowledge, and reflective experiences [40]. In such thinking process, an individual is competent enough to justify problems, recognize interrelationships between problem and its related components, validate and analyze facts in relation to problem, and infer a convincing conclusion, so that the problem could be resolved, and proper inferences of what to do in future can be made [4, 40].

7. Role of collaborative learning in critical thinking

Collaborative learning is one of the educational approaches in which students discuss ideas, learn from each other, and solve problems together by working in groups. Through active participation, collaboration, and communication, this strategy helps students develop their critical thinking abilities. Students come across a variety of ideas and perspectives when working in groups, which challenges their preconceptions and compels them to consider the topic more carefully. Students can develop their ability to analyze arguments, make wise decisions, and critically evaluate information through debates and discussions [15]. Thus for improving learners' critical skills, collaborative learning has a positive impact [41, 42]. Furthermore, collaborative learning is considered to be helpful for advancing critical studying skills e.g. decision-making, problem-solving, higher-order metacognitions, and critical thinking, which cause motivation in learning, prompts students' involvement, positive attitudes, deeper learning, and eventually improves the academic performance [41]. So, in order to enhance the critical thinking skills collaborative learning is beneficial.

8. Factors influencing the effectiveness of collaborative learning

Several factors influence the effectiveness of collaborative learning, such as the size and composition of group, complexity of task, teacher facilitation, student's motivation, classroom environment, and cultural norm [15].

8.1 Group size

Smaller groups (typically 3–5 students) are often more effective for collaborative learning. They allow greater engagement and interaction among students, which directs to deeper learning experience.

8.2 Group composition

Group composition impact the efficiency of collaborative learning. When forming groups, it's essential to consider factors like student's learning styles, ability level, and cultural background to ensure everyone can contribute and benefit from the group work.

8.3 Task complexity

Collaborative learning is more effective when the given task is complex and demands critical thinking. Such tasks promote cooperation among students to resolve the complexity and increase their critical thinking skills.

8.4 Teacher facilitation

The teacher's facilitating role is very crucial in collaborative learning. The teacher should monitor group progress, provide clear instructions, guidance, and give feedback to keep all the students engaged.

8.5 Student's motivation

Student's motivation plays a key role in the effectiveness of collaborative learning. Teachers can boost motivation by assigning challenging and meaningful tasks, fostering optimistic classroom culture, rewarding and recognizing student's contributions.

8.6 Class environment

The inclusive and supportive classroom environment impacts the efficiency of collaborative learning. It promotes optimistic student's interactions and increase social adaptability.

8.7 Cultural norms

The effectiveness of collaborative learning is influenced by cultural norms. It is necessary to acknowledge cultural differences and give opportunity to students so as to facilitate them in sharing their experiences and perspectives inclusively and respectfully.

9. Barriers in implementing collaborative learning

Despite several benefits of collaborative learning, certain barriers may still affect its accomplishment and efficacy. Some obstacles relevant to collaborative learning are given below:

9.1 Difficulties in distributing tasks and responsibilities

In collaborative learning, duties should be divided fairly and equitably among group members; however, it can be challenging to assign duties and responsibilities in a way that takes into account the skills and abilities of each group member. As a result of this, members of the group may feel treated unfairly and unsatisfied.

9.2 Problems in time management

In collaborative learning, time management difficulties often arise, particularly if group members have disparate schedules. This may result in poorly completed or incomplete assignments.

9.3 Problems in communication

In collaborative learning, group members' ability to communicate effectively is essential. However, communication issues can occasionally arise, including misinterpretations of information, disregard for divergent viewpoints, and ineffective communication skills.

9.4 Lack of student engagement

While the goal of collaborative learning is to boost student participation, there are situations in which students must take an active role in group projects. This may highlight the value of collaboration and the requirement for increased incentive to fulfill tasks and obligations. Effective collaboration requires that each member of the group understand their specific roles and responsibilities. But in group activities, it's often necessary to have defined roles and duties, so each member of the group must decide what to do.

Barriers in implementing collaborative learning must be overcome so that it can run efficiently and give students maximum benefits. To overcome the barriers, one should strengthen one's awareness regarding the importance of collaboration, giving adequate resources, describing clear responsibilities/tasks and roles, promoting an inclusive culture, and encouraging student involvement [15].

DOI: http://dx.doi.org/10.5772/intechopen.1007316

10. Conclusion

Collaborative learning is one of the educational approaches in which students discuss ideas, share information, solve problems, and learn from each other by working together in a group. This assists the students to develop a deeper understanding regarding any matter as it encourages active participation among students. When students work in groups, they share different ideas, thoughts, and opinions, which sometimes cause intellectual disagreements as well as disharmony in groups; but as a result of this, students learn how to solve issues/conflicts, how to communicate effectively, and how to work with individuals of different backgrounds. As these skills are vital not only in educational settings but also in workplace and everyday life. When students are engaged in collaborative learning, they involve themselves in a learning process as how to analyze arguments, their ideas and thoughts become clearer via debates and discussion, they resolve issues/problems and make decisions; hence, they develop good problem-solving and critical thinking skills. Thus overall, it is deduced that, collaborative learning as compared to individualistic learning has countless benefits so it is necessary for educational platforms to practice collaborative learning to achieve its various benefits.

Acknowledgements

Even though the institutions did not provide us with any funding, we still acknowledge contribution to the institutions. Our environments at the Universities of Gujrat, Gujrat, Pakistan, and Narowal, Pakistan, provide us with the opportunity to contribute to this chapter while handling other professional obligations. We dedicate this work to our friends, instructors, and parents who always supported us in writing creatively for the community.

Conflict of interest

No conflicts of interest have been declared by the writers.

Notes/thanks/other declarations

We are grateful to our families and the universities that supported us in contributing to this chapter in the top publication in the world: University of Gujrat, Gujrat, Pakistan; and University of Narowal, Narowal, Pakistan. We also express our gratitude to the "Intech Open" publisher and its staff, who provided us with this chance and helped us at every turn when we needed it.

Acronyms and abbreviations

TPS	Think-Pair-Share
PBL	problem-based learning

Author details

Zanub Ansari[1*] and Sabila Naseer[2]

1 Department of Psychology, University of Gujrat, Gujrat, Pakistan

2 Allied Sciences Department, University of Narowal, Narowal, Pakistan

*Address all correspondence to: zanub.mphil14@gmail.com; zanub.ansari@gmail.com

References

[1] Koesnandar A. Pembelajaran Kolaboratif di Era dan Pasca Pandemi, Mengapa Tidak? 2021. Available from: https://pusdatin.kemdikbud.go.id/pembelajarankolaboratif-di-era-dan-pasca-pandemi-mengapa-tidak/

[2] Sidgi LFS. The benefits of using collaborative learning strategy in higher education. International Journal of English Literature and Social Sciences. 2022;**7**(6):217-224

[3] Koretsky MD, Vauras M, Jones C, Iiskala T, Volet S. Productive disciplinary engagement in high- and low-outcome student groups: Observations from three collaborative science learning contexts. Research in Science Education, Supplement. 2021;**1**(1):159-182. DOI: 10.1007/s11165-019-9838-8

[4] Warsah I, Morganna R, Uyun M, Hamengkubuwono, Afandi M. The impact of collaborative learning on learners' critical thinking skills. International Journal of Instruction. 2021;**14**(2):443-460. DOI: 10.29333/iji.2021.14225a

[5] Dewi CA, Erna MM, Haris I, Kundera IN. The effect of contextual collaborative learning based ethnoscience to increase student's scientific literacy ability. Journal of Turkish Science Education (TUSED). 2021;**18**(3):525-541

[6] McHugh D, Hall JM, McLeod KM, Kovelowski CJ, Payne AM. Twelve tips for developing and implementing curriculum in dedicated collaborative classroom. Medical Teacher. 2020;**42**(3):266-271

[7] Morgan BM. Cooperative learning in higher education: Undergraduate student reflections on group examinations for group grades. College Student Journal. 2003;**37**(1):40-50

[8] Azar AS, Keat OB, Arutus JS. Collaborative learning in the classroom: The study of Malaysian university students' attitude. Ilkogretim Online-Elementary Education Online. 2021;**20**(4):272-284

[9] Mandusic D, Blaskovic L. The impact of collaborative learning to critically thinking. Trakia Journal of Sciences. 2015;**13**(1):426-428

[10] Hadwin AF, Bakhtiar A, Miller M. Challenges in online collaboration: Effects of scripting shared task perceptions. International Journal of Computer-Supported Collaborative Learning. 2018;**13**(3):301-329

[11] Strijbos JW. Assessment of collaborative earning. In: Brown GTL, Harris L, editors. Handbook of Social and Human Conditions in Assessment. New York: Routledge; 2016. pp. 302-318

[12] Barkley EE, Major CH, Cross KP. Collaborative Learning Techniques: A Handbook for College Faculty. 2nd ed. San Francisco, CA: Jossey-Bass; 2014

[13] Reeve J, Lee W. Students' classroom engagement produces longitudinal changes in classroom motivation. Journal of Educational Psychology. 2014;**106**(2):527-540

[14] Laal M, Laal M. Collaborative learning: What is it? Procedia Social and Behavioral Sciences. 2012;**31**(2011):491-495. DOI: 10.1016/j.sbspro.2011.12.09

[15] Pujiati A. Exploring the connection between collaborative learning and

students' critical thinking and social adaptation skills. Stipas Tahasak Danum Pambelum Keuskupan Palangkaraya. 2023;**1**(3):108-125

[16] Daniel BK, Harland T. Higher Education Research Methodology: A Step-By-Step Guide to the Research Process. Routledge; 2017

[17] Nasution FS, Surya E. Efforts to increase student learning results with cooperative learning type learning model think pair share on the cube and beams materials in class VIII SMP Kartika I-1 Medan. International Journal of Sciences: Basic and Applied Research (IJSBAR). 2017;**33**(3):280-290

[18] Nelson SJ. Enhancing transfer of learning from seminary classes to pastoral ministry. The Wabash Center Journal on Teaching. 2021;**2**(2):179-198

[19] Hanseth O, Aanestad M, Berg M. Guest editors' introduction: Actor-network theory and information systems. What's so special? Information Technology & People. 2004;**17**(2):116-123

[20] Chang YH, Yan YC, Lu YT. Effects of combining different collaborative learning strategies with problem-based learning in a flipped classroom on program language learning. Sustainability. 2022;**14**(9):5282

[21] Reynolds RB. Relationships among tasks, collaborative inquiry processes, inquiry resolutions, and knowledge outcomes in adolescents during guided discovery-based game design in school. Journal of Information Science. 2016;**42**(1):35-58

[22] Chang CJ, Chang MH, Chiu BC, Liu CC, Chiang SHF, Wen CT, et al. An analysis of student collaborative problem solving activities mediated by collaborative simulations. Computers & Education. 2017;**114**:222-235

[23] Depaz I, Moni RW. Using peer teaching to support co-operative learning in undergraduate pharmacology. Bioscience Education. 2008;**11**(1):1-12

[24] Corden R. Group discussion and the importance of a shared perspective: Learning from collaborative research. Qualitative Research. 2001;**1**(3):347-367

[25] Eaton CD, Wade S. Collaborative learning through formative peer review with technology. Primus. 2014;**24**(6):529-543

[26] Mengduo Q, Xiaoling J. Jigsaw strategy as a cooperative learning technique: Focusing on the language learners. Chinese Journal of Applied Linguistics (Foreign Language Teaching & Research Press). 2010;**33**(4):113

[27] Marcos-Garcia JA, Martinez-Mones A, Dimitriadis Y, Anguita-Martinez R. A role-based approach for the support of collaborative learning activities. e-Service Journal. 2007;**6**(1):40-58

[28] Sharan S. Large classes, small groups: A social systems approach. In: Cooperative Learning. Routledge; 2003. pp. 210-223

[29] Lyons KM, Lobczowski NG, Greene JA, Whitley J, McLaughlin JE. Using a design-based research approach to develop and study a web-based tool to support collaborative learning. Computers & Education. 2021;**161**:104064

[30] Sumadyo M, Santoso HB, Sensuse DI, Suhartanto H. Metacognitive aspects influencing help-seeking behavior on collaborative online learning environment: A systematic literature

review. Journal of Educators Online. 2021;**18**(3):78-89

[31] Lu HS, Smiles R. The role of collaborative learning in the online education. International Journal of Economics, Business and Management Research. 2022;**6**(6):125-137

[32] Balta N, Hamza M. The effect of student collaboration in solving physics problems using an online interactive response system. European Journal of Educational Research. 2017;**6**(3):385-394. DOI: 10.12973/eu-jer.6.3.385

[33] Johnson DW, Johnson RT, Holubec EJ. Cooperation in the Classroom. Edina, Minnesota, USA: Interaction Book Co. publishing; 1984

[34] Johnson DW, Johnson RT. Cooperation and Competition Theory and Research. Edina, Minnesota, USA: Interaction Book Co. publishing; 1989

[35] Panitz T. Benefits of cooperative learning in relation to student motivation. In: Theall M, editor. Motivation from within: Approaches for Encouraging Faculty and Students to Excel, New Directions for Teaching and Learning. San Francisco, CA, USA: Josey-Bass publishing; 1999

[36] Laal M, Ghodsi SM. Benefits of collaborative learning. Procedia Social and Behavioral Sciences. 2012;**31**:486-490

[37] Thanh PTH, Gillies R, Renshaw P. Cooperative learning (CL) and academic achievement of Asian students: A true story. International Education Studies. 2008;**1**(3):82-88. Available from: https://eric.ed.gov/?id=EJ1065440

[38] Du C. The effect of cooperative learning on students' attitude in first-year principles of accounting course. Business Education Innovation Journal. 2015;**7**(2):107-116

[39] Johnson DW, Johnson RT, Roseth C, Shin TS. The relationship between motivation and achievement in interdependent situations. Journal of Applied Social Psychology. 2014;**44**(9):622-633. DOI: 10.1111/jasp.12280

[40] Howard LW, Tang TLP, Austin MJ. Teaching critical thinking skills: Ability, motivation, intervention, and the pygmalion effect. Journal of Business Ethics. 2015;**128**(1):133-147. DOI: 10.1007/s10551-014-2084-0

[41] Han F, Ellis RA. Patterns of student collaborative learning in blended course designs based on their learning orientations: A student approaches to learning perspective. International Journal of Educational Technology in Higher Education. 2021;**18**(1):1-16. DOI: 10.1186/s41239-021-00303-9

[42] Kurniasih R, Sujadi I, Pramesti G. The implementation of collaborative learning using AfL through giving feedback strategy for improving students' attention to mathematics lesson. Journal of Physics: Conference Series. 2016;**693**(1):012018. DOI: 10.1088/1742-6596/693/1/012018